IMMORALITY

*

STUDIES IN MORAL, POLITICAL,
AND LEGAL PHILOSOPHY

✳ ✳ ✳

General Editor: Marshall Cohen

IMMORALITY

* * *

Ronald D. Milo

PRINCETON UNIVERSITY PRESS
PRINCETON, NEW JERSEY

Copyright © 1984 by Princeton University Press

Published by Princeton University Press, 41 William Street,
Princeton, New Jersey 08540

In the United Kingdom: Princeton University Press, Guildford, Surrey

All Rights Reserved

Library of Congress Cataloging in Publication Data will be found on
the last printed page of this book

ISBN 0-691-06614-0

Publication of this book has been aided by a grant from The Whitney
Darrow Fund of Princeton University Press

This book has been composed in Linotron Palatino and Cartier

Clothbound editions of Princeton University Press books are printed on
acid-free paper, and binding materials are chosen
for strength and durability.

Printed in the United States of America by Princeton University Press
Princeton, New Jersey

To My Parents
ELIAS AND EVA
*

CONTENTS

*

PREFACE

＊

It is surprising that, apart from Aristotle's suggestion that there are two basic types of immorality (wickedness and moral weakness), hardly anything has been written about the typology of immorality. It is also curious that so much more has been written about the nature of moral goodness than about the nature of moral badness. Kant, for example, has a great deal to say about what a Good Will (or morally good character) consists of, but very little to say about what wickedness consists of. Recently there have been many discussions of moral weakness, but wickedness has been largely ignored. Insofar as it is discussed at all, the Aristotelian conception of it is accepted without question. Aristotle conceived of the agent of a wicked act as believing that what he does is right—because, Aristotle suggests, he is ignorant of the moral principle according to which his act is wrong. I shall argue that this conception of wickedness misconstrues our ordinary understanding of this notion. As we ordinarily conceive of wickedness, the agent of a wicked act does not believe that what he does is right; rather, he does something that he believes to be wrong because he prefers some other end (or his own self-interest, in general) to the avoidance of moral wrongdoing. (I shall refer to Aristotle's view as the conception of wickedness as *perverse wickedness* and to my view as the conception of wickedness as *preferential wickedness*.)

In addition to this misconception of the nature of wickedness in the philosophical literature, there has also been a failure to appreciate the variety of immorality. I argue that

ix

the simple dichotomy between wickedness and moral weakness is inadequate for a full understanding of the nature of immorality. For this it is necessary to recognize a number of logically distinct forms of immoral behavior. Besides wickedness (which, as I have already suggested, may be conceived of in two quite different ways) and moral weakness, we must also recognize the following: moral negligence, which Aristotle and others fail to distinguish from moral weakness; and amoral wrongdoing, which I further subdivide into amoral wrongdoing proper and morally indifferent wrongdoing. This book is primarily devoted to a discussion of these different kinds of immoral behavior, each of which is discussed in considerable detail and distinguished from the others. In addressing itself to this topic, this book treats an aspect of ethical theory that, as I hope to show, has been insufficiently explored in the literature. I shall also try to show that those forms of immoral behavior that have been recognized—namely, wickedness and moral weakness—have often been misconstrued.

Although the primary aim of this book is to make clear the nature and variety of immoral behavior, the secondary aim is to criticize certain contemporary accounts of the nature of moral beliefs and judgments. I argue that purely noncognitivist accounts of moral beliefs—i.e., those that identify them with some conative or affective mental state—make it difficult or impossible to account for certain kinds of immorality. And I argue that this is a reason for rejecting such accounts. For example, all such accounts rule out the possibility of moral indifference (i.e., wrongdoing due to the fact that the agent simply does not care if what he does is morally wrong), and certain of these accounts (those that make overridingness, or dominance, a defining characteristic of moral beliefs) also force us to construe wickedness as perverse rather than preferential in character. Thus, some of the arguments designed to establish the possibility of certain forms of immorality are, at the same time, arguments designed to show the inadequacies of certain meta-ethical theories.

This study also has implications for theories of moral education and development because, as will become clear, a study of the typology of immorality is, at the same time, a study of the causes of immorality. My study leads to the conclusion that there are three principal sources of immoral behavior: lack of moral concern—the cause either of morally indifferent or amoral wrongdoing, depending on whether the agent is conscious or unconscious of his own wrongdoing; bad preferences (or values)—the cause of wickedness, whether conceived of as perverse or as preferential wickedness; and lack of rational self-control—the cause of either moral weakness or moral negligence, depending on whether the agent's desires and emotions prevent him from acting on his moral judgment or prevent him from seeing (or judging) that his act is wrong in the first place.

I should like here to express my gratitude to all those who have helped to make this book possible. Among my teachers, A. I. Melden is most responsible for having stimulated and nurtured my interest in ethical theory, and David Keyt helped me to understand and appreciate Aristotle's ethical theory. My interest in the topic of immorality grew out of my doctoral study of Aristotle's account of weakness of will. Over the years conversations with my students and colleagues have helped me to develop and clarify my thoughts on this topic. I am especially grateful to my colleagues, Joel Feinberg and Henning Jensen, and to my former colleague, Jeffrie G. Murphy, for many valuable and enjoyable conversations on various topics treated in this book, as well as for reading and commenting on various parts of it. Kurt Baier and William K. Frankena read the manuscript in its entirety. I am indebted to them for a number of perceptive suggestions for revision. The University of Arizona granted me a sabbatical leave during the first semester of the 1982-1983 academic year, and this gave me the opportunity to complete and put the finishing touches on this book. Finally, I am grateful to my wife, Shery, who is also a teacher of philosophy, not only for her love, support, and encouragement, but also for valuable philosophical conversations that helped me to clarify my ideas.

Some of the material in this book has been published elsewhere. An earlier version of Chapter Two appeared in *American Philosophical Quarterly*, vol. 20 (1983), and an earlier version of Chapter Three appeared in *Mind*, vol. 92 (1983). An earlier version of part of Chapter Six was published by *The Monist*, vol. 64 (1981). I am grateful to these journals for permission to reprint this material here.

One further acknowledgment seems called for. I would not have been able to write a book on this subject had I not had the opportunity to supplement my vast introspective findings with the observation of the behavior of my friends and colleagues. For this I express my deepest gratitude.

IMMORALITY

✳

O N E

* * *

IMMORALITY:

LET ME COUNT THE WAYS

What does immorality consist in? Immoral behavior does not consist merely in the performance of morally wrong acts, for morally wrong acts are not always blameworthy and immoral behavior is blameworthy. But the question I wish to consider here is not—or, at least, not primarily— about the conditions under which morally wrong acts are blameworthy. For even when we are in agreement about this it is still possible to conceive of immorality in different ways, or to conceive of immoral behavior as taking on different forms.

For example, Aristotle distinguishes between two types of immorality: wickedness and weakness. He compares the morally weak person to a state that has good laws but fails to apply them and the wicked person to a state that applies its laws but has bad laws. This suggests that there are two quite different forms of immoral behavior: (1) cases where the agent has good moral principles but fails to act on them and (2) cases where the agent acts on bad moral principles.[1]

---

[1] See Aristotle, *Nicomachean Ethics*, Book VII, Chapter 10. Cf. Nowell-Smith, *Ethics* (Baltimore: Penguin Books, 1954), p. 265. Whereas Aristotle treats wickedness and weakness as attributes of persons—as types of bad character—I shall be primarily concerned with them as attributes of ac-

In both cases we have morally wrong behavior that is also blameworthy—i.e., morally wrong behavior done in the absence of excusing conditions. The difference lies in the fact that whereas the agent of a morally weak act believes that what he does is wrong, the agent of a wicked act believes that what he does is right—i.e., he believes either that it is the sort of act that one ought to do or, at least, that it is not the sort of act that is wrong.[2] Thus, whereas the morally weak agent is inclined to feel remorse and condemn himself, the wicked agent is not.

Aristotle's distinction between wickedness and moral weakness involves a distinction between cases of wrongdoing where the agent fails to believe that what he does is wrong (believing instead that it is right) and cases where the agent believes that it is wrong but does it nevertheless. But are all cases of unconscious wrongdoing cases of wickedness, and are all cases of conscious wrongdoing cases of moral weakness?

1. Conscious Wrongdoing

Let us first consider those cases of immoral behavior where the agent himself believes that what he does is wrong. If a person does something that he himself believes to be morally wrong, must we suppose that this could be so only because he has a weak will (and thus has succumbed to temptation) or else because he was subject to some form of compulsion (and hence is not blameworthy)? Or is it

---

tions, i.e., as types of immoral behavior. A person who is not, in general, weak-willed can, on occasion, act in a morally weak manner; and even a good man may sometimes act wickedly. It is with the nature of these forms of behavior that I shall be concerned in this book.

[2] Both Aristotle and Nowell-Smith describe the agent of a wicked act as believing that he ought (is morally required) to act as he does rather than as merely believing that what he does is morally permissible. However, I can see no good reason for excluding the latter belief as characterizing the agent of a wicked act. This point will be discussed in Chapter Three.

also possible for a person to do something that he believes to be morally wrong simply because he is indifferent to (does not care about) the fact that it is morally wrong? If so, we shall have to recognize another form of immoral behavior that is logically distinct from both wicked and morally weak behavior. I shall refer to such behavior as morally indifferent behavior (*moral indifference*). In cases of moral indifference the agent of course feels no remorse or guilt for what he does. In this respect he is like the agent of a wicked act and unlike the agent of a morally weak act. But, unlike the agent of a wicked act and like the agent of a morally weak act, the morally indifferent agent does believe that what he does is wrong.

Could it not also be the case that a person does something that he himself believes to be wrong, not because he has a weak will or because he is indifferent to the moral wrongness of his acts, but rather because, although he has some desire to avoid moral wrongdoing (some con-attitude toward acts he believes to be morally wrong), he prefers the realization of some desired end—or, in general, the pursuit of his own good— to the avoidance of moral wrongdoing when these conflict? If so, then we must recognize still another logically distinct form of immoral behavior. For here again the agent cannot be described as yielding to temptation or as acting against his better judgment. Rather, he thinks that it is better to pursue a certain end than to avoid moral wrongdoing. Thus, he is not inclined to feel remorse for what he has done. On the other hand, unlike the agent of a wicked act—as we have so far characterized wickedness—he does not fail to believe that what he does is wrong. But if he deliberately and knowingly does what is morally wrong without being subject to any sort of compulsion, should we not describe his behavior as wicked?

This raises the question of just how we should conceive of wicked, as opposed to morally weak, behavior. Aristotle's analogy between the wicked person and the state that has bad laws suggests that the agent of a wicked act acts in accordance with his own moral principles and hence does not himself believe that what he does is wrong. But this Aristotelian, or Greek, conception of wickedness differs markedly from the way in which many of us are inclined to conceive of wickedness. According to what might be called (for want of a better term) the Christian conception of wickedness, wickedness is a more evil or blameworthy form of immoral behavior than moral weakness, because it consists in deliberately and knowingly doing what is morally wrong without any compunction or scruple. Wicked behavior results not from a lack of knowledge or from a failure to believe that one's act is wrong, but rather from one's lacking a desire to avoid moral wrongdoing or from one's preferring, say, the pursuit of one's own good to the avoidance of moral wrongdoing.[3]

In cases of truly wicked behavior the agent afterwards feels no remorse or guilt for what he has done. On this score, the Aristotelian and the Christian conceptions of wickedness are in agreement. But Aristotle suggests that this is because the wicked agent does not himself believe his act to be wrong. He is ignorant that acts of this sort are wrong and mistakenly believes them to be right.[4] According to the Christian conception of wickedness, on the other hand, the agent feels no remorse or guilt afterwards, not because he is ignorant that what he does is wrong, but rather because the fact that his act is morally wrong is a matter of complete indifference to him (he is concerned, say, only to promote his own advantage), or else because, although he has some concern to avoid moral wrongdoing, he prefers the pursuit of his own good (or the realization of some particular desired end) to the avoidance of moral wrongdoing. This is what makes his behavior so bad and even "more immoral" than that of the morally weak agent. Aristotle, on the other hand, suggests that if the wicked

---

[3] The Christian will be inclined to equate lack of moral concern with a turning away from God, and preferring one's own good to the avoidance of moral wrongdoing with the sin of pride. But one need not accept these, or any other, theological views in order to accept this conception of wickedness.

[4] See *Nicomachean Ethics*, Book III, Chapter 1.

agent did believe his act to be wrong, he would not be inclined to do it. Thus, the wicked agent, as characterized by Aristotle, has at least the saving grace of conscientiousness.

According to the Christian conception, however, the wicked agent does not fail to believe or know that what he does is wrong; hence he cannot be said to have the saving grace of conscientiousness. Indeed, the most extreme form of wickedness, according to this conception, is exemplified by Satan, who is sometimes conceived of as doing what is morally wrong just because he believes it to be wrong.[5] Thus, the worst form of immoral behavior—what might be called "satanic wickedness"—is the exact opposite of Kantian moral goodness. For morally good behavior consists, according to Kant, in doing what one morally ought to do just because one believes that one ought to do it. One hopes, however, that satanic wickedness is an "ideal" form of wickedness that is realized only by Satan and not by mere human beings. The wickedness of mere human beings seems to result—at least in normal cases—not from their having a direct desire to do what is morally wrong for its own sake, but rather from their lacking a desire to avoid moral wrongdoing (because, say, they lack a concern for the welfare of others) or from their preferring, say, the pursuit of their own good when these conflict.[6]

How, then, shall we conceive of wickedness? Shall we conceive of the agent of a wicked act as desiring to avoid moral wrongdoing but failing to believe or know that what he does is wrong (as Aristotle suggests), or as believing that what he

[5] "To do aught good never will be our task, but ever to do ill our sole delight, as being contrary to His high will whom we resist." Satan in Milton's *Paradise Lost*, Book I, lines 159-162.

[6] W. D. Ross also remarks of human beings that "it seems very doubtful whether they are ever attracted by the mere thought of the wrongness of an act," and he suggests that " 'Evil, be thou my good' is the maxim not of a man but of a devil." See his *The Right and the Good* (Oxford: Clarendon Press, 1930), p. 163. And, as Milton shows us, even Satan can be made more human by supposing that he does what is morally wrong not for its own sake, but rather in order to spite God and thwart his will. I shall discuss this matter further in Chapter Eight.

does is wrong but either being indifferent to this or else preferring some other end to the avoidance of moral wrongdoing? Or should we perhaps recognize two different kinds of wicked behavior? Without at this point intending to beg any of these questions, let us refer to that form of immoral behavior that consists in an agent's doing what is morally wrong because he has bad moral principles (i.e., because he fails to believe that such acts are wrong and believes instead that they are right) as *perverse wickedness*. Let us then refer to that form of immoral behavior that consists in an agent's doing what is morally wrong because he prefers some other end to the avoidance of moral wrongdoing as *preferential wickedness*. Finally, let us (as I have already suggested) refer to that form of immoral behavior that consists in doing what is morally wrong because doing it promotes some desired end and one is completely unmoved by its moral wrongness as *moral indifference*.[7] Each of these forms of immoral behavior may be thought

[7] I shall not treat satanic wickedness as a distinct type of immorality. Instead, I shall interpret the notion of moral indifference broadly enough to include satanic wickedness. Thus, I shall characterize the agent of a morally indifferent act merely as failing to have any sort of con-attitude toward his act in virtue of its being morally wrong—and not as having neither a pro- nor con-attitude toward it in virtue of its wrongness. There is a sense in which even the sadist, who directly desires to inflict pain or suffering on others, may be said to be indifferent to (or unconcerned about) the suffering of others. He is indifferent to the suffering of others not in the sense that he has neither a pro- nor con-attitude toward this, but rather in the sense that, unlike normal persons, he lacks a con-attitude toward the suffering of others. In this sense both the sadist and the person who pursues his own advantage, no matter what the cost in terms of suffering to others, may be said to be indifferent to the suffering of others. Similarly, both the agent who does not care one way or the other whether what he does is wrong and the agent who directly desires to do what is wrong may be said to be indifferent to the moral wrongness of acts, in the sense that both, unlike normal persons, lack a con-attitude toward acts they believe to be morally wrong. My reason for thus subsuming satanic wickedness under moral indifference is that the chief philosophical issue raised by each of these notions is whether it is possible for a person to fail to have a con-attitude toward acts that he himself believes to be wrong.

of as forms of wickedness in a broad sense of that term, which refers to immoral behavior that is not due to weakness of will but done without compunction. However, whereas in cases of perverse wickedness the agent does not believe that what he does is wrong, in cases of preferential wickedness and moral indifference the agent (like the agent of a morally weak act) does believe this.

2. Unconscious Wrongdoing

Let us now consider those cases of immoral behavior where the agent fails to believe that what he does is wrong. Are all such cases instances of perverse wickedness, or are there other forms of immoral behavior satisfying this description? The first thing to note is that a person may fail to believe that what he does is wrong either because he fails to believe (or is ignorant) that acts of such and such a kind (of which his act happens to be an instance) are wrong or because, although believing such acts to be wrong, he is ignorant that his act is an act of this kind. The former kind of ignorance—ignorance of moral principles—never excuses one, according to Aristotle, whereas the latter sort of ignorance—ignorance of particular facts—sometimes does (i.e., if the agent could not reasonably be expected to have avoided it). But Aristotle acknowledges that ignorance of particular facts does not excuse if it is the result of carelessness or negligence.[8]

Suppose, for example, that a person does something that is morally wrong—say, he deeply embarrasses and humiliates someone, not because he is ignorant or fails to believe that such acts are wrong, but because he is ignorant that his particular act (making a certain remark) is an act of this sort. Suppose, moreover, that his ignorance is due to negligence; he simply fails to consider how his remark might affect this person when he could and should have

---

[8] See *Nicomachean Ethics*, Book III, Chapter 5.

done so. If we consider his act blameworthy, then it appears that we must recognize still another form of immoral behavior. I shall refer to this form of immorality as *moral negligence*. Unlike the agent of a perversely wicked act, the agent of a morally negligent act does not fail to believe that acts of this sort are wrong, although he fails to believe that his particular act is an act of this sort and hence wrong. Moreover, since he does believe that acts of this sort are wrong, he will be inclined—if and when he realizes that the act he has done is an act of this sort—to feel remorse.[9] In this respect again, he is unlike the agent of a perversely wicked act and like the agent of a morally weak act. Aristotle does not recognize moral negligence as a distinct form of immoral behavior, but seems rather to confuse it with moral weakness; for Aristotle suggests that in typical cases of moral weakness the agent does not really realize, at the time he acts, that his particular act is wrong, although he does believe that acts of this sort are wrong.[10]

The second thing to note is that Aristotle characterizes the agent of a (perversely) wicked act not merely as being ignorant (or as failing to believe) that his act is wrong, but also as falsely believing that it is right. At least, this is what is suggested by his analogy between the wicked person and the state that has bad laws. His failure to avoid doing what is morally wrong is attributable not to the fact that he has no moral principles at all (in which case he would be more like an anarchical society), but rather to the fact that he has bad moral principles. According to his moral principles, it is permissible—perhaps even required—to act as he does. This is why I have suggested that we refer to this sort of immoral behavior as perverse wickedness.

[9] I am assuming here that his wrongdoing is due to his ignorance and not because he lacks a con-attitude toward morally wrong acts or prefers the pursuit of some end to the avoidance of moral wrongdoing.

[10] In Chapter Four I shall argue that Aristotle's notion of *akrasia* covers both moral weakness and moral negligence, but that Aristotle does not clearly distinguish them.

But now suppose that a person fails to avoid doing something that is morally wrong, not because he believes that such acts are right (i.e., not because such acts are in accordance with his moral principles), but because he has no moral principles at all—at least, none pertaining to acts of this sort. Like the agent of a perversely wicked act, he fails to believe that what he does is wrong; but, unlike the perversely wicked agent, neither does he believe that it is right. An agent who has no moral principles at all cannot be said to believe or judge that his act is not wrong (as opposed to merely failing to believe that his act is wrong), since to say that a person believes that a certain act is not wrong is to say that he believes that it does not violate any moral principles (i.e., moral principles that, we believe, he himself accepts). The agent of a perversely wicked act does believe that his act is not wrong, for he has, at least, bad moral principles. (Indeed, he may even believe that it is wrong not to act as he does—that what he does is not merely permissible but required.) Perhaps, then, we should also distinguish between perversely wicked behavior and behavior that seems more appropriately described as a kind of amoral behavior. Let us, then, refer to morally wrong behavior done by an agent who neither believes that what he does is wrong nor believes that it is right (not wrong)—i.e., by an agent who has no moral principles at all pertaining to acts of this sort—as amoral behavior (*amorality*). If such behavior can sometimes be blameworthy, as I shall argue in Chapter Three, then amorality will be still another possible form of immorality.

Beginning with our original twofold classification of immorality (wickedness and weakness), we have now been led to consider six main types of immoral behavior. However, they still fall into two main groups. In cases of *perverse wickedness, moral negligence,* and *amorality,* the agent fails to believe (or is ignorant) that what he does is wrong. In cases of *preferential wickedness, moral weakness,* and *moral indifference,* the agent believes (or knows) that what he does is wrong. This twofold classification reflects the common-sense view that there are two main reasons why a person might fail to avoid doing something that is morally wrong. One is lack of conviction (or knowledge)—i.e., because he himself does not believe (or know) that it is wrong. This is clearly true in cases of perverse wickedness and cases of amorality. In cases of moral negligence the agent does believe that the kind of act he performs is wrong, but he fails to believe that his particular act is wrong since he fails to realize that it is an act of this kind. The other main reason why persons fail to avoid doing what is morally wrong is that they are lacking in (sufficient) motivation. In cases of moral indifference the agent fails to avoid doing that which he believes to be wrong because the fact that his act is wrong is, in itself, of no concern to him—i.e., because his belief that his act is wrong fails completely to motivate him. In cases of moral weakness the agent does not lack the desire to avoid moral wrongdoing, but he may nevertheless be thought to lack sufficient motivation; for his desire to perform the particular act in question (in virtue of certain other features of it) seems to be motivationally stronger than his desire to avoid moral wrongdoing—even though he rationally prefers the avoidance of moral wrongdoing to the realization of the conflicting desired end. In cases of preferential wickedness the agent has some desire to avoid his act in virtue of its moral wrongness, but he prefers the realization of a certain end (or, in general, the pursuit of his own good). Thus, in cases where these conflict, he is not motivated, given his preference, to avoid moral wrongdoing. He acts in accordance with his rational preferences, though not in accordance with his moral principles.

3. Cognitivist versus Noncognitivist Perspectives

Could it be that philosophers have been blind to the variety of immorality? Are all of these types of immorality possible, or do some of them turn out, after philosophical analysis, to be logically impossible or not really logically distinct from some other type? For example, Socrates denied that moral weakness was possible, and present-day philosophers continue to puzzle themselves about how the notion of moral weakness can be made conceptually coherent. But the other kinds of immorality—with the possible exception of moral negligence—seem equally problematic.

Consider, for example, morally indifferent behavior. Is it logically possible for a person to be indifferent to acts he believes to be morally wrong? Or is it paradoxical to suppose that a person could believe that an act is wrong and yet have no con-attitude whatsoever toward anyone's performing such acts? What about preferential wickedness? Is it possible for a person to believe that what he does is morally wrong and yet choose to do it nevertheless because he prefers the pursuit of some other end to the avoidance of moral wrongdoing? Or is his having such a preference logically incompatible with his believing that what he does is morally wrong?

If we reject moral indifference and preferential wickedness as logically possible types of immoral behavior, then it seems that we must identify wickedness with perverse wickedness or with blameworthy amorality. However, these notions do not seem to be free of conceptual difficulties either. Does it really make sense to suppose that a person might believe that such acts as killing, injuring, and deceiving others are morally right—that such acts are not even *prima facie* wrong but are perfectly permissible, perhaps even morally required? Or is having such beliefs incompatible with understanding what "morally wrong" means? Indeed, is it even possible for a person who knows what "morally wrong" means to *fail to believe* that such acts are *prima facie* morally wrong—at least, if he considers the question of whether they are wrong? Finally, is it possible for a person who knows what "morally wrong" means to have no moral principles at all—or to believe that nothing (i.e., no possible kind of human behavior) is morally wrong?

How one answers these questions—and thus how one conceives of immorality—will depend on what sort of meta-ethical theory one adopts. Much hinges on whether one decides to adopt a cognitivist or noncognitivist analysis of moral beliefs and on the closely related issue of whether to adopt an internalist or an externalist account of the relation between moral beliefs and motivation.[11] If, for example, one holds that having a moral belief does not consist (merely) in accepting some proposition as true and holds that it is a necessary condition of believing an act to be wrong that one have some con-attitude toward it, one must reject moral indifference as a possible form of immoral behavior. And it has been suggested that if one adopts a certain kind of noncognitivist analysis of moral beliefs moral weakness becomes difficult, if not impossible, to explain. R. M. Hare, for example, is led to conclude that in cases of moral weakness it is psychologically impossible for an agent to have acted otherwise.[12] But, if so, how can morally weak behavior be considered blameworthy and, hence, a form of immoral behavior?[13]

How one answers these questions also depends, in some cases, on how one distinguishes moral beliefs and princi-

[11] As I shall employ the terms "internalism" and "externalism," internalism is the thesis that having some motivation to act on one's moral beliefs is logically internal to them (whereas externalism consists in the denial of this). The internalist holds, for example, that it is a necessary condition of believing an act to be wrong that one have some con-attitude toward it. This definition of "internalism" is narrower than that proposed by Frankena in his "Obligation and Motivation in Recent Moral Philosophy," in A. I. Melden, ed., *Essays in Moral Philosophy* (Seattle: University of Washington Press, 1958), pp. 40-81. I shall discuss this thesis in Chapter Six.

[12] See his *Freedom and Reason* (Oxford: Clarendon Press, 1963), Chapter 5.

[13] However, as I shall argue in Chapter Five, it is a mistake to think that moral weakness will appear problematic only if one adopts a non-cognitivist analysis of moral beliefs. It is problematic even for one who adopts a cognitivist analysis of moral beliefs—although certain kinds of noncognitivist analyses make it seem especially paradoxical.

14

ples from nonmoral ones—specifically, on whether one distinguishes moral beliefs and principles from nonmoral ones in terms of their "formal" characteristics or in terms of their "material" characteristics (or "content"). For example, if one holds that any principle can be accepted as a moral principle just in case one is prepared to *prescribe* it *universally* and to accept it as *overriding* (these "formal" features being taken to be necessary and jointly sufficient conditions of accepting a principle as a moral one), then one will be led to reject preferential wickedness as a possible form of immoral behavior. For, according to this view, it is a necessary condition of accepting a principle as a moral principle that one be unwilling to allow it to be overriden by other principles or considerations (overridingness being an essential or defining characteristic of moral principles). Thus, one could not both believe that one's act is morally wrong (and hence violates a principle that one accepts as a moral principle) and yet do it nonetheless because one prefers, say, the pursuit of one's own good to the avoidance of moral wrongdoing; for if one were willing to allow the principle forbidding such acts to be overridden in this way, this would mean that one did not accept it as a *moral* principle (and hence did not believe one's act to be *morally* wrong). Indeed, if one were willing to prescribe universally, and accept as overriding, a principle directing each person to pursue his own good—no matter what the cost in terms of harm or suffering to others—then one could be described (on this view) as believing that one is morally required to act in this way.[14]

If, on the other hand, one holds that whether or not one accepts a principle as a moral one depends on what descriptive characteristics of the acts forbidden or required by the principle one takes to be reasons for holding that

[14] This view has been defended by Nowell-Smith, *Ethics*, and Hare, *Freedom and Reason*. I shall discuss this view further in Chapters Two and Seven.

such acts are wrong or ought to be done, then one may find certain cases of perverse wickedness to be paradoxical. For example, proponents of this latter sort of view (which is said to define moral principles in terms of their "content") have made such suggestions as the following: that one accepts a principle as a moral one only if one holds that the acts prescribed (or proscribed) by the principle are such that, if universally done (or avoided), this will promote social harmony—or maximize the general happiness, or minimize harm, or be for the good of everyone alike.[15] If one adopts this sort of view, one will find it paradoxical to suppose that a person could believe that one is morally required—or even that it is morally permissible—to pursue one's own good or advantage no matter what the cost in terms of suffering or harm to others (even if we suppose that someone is perverse enough to be willing to prescribe universally a principle requiring this and to accept it as overriding). On such a view it would be absurd to explain a person's failure to avoid wrongdoing on the ground that he himself believes that one is morally required (or, at least, that it is morally permissible) to kill (or injure or deceive) others for the sake of promoting one's own advantage. Indeed, it is just because they are convinced that it is absurd or paradoxical to suppose that a person could believe (without incoherence) such behavior to be morally required or permissible, that these philosophers do adopt such a "material" or "content-based" conception of morality.

Thus, the question we are considering—"What does immorality consist in?"—raises issues that lie at the very center of contemporary ethical theory. If it is true that different answers to this question are entailed by different metaethical theories, then perhaps one way of testing these theories is by seeing whether or not their implications are compat-

[15] Views of this sort have been defended by: Philippa Foot (in "Moral Arguments," *Mind*, vol. 67, 1958, pp. 502-13); Kurt Baier (in *The Moral Point of View*, Cornell University Press, 1958); and G. J. Warnock (in *Contemporary Moral Philosophy*, London: Macmillan and Co., 1967).

ible with our preanalytical intuitions about what immoral behavior consists in. For example, if one is convinced, as I am, not only that it is perfectly possible for a person to realize that a certain kind of act is morally wrong and yet either fail to have a con-attitude toward the performance of such acts or else prefer the pursuit of his own good to the avoidance of such acts, but also that immoral behavior sometimes results because of this, then one will be led to question the assumptions behind those metaethical theories which imply that moral indifference and preferential wickedness are not really possible. I believe that it is our common-sense conviction that the most serious, or blameworthy, form of immoral behavior consists in just this sort of behavior. We do not suppose, as Aristotle suggests, that the agent of a wicked act is unaware of his own wrongdoing or wickedness—that he himself does not believe (or know) that what he does is morally wrong.[16]

Thus, I shall be concerned (in the course of this book) not only to explore the nature and variety of immoral behavior; I shall also argue for certain metaethical views. In particular I shall argue that our pretheoretical intuitions about what immoral behavior consists in can best be accounted for and systematized if we adopt a cognitivist analysis of moral beliefs, together with an externalist account of their relation to motivation, and a "material" or "content-based" criterion for distinguishing between moral and nonmoral beliefs. And I shall argue that the reasons typically given for rejecting these views are misguided. However, many of the issues that I shall discuss transcend these metaethical disputes—especially those that arise in connection with moral negligence and moral weakness. And I shall argue that there are certain broad distinctions (re-

---

[16] In Chapter 8 of Book VII of his *Nicomachean Ethics*, Aristotle claims that "incontinence [moral weakness] and vice [wickedness] are different in kind; vice is unconscious of itself, incontinence is not."

garding immoral behavior) that one will want to draw, regardless of one's particular metaethical views.

4. Immorality and Wrongness

I have been assuming that for an act to be immoral it must be wrong. But is it necessary that it actually be wrong, or is it sufficient that the agent believes it to be wrong? Suppose, for example, that someone promises a friend that he will help him repair his automobile next Tuesday (a job requiring two persons). Afterwards he is confused and thinks that he has promised to help his friend on Monday. On Monday an opportunity occurs to do something he very much wants to do, but he thinks that to take advantage of this opportunity will mean breaking his promise. He chooses to take advantage of the opportunity. Now, since he does not really break his promise (indeed, once he realizes his mistake, he can still keep it), his act is not objectively wrong— or so it might be argued. Nevertheless, if no excusing conditions obtain, his act would seem to be blameworthy. Although he does not perform an objectively wrong act, he does act wrongly and is guilty of wrongdoing. For, in acting as he does he intentionally does something that he believes involves breaking a promise in circumstances where this cannot be justified. Moreover, the fact that this belief is false does not excuse him from the charge of having made a morally wrong choice. Thus, I am inclined to think that it is not necessary that an immoral act be objectively wrong. If the agent is mistaken about a matter of fact, and, if, had the facts been as he supposed, his act would be wrong, then, unless there are excusing conditions, his act is blameworthy and immoral.

Suppose, however, that the agent is mistaken, not about a matter of fact, but rather about a matter of moral principle. Suppose that he believes his act to be wrong because he believes that acts of such and such a kind are wrong; but suppose that there is in fact nothing wrong about such acts. Perhaps he has been told, and simply accepts this on authority, that homosexual behavior is wrong. In this case it is not so clear that we have an instance of immoral behavior. If we are convinced that there is nothing at all wrong about homosexual behavior, then it would seem to be misleading to say of someone who engages in such behavior that he acted wrongly—even if he himself believes it to be wrong. But why? How does this case differ from the previous one? In both cases the agent does something that he believes to be wrong, and in both cases the act manifests a lack of conscientiousness on the agent's part— something we consider to be a moral defect. What, then, is the difference? It seems to be this. In the first kind of case *what the agent takes himself to be doing*—e.g., breaking a promise because one would rather do something else— is something that is wrong, whereas in the second kind of case what the agent takes himself to be doing—e.g., engaging in homosexual activity—is not something that is morally wrong. Thus, although there is something morally defective about the agent in the second case (and in this respect we may consider him blameworthy), it is at least questionable whether he can be described as acting immorally. I am inclined to think that in order for us to consider someone's behavior a case of immorality, although we need not think that what he does is objectively wrong, we must at least think that what he takes himself to be doing is wrong.[17]

Some philosophers have suggested that, in order for an act to be immoral, it is not even necessary that an act be believed by the agent to be wrong. An act which is not only believed by the agent to be right, but actually is, can nevertheless be blameworthy, they contend, if it is done

[17] It is important that we do not interpret "what he takes himself to be doing" in such a way that it includes "doing something that is wrong"; for then we would not be able to distinguish these two cases. We must interpret it as referring to that description of the act which, according to him, makes it wrong.

from the wrong motive. R. B. Brandt gives the following example:

> Suppose I have promised to take my son to the circus. Subsequent to the promise, I deliberate about whether to keep my promise and tentatively decide not to do so. But, on learning that another philosopher is going, and that he and I can sit together and discuss philosophy during the circus, I decide to keep my promise after all. My intention, in taking my son to the circus, then, includes causing him enjoyment, keeping my promise to him, and talking philosophy with my friend. Therefore, it would seem, my deed must be laudable or at least not questionable. Not so, however. If it is really true that I am *motivated* solely, or almost solely, by the chance to talk philosophy, and but for this would not have taken my son to the circus even though I promised to, my action may very well be reprehensible—on account of what did and didn't *motivate* it.[18]

Here again, although there is something morally defective about the agent, it does not seem correct to describe him as acting immorally. He may be blameworthy, but he is not blameworthy for having performed this act. What he is blameworthy for is a lack of conscientiousness. But this is not a defect that is manifested in his act, in the sense of being the cause of his doing it (as, for example, a person's committing adultery might manifest weakness of will). Indeed, this moral defect could have been revealed either by his choosing not to keep his promise or by choosing to keep it for the wrong reason. Moreover, not only is his act not objectively wrong, it is not even the case that what he

[18] R. B. Brandt, *Ethical Theory* (Englewood Cliffs, N.J.: Prentice-Hall Inc., 1959), pp. 462-63. For another example see C. D. Broad, "Some of the Main Problems of Ethics," in Feigl and Sellars, eds., *Readings in Philosophical Analysis* (New York: Appleton-Century-Crofts, Inc., 1949), p. 559. Reprinted from *Philosophy*, vol. 21, 1946.

takes himself to be doing is wrong. Thus, he cannot be said to have acted wrongly or to be guilty of wrongdoing.

I am inclined to think, then, that although it is not necessary to perform an objectively wrong act in order to act immorally, it is necessary to act wrongly (be guilty of wrongdoing). A person may be said to act wrongly just in case what he takes himself to be doing is a wrong act. Just as a person need not be blameworthy for having done a wrong act, so a person can be blameworthy even though he performs no wrong act (and even if he does not act wrongly). A person may not be blameworthy for an act that violates moral requirements if there are excusing conditions (such as ignorance or duress); and a person may be blameworthy even if he does the right thing, since his motivation for doing it may indicate that he has a morally defective character. However, a person cannot act wrongly, or be guilty of wrongdoing, without being blameworthy; for to say that a person acts wrongly is to pass judgment on both the act and the agent.[19] If we believe that an agent should be excused for having performed a wrong act, then we must withdraw the charge that he acted wrongly. And although saying that a person acted wrongly does not imply that his act is objectively wrong, it does imply that it is subjectively wrong—i.e., that what he took himself to be doing in so acting is a wrong act.

One might go even further, in attempting to establish a connection between immorality and wrongness, by calling into question the notion of objective wrongness that we have been employing. In many respects this notion seems more misleading than useful. It is misleading in that when we say, as we have said, that, although the agent's act was subjectively wrong, it was not objectively wrong, this suggests that there is at least some sense in which what the agent did is something that it is all right to do. But in those

[19] As Michael Stocker points out. See his "Act and Agent Evaluations," *Review of Metaphysics*, vol. 27, 1973, p. 55.

cases where it seems appropriate to say that what the agent did is subjectively but not objectively wrong (since he did not actually break his promise, for example), is there really any sense in which we want to say that what the agent did was all right?

Our primary purpose in passing moral judgments on our actions is to enable us to guide our choices about how to act. For this purpose the notion of objective wrongness seems to be of little use. Consider the following example. Jones dislikes Smith because Smith is his rival for a promotion. Jones thinks—mistakenly, as it turns out—that their employer is a political conservative and hates liberals. Jones therefore tells their employer that Smith is a strong supporter of liberal causes (which he knows to be true), thinking that this will lead their employer to give the promotion to him rather than to Smith. But since their employer is actually a liberal, he gives the promotion to Smith. Now Jones certainly acted wrongly. But is what he did objectively wrong? A strong case can be made for saying that it is—or, at least, that no important distinction between subjective and objective wrongness can be made here. It is not as if Jones attempted to do something he believed to be wrong (get Smith unfairly passed over) but failed to succeed. Although he did not succeed in getting Smith unfairly passed over, he did "succeed" in doing something wrong, for what he chose to do was the wrong thing to choose to do. Suppose we pose the following question: If one has reason to believe that one's employer will unfairly pass over one's rival if one reveals certain information about him, is it all right to do this? The answer is: "No, this would be wrong." The fact that one's belief is mistaken no more rebuts the charge that one made the wrong choice in these circumstances than it rebuts the charge that one is blameworthy for having given this information. The fact that Jones did not succeed in doing what he attempted to do—cause Smith to be unfairly passed over—does not seem to make his act not wrong in any important sense, for it is relevant neither to the question of whether Jones made the right choice in the circumstances nor to the question of whether he is to blame for acting as he did.

Recall now the case considered earlier regarding the person who mistakenly believes himself to be breaking a promise in choosing to take advantage of a certain opportunity. There it seemed natural to speak of the act as being subjectively but not objectively wrong, because, although the agent believes himself to be breaking a promise, he does not actually do so. Thus, it seems that his act does not actually violate the moral requirement to keep one's promises. But there is another way of looking at the matter. Although he does not break his promise, he does break the moral rule against promise-breaking. One can say, that is, that his act violates the moral rule directing us to keep our promises, since he intentionally does something that he believes involves breaking a promise. And this is really all that is important. There is no important sense in which what is done is something that it is all right to do. The notion of objective wrongness is not only misleading; it fails to be useful either for guiding our choices—i.e., to the question of what it would be right to do, given the circumstances and the information available to one—or for fixing blame—i.e., to the question of whether the agent is blameworthy or to be excused for what he has done. Thus, the notion of objective wrongness is relevant neither to prospective judgments about what it would be right to do nor to retrospective judgments about whether the agent is to be blamed for his act.

Those philosophers who thought it important to draw a distinction between subjective and objective wrongness were not concerned with the kinds of cases we have been considering. They were more concerned with cases where it seems that the action is in some sense wrong, but the agent justifiably believes it to be right and is therefore not blameworthy—i.e., with cases where the act is objectively wrong but not subjectively wrong. Consider the following example given by C. D. Broad:

Suppose, e.g., that a person receives a letter purporting to come from his old nurse and that he is moved to send her a postal money-order in the belief that she is in want and with the expectation that it will enable her to buy comforts. It may be that in fact the nurse has died, that the letter has been written in her name by a dishonest relative, and that the money will be spent by him on drink. What this man intended to do was to bring relief to his old nurse; what he in fact did was to enable a dishonest stranger to get drunk.

Now, if we consider the agent's intention in this example, we are inclined to say that he acted rightly. But, if we consider the actual facts of the situation and the consequences, we are inclined to say that he acted wrongly and that the right action would have been to refuse to send money and to have reported the matter to the police.[20]

But, here again, although it is clear in what sense the agent acted rightly, in what sense did he act wrongly? Indeed, in what important sense can it even be said that what was

[20] C. D. Broad, "Some of the Main Problems of Ethics," p. 556. (My notion of subjective rightness and wrongness includes both what Broad calls "subjective" and what he calls "formal" rightness and wrongness.) For another way of drawing the distinction between subjective and objective rightness and wrongness, see Bertrand Russell, "The Elements of Ethics," in Sellars and Hospers, eds., *Readings in Ethical Theory* (New York: Appleton-Century-Crofts, Inc., 1952), pp. 11-18. Reprinted from Russell's *Philosophical Essays*. Russell (correctly, in my view) identifies the objectively right act with what he calls the "wisest," as opposed to the "most fortunate" act. "The *objectively right* action, in any circumstances, is that action which, of all that are possible, gives us, when account is taken of all available data, the greatest expectation of probable good effects, or the least expectation of probable bad effects. The *subjectively right* or *moral* action is that one which will be judged by the agent to be objectively right if he devotes to the question an appropriate amount of candid thought, or, in the case of actions that ought to be impulsive, a small amount" (p. 18). Notice that Russell (also correctly) defines the subjectively right act in such a way that what I have called a morally negligent act is not subjectively right or moral.

done is wrong? Broad suggests that the act is wrong in the sense that it does not actually succeed in fulfilling any of the agent's obligations (e.g., the obligation he has to his old nurse) but instead fails to fulfill an obligation "to refuse to send money and report the matter to the police." But, given the circumstances and information available, is there such an obligation? Again, the agent makes the right decision in the circumstances, and this is all that is important.

However, this denial of the importance of this particular notion of objective wrongness is not meant to imply that no important distinction can be drawn between what is believed to be right (or wrong) and what is right (or wrong). Of course an agent can mistakenly believe that what he does is right, either because he is mistaken about a matter of fact or (as some would allow) a matter of moral principle. If it is reasonable to expect him to have avoided this mistake, then his act will be blameworthy. It will be a case of either moral negligence or perverse wickedness; and it will be a case both of a wrong act and of acting wrongly. The act is wrong because, given the circumstances and available information, it was wrong to choose to act in that way; the agent is simply negligent in not availing himself of this information. However, if the mistake could not have been avoided by any reasonable efforts or precautions, the act is not blameworthy. In this case what we have is neither a case of acting wrongly nor a wrong act. When ignorance or mistake functions as a valid excuse, it wipes away not only the charge of blameworthiness (acting wrongly) but also the charge that the act was wrong; for, if the excuse is valid, the agent made the right (at least, not wrong) choice, given the information available.

5. The Typology of Immorality

My chief concern in this book is with the typology of immorality. However, the investigation of types of immoral behavior here undertaken is a philosophical rather than an empirical one. No attempt will be made to describe how human beings actually behave or to classify their behavior in such a way as to gain a better psychological understanding of it. Rather, the purpose here is to come to a better understanding of the concept of immorality. Thus, insofar as I am concerned with types of immoral behavior, I shall be concerned with the logical possibility of various types of immoral behavior, rather than with their instantiation or incidence. Thus, questions like, "Was Hitler's behavior wicked or amoral?" "Is amoral behavior characteristic of anyone but a psychopath?" "Is most immoral behavior a case of weakness of will rather than wickedness?" will not be considered here. Insofar as the purposes of this investigation are concerned, it will not make any difference if it turns out that no one's behavior is truly wicked, so long as the notion of wickedness (however we construe it—as perverse or as preferential wickedness) is a coherent and logically distinct notion.

As I have already pointed out, the sorts of question that will here be our concern are questions that have a bearing on so-called metaethical theory. Thus, I shall be concerned with questions like the following: Is it possible for a person to believe that it is morally wrong to do such and such and yet be completely indifferent to this? Can one think that it is morally wrong to do such and such and yet think that one ought, all things considered, to do it? Can an act be both amoral and immoral, or does the ascription of amorality necessarily preclude the ascription of immorality? Is genuine moral weakness possible, or are all cases of weakness of will cases of psychological impossibility? However, although my primary concern will be with such conceptual questions as these, it would be a mistake to think that how one answers them has no relevance to more practical and empirical concerns, and I do not wish to give the impression that this is so. For one thing, being aware of all the logical possibilities (and thus having a better understanding of the concept of immorality) may lead us to notice or look for certain kinds of behavior that might otherwise be overlooked. And if some logically possible form of immoral behavior fails to be instantiated (as some might think about what I have called morally indifferent behavior), this will be an important piece of information about the nature of human beings.

Moreover, as will become clear, a study of the different possible types of immoral behavior turns out to also be a study of the different sources of immorality. Some philosophers have suggested that what makes immoral behavior bad or blameworthy is the fact that it always presupposes some bad desire or intention on the part of the agent—or, either this or the lack of some good desire or intention. I shall suggest that this view is an oversimplification (to say the least) and that conceptual clarity is best preserved if we recognize three principal sources of immoral behavior: bad preferences (or values), lack of moral concern (which, I shall suggest, translates into a lack of concern for the interests of others), and lack of rational self-control. The first of these is the cause of wickedness, whether conceived of as perverse or a preferential wickedness. The second is the cause of either amoral or morally indifferent wrongdoing, depending on whether lack of moral concern accounts for one's not bothering to make any moral judgment or for one's not acting on one's judgment. Finally, I shall argue that lack of self-control can be the source either of moral negligence (if one fails to prevent one's desires and emotions from obscuring or distorting one's judgment) or of moral weakness (if one allows them to prevent one from acting on one's judgment).

Here again, however, I intend to make no claims about the instantiation or incidence of these three main moral defects. Nevertheless, whether or not this aspect of my theory is true may well be relevant to theories of moral education and development—especially since some of these theories seem to concentrate on lack of concern for the

interests of others to the exclusion of the other two defects.[21] Thus, although this book is intended to be an essay
in ethical theory and will not directly answer empirical
questions or more practical ones (such as how best to ed-
ucate our children morally), what will be said does have
an important bearing on these matters.

[21] See, for example, John Wilson, Norman Williams, and Barry Sugarman, *Introduction to Moral Education* (Baltimore: Penguin Books, 1967),
and Norman and Sheila Williams, *The Moral Development of Children* (London: Macmillan and Co., 1970).

TWO

* * *

PERVERSE WICKEDNESS

As we have seen, wickedness, defined as deliberately doing something that is morally wrong without any compunction or scruple, can be conceived of in two quite different ways. According to the conception of it as perverse wickedness, the agent himself believes that acts of this sort are right—either morally required or, at least, morally permissible. According to the conception of it as preferential wickedness, the agent believes that what he does is wrong, but does it nevertheless because he prefers the realization of some end to the avoidance of moral wrongdoing. According to both conceptions, the agent of a wicked act willingly chooses to do something that is in fact morally wrong—for example, he chooses to kill someone in order to take his money. But the agent of a perversely wicked act does not himself believe that such acts are wrong. Thus, insofar as we conceive of wickedness as perverse wickedness, we have no reason to suppose that the agent of a wicked act is lacking in conscientiousness. Indeed, he may be motivated to act as he does by a sense of duty; for he may believe that one is morally required to act as he does. On this conception the wrongdoing is due not to lack of a con-attitude toward moral wrongdoing, but rather to lack of the belief that one's act is morally wrong.

Let us now examine this conception of wickedness in

detail. Why is it that the agent is ignorant of, or fails to believe, that acts of this sort are morally wrong? If he is ignorant that such acts are wrong, why is not this ignorance excusing? Moreover, how has it come about that he not only fails to believe that what he does is wrong, he also believes that what he does is right? How can we account for such perverse moral beliefs as that it is all right (perhaps even required) to kill anyone who stands in one's way? Indeed, can we even make sense of such beliefs? How one answers these questions may depend on what analysis one adopts of the nature of moral beliefs. Thus it is important to notice that perverse wickedness may be conceived of from either a cognitivist or a noncognitivist perspective.

According to the cognitivist version, the agent of a perversely wicked act does something that is morally wrong because he is ignorant that acts of this sort are morally wrong and falsely believes that such acts are right (at least in the sense of being morally permissible). Now, in speaking of the agent as being *ignorant*, one is assuming that there is such a thing as moral knowledge. And in speaking of the agent as acting on a *false* belief, one is implying that his believing that what he does is right consists in his accepting as true some false proposition. Insofar as one who adopts a noncognitivist analysis of moral beliefs rejects these assumptions, this conception of wickedness is not one that he can accept. Nevertheless, one can conceive of perverse wickedness from a noncognitivist perspective. According to the noncognitivist version, a perversely wicked act consists in doing what is morally wrong because of one's acceptance of a *bad* moral principle. This version of perverse wickedness is in keeping with the analogy drawn by Aristotle between the wicked person and the state that has bad laws, but it rejects the notion that the agent of a wicked act acts in ignorance. This is because the noncognitivist views basic moral principles not as objects of knowledge nor as propositions to be discovered by the intellect, but as objects of the will—i.e., as expressions of attitudes or decisions of principle.

I shall first consider each of these versions of perverse wickedness separately, since somewhat different issues are raised in each case. Then I shall examine the common assumptions that lie behind both versions of perverse wickedness. I shall try to show that these assumptions are dubious and hence that it is better to conceive of wickedness as preferential wickedness. However, the argument must at this point remain incomplete. I shall not be in a position to complete it until further groundwork for this has been laid in some of the later chapters.[1]

1. *The Cognitivist Version*

According to the cognitivist version of perverse wickedness, the agent of such an act does what is morally wrong because he is ignorant of the moral principle according to which his act is wrong and mistakenly believes that what he does is right. Nevertheless, his ignorance is thought not to excuse him. Aristotle holds that, unlike ignorance of particular facts, ignorance of a moral principle is never an excusing condition. This is because the cause of such ignorance always lies within the agent himself, whereas the cause of ignorance of particular facts sometimes lies in external circumstances—i.e., in certain facts being inaccessible or difficult to ascertain. When the cause of factual ignorance lies wholly in the external circumstances, the ignorance is said to be unavoidable, and the agent is not held morally responsible or blameworthy for acts due to such ignorance. When factual ignorance is avoidable—i.e., when the agent could have avoided being ignorant by taking certain precautions or making certain investigations— then the question arises as to whether it is reasonable to

---

[1] I shall complete the defense of the conception of wickedness as preferential wickedness in Chapter Seven.

expect him to have taken such measures in order to avoid his ignorance. If it is reasonable to expect him to have taken such measures, then his ignorance does not excuse him and, if no other excusing condition obtains, he is blameworthy. For in this case the cause of his ignorance is internal. His act is due to carelessness or negligence. In a case of moral ignorance, however, the cause of ignorance is always internal. It consists in a person's having certain bad character-traits or bad desires. And, it is supposed, the agent not only should have but could have taken certain measures to foster in himself good character-traits and desires. Thus, unlike ignorance of particular facts, ignorance of moral principles is always avoidable and hence never excusing.[2]

Others have disagreed with Aristotle on this point. Richard B. Brandt suggests that in some cases a person "may have failed to do what he ought because of *an excusable mistake of moral principle.*" And he argues that "within a certain range, absence of belief that an act is wrong (or positive belief that it is a duty) serves as an excuse in morals; we hardly condemn a Mormon for practising polygamy, and we partly if not wholly excuse a Christian Scientist who refuses to take an ill child to the hospital."[3] But Brandt agrees that ignorance of *certain* moral principles could not possibly be considered an excusing condition. This is because "there are some things no decent person will believe to be right (we think), and if we must defend our act by saying we believed what no decent person would believe, we may have condemned ourselves more than excused ourselves."[4] John Hospers reasons similarly:

> What if one were to argue, "Yes, I knew that the gun was loaded, and I shot him deliberately, but I had

---

[2] See *Nicomachean Ethics*, Book III, Chapter 5.

[3] See his *Ethical Theory* (Englewood Cliffs, N.J.: Prentice-Hall, Inc., 1959), pp. 458 (emphasis added) and 487. See also John Hospers, *Human Conduct* (New York: Harcourt, Brace & World, Inc., 1961), pp. 218-19, 271-72.

[4] *Ibid.*, p. 473.

no idea that killing was wrong." . . . Such pleas may in fact boomerang against the user: we may think it worse for a man to kill in the belief that unprovoked killing is all right, than for him to believe that it is wrong and do it anyway in the heat of passion. . . . *A man who believes that unprovoked killing is right and acts on this belief, does not lack conscientiousness, but he is an even worse person than one who has better moral principles and lapses from them occasionally in his practice."*[5]

But now what is it about certain moral principles such that being ignorant of them (or believing their contradictories) shows one to be a person of bad moral character? Can having a bad moral character consist merely in being ignorant of certain moral principles—or in falsely believing certain kinds of acts to be morally right? Or is it that only a person of bad moral character could be ignorant of such principles or believe their contradictories? If one adopts a purely cognitivist account of the nature of moral beliefs— i.e., if one holds that to believe that a certain act is wrong is to accept as true a proposition to this effect—then how does one explain why having a bad character (or, at least, some bad character-trait) prevents a person from grasping the truth of this proposition? If one adopts a modified cognitivist account, according to which believing that a certain kind of act is morally wrong consists both in accepting as true a proposition to this effect and in having a con-attitude toward (or being inclined to universally prescribe the prohibition of) acts of this kind, then one might be able to explain why having the kind of character that would dispose one to refrain from acts of this kind would be a necessary condition of believing (and hence knowing) that such acts are morally wrong. But still, why should having a bad character prevent one from accepting as true the proposition that such acts are morally wrong? Why could not a person of bad character have (as Frankena puts it) at least "a bare intellectual apprehension" of the moral

---

[5] See his *Human Conduct*, p. 482 (emphasis added).

wrongness of such acts?[6] Or is there something peculiar about the truth of the propositions expressed by these moral principles, such that only a person of good character can grasp such truths? This seems to me to be the fundamental question facing anyone who wishes to adopt the cognitivist verson of perverse wickedness.

The answer suggested by Aristotle is that a person of bad moral character has a personality (or soul) that is in an unhealthy or diseased condition—a state of internal disharmony. Just as when one's body is in a diseased condition this may affect one's sensory capacities (for example, make sweet things taste bitter or blur one's vision), so, when one's soul is in a "diseased" condition, this may affect one's intellectual capacities (for example, make certain true propositions appear to be false or blur one's intuitive apprehension of them).[7] But, whereas we have some understanding of how a diseased or drug-induced condition of the body can affect one's sensory capacities, it is far from clear how bad character-traits (diseases of the soul) can make one ignorant (or believe the contradictories) of the propositions expressed by moral principles.

Suppose that a certain person is utterly self-centered, having no direct concern whatsoever for the welfare of others. One can understand why such a person would not care whether or not his acts were harmful to others. But why should this lack of concern prevent him from acknowledging the truth of the proposition that it is morally wrong to cause harm to others? Why should it make him think that it is false? Or, given that he has some concern for the welfare of others but nevertheless prefers the pursuit of his own welfare—no matter what the cost in terms of harm to others—why should his having such a preference prevent him from acknowledging that this is morally

---

[6] See William K. Frankena, "Obligation and Motivation in Recent Moral Philosophy," in A. I. Melden, ed., *Essays in Moral Philosophy* (Seattle: University of Washington Press, 1958), p. 66.

[7] See *Nicomachean Ethics*, Book III, Chapter 4.

wrong, rather than simply making him unwilling to sacrifice his own good in order to avoid a moral wrongdoing
which he himself acknowledges?

It might also be suggested that we could explain the
agent's ignorance of the moral principle according to which
his act is wrong by the fact that the agent failed to make
the intellectual effort required in order to grasp or discover
this principle. This would also explain why we hold the
agent morally responsible for his ignorance and why, therefore, it is not excusing. For the failure to make this effort
is not a mere intellectual fault, like the failure to exert the
effort necessary to grasp the principles of geometry. Since
the possession of moral knowledge is necessary in order
to be sure of avoiding moral wrongdoing, the failure to
make the effort required to obtain this knowledge is a moral
fault.

But how can we explain why the wicked agent fails to
make the intellectual effort required in order to discover
the moral principle according to which his act is wrong?
In the next chapter I shall suggest that one kind of amoral
wrongdoing can be explained as being due to the fact that
the agent simply does not care whether what he does is
right or wrong, and so does not even bother to consider
the question of the rightness or wrongness of what he does.
Unlike the perversely wicked agent, the amoral agent has
no moral principles at all, and neither believes that what
he does is wrong nor believes that it is right. His ignorance
that what he does is wrong is due to a lack of moral concern,
which is clearly a fault of character. Hence, his ignorance
is blameworthy. But the agent of a perversely wicked act
is not described by those who conceive of wickedness in
this way as lacking in moral concern. This is not supposed
to be the cause of his wrongdoing. Rather, it is suggested
that if he himself believed that what he does is wrong he
would be inclined not to do it. This is why he is characterized not only as being ignorant that such acts are wrong,
but also as believing that such acts are right. But if he is

not lacking in conscientiousness, then why does he not make the effort required in order to determine whether or not such acts are wrong? And if he *is* lacking in conscientiousness, and hence does not even consider the question of the wrongness of such acts, then he will neither believe that such acts are wrong nor believe that such acts are right.

2. *The Noncognitivist Version*

These difficulties can be avoided, however, if one adopts the noncognitivist version of perverse wickedness. For, according to the noncognitivist, believing an act to be morally wrong is not to be identified with accepting a proposition to this effect, although it may (and the more sophisticated noncognitivists would say "must") involve accepting certain other propositions about such acts—namely, those that one takes to be reasons for judging such acts to be morally wrong. Believing an act to be morally wrong consists, rather, in having a certain kind of con-attitude toward it, or in accepting a (universalizable and overriding) prescription to the effect that such acts not be done. But for the noncognitivist there is no proposition (true or false) expressed by any moral principle; and thus there is nothing to be ignorant of or to falsely believe. (On this view moral beliefs are more appropriately assessed as good or bad, rather than true or false.) Thus, the problem of how a bad character-trait can affect one's apprehension of the truth of a moral principle does not arise for the noncognitivist.

Moreover, since believing a certain kind of act to be morally wrong necessarily involves having a con-attitude toward acts of that sort, it is easy to see how having certain character-traits or desires might affect one's moral beliefs. Indeed, some noncognitivists see the relationship between one's character-traits and one's moral principles as extremely intimate. Nowell-Smith, for example, views both traits of character and moral principles as dispositions to choose, which imply pro-attitudes. And he suggests that how a person conducts himself may reveal, at the same time, both his character-traits and his moral principles. This will be especially true in certain cases of wrongdoing.

> These are cases of wickedness, cases in which a man, so far from struggling with temptation, neither tries nor thinks that he ought to try to do anything other than what he does. He may, of course, know that he ought not to do what he does in the sense that he knows that the practice is morally condemned by others. But he does not believe that he ought not to do it in the verdict-giving sense of "ought"; on the contrary his action is an expression of the moral principle that he espouses. . . . If a man consistently, and over a long course of years, tries to get the better of his fellows in all the transactions of daily life or if he is never moved by the consequences of his actions for other people, we might say, colloquially, that "he has no moral principles." But this clearly means, not that he has good ones and continually succumbs to temptation to act against them, but that he has *bad* moral principles.[8]

Such a person's behavior shows, Nowell-Smith goes on to argue, not only that he is a selfish person who is indifferent to the welfare of others; it also shows that he believes that this is how one morally ought to act. It would be absurd to say of such a person that he himself believes his acts to be morally wrong.[9]

But why must we conclude that such persons cannot believe that their acts are morally wrong? Let us grant that they act deliberately and that they feel no remorse or regret afterwards. Thus, they cannot be said to be acting in a morally weak manner. But why should we suppose that

[8] *Ethics* (Baltimore: Penguin Books, 1954), pp. 266-67.
[9] *Ibid.*, pp. 306-10.

the only alternative is to say that they believe that they (morally) ought to act as they do? Perhaps they do believe that what they do is morally wrong but simply do not care that what they do is wrong. Or perhaps, although they believe that what they do is wrong, they simply prefer the pursuit of their own interests to the avoidance of moral wrongdoing. Perhaps they do act on bad principles. But why should we describe their principles as *bad moral* principles rather than as *morally bad* principles? Indeed, is it not paradoxical to suppose that a person who knows what "morally wrong" means could fail to believe that it is morally wrong to act selfishly and thereby harm others? And is it not even more paradoxical to suppose that a person who knows what "morally wrong" means could believe that it is morally permissible—let alone morally required— to act selfishly so as to harm others?

The chief question, then, that arises when we consider the noncognitivist version of the notion of perverse wickedness is this: why should we describe a person who harms others because he has a universalizable and dominant pro-attitude toward the pursuit of his own interests (regardless of the consequences for others) as believing that one is morally required (or even that it is morally permissible) to advance one's interests at the expense of harm to others, rather than as believing that what he does is morally wrong but either not caring that it is morally wrong or else preferring the pursuit of his own interests to the avoidance of moral wrongdoing?

3. Moral Ignorance

In spite of the differences between them, the cognitivist and noncognitivist versions of perverse wickedness rest on some common assumptions. First, both assume that it is possible to believe of any act whatsoever either that it is morally wrong or that it is morally right. Thus, both assume that it is possible to believe (without incoherence or self-contradiction) such things as that it is morally right to kill others or to cause suffering and that it is morally wrong to help others or to alleviate suffering. Moreover, both versions assume that it is possible for a person who knows what it means to say that an act is morally wrong to fail to believe such things as that it is morally wrong to harm or deceive others. They assume that there is no kind of act such that knowing what it is for an act to be morally wrong (or knowing what "morally wrong" means) entails believing that such acts are morally wrong. It is these assumptions that I should now like to question.

Let us begin with the second of these assumptions. Is it possible for a person who knows what "morally wrong" means to fail to believe such things as that it is morally wrong to cause suffering to others—even if we also suppose that he has considered the question of whether such acts are wrong and also knows what suffering is? Is it possible to know what it is for an act to be morally wrong (or what it means to say that an act is morally wrong) without knowing of certain kinds of acts that they are morally wrong? Although both versions of perverse wickedness assume that this is possible, the fact that the agent fails to believe that what he does is wrong is given greater emphasis by the cognitivist version (which puts the blame on the fact that the agent is morally ignorant), whereas the noncognitivist version emphasizes the fact that the agent himself believes that what he does is right (putting the blame on the fact that the agent accepts a bad moral principle).

According to the cognitivist version of perverse wickedness, certain immoral acts occur because the agent is ignorant that acts of this sort are morally wrong. This way of viewing the matter concedes that ignorance of basic moral principles is possible but insists that such ignorance does not excuse since it reflects a bad character-trait. But there is another way of looking at it. What the cognitivist should say, I shall argue, is that ignorance of certain moral principles could not possibly excuse the agent because one could not possibly be ignorant of such principles, given that one knows what it means to say that an act is morally wrong. In order to see this, we must first notice that the kind of ignorance that is supposed to characterize the agent of a perversely wicked act must be ignorance of *basic* moral principles—i.e., those which are not derived from more general moral principles together with certain factual (or nonmoral) assumptions.

Consider again the case of the Christian Scientist who, we suppose, is ignorant that it is morally wrong to refuse to allow one's seriously ill child to be given medical treatment. Why do Brandt and Hospers suggest that his ignorance may excuse him, whereas the ignorance of one who fails to know that it is morally wrong to kill another human being does not excuse? Is it because they do not suppose the Christian Scientist to be ignorant of the more general principle that it is morally wrong to harm one's child or do what is detrimental to his welfare? Perhaps they suppose him to be merely ignorant that refusing to allow one's sick child to be given medical attention is detrimental to the child's welfare, because he believes that medical treatment is not really efficacious and other ways of treating the sick (say, "spiritual healing") are. But if so, then they do not suppose him to be ignorant of the basic moral principle according to which his act is wrong. Indeed, he is only ignorant of the derivative moral principle that it is morally wrong to refuse to allow one's seriously ill child to be given medical treatment, because he is ignorant of the fact that this would be harmful to one's child. Now ignorance of derivative moral principles may sometimes excuse, because ignorance of derivative moral principles may sometimes be reducible to excusable ignorance of matters of fact. Thus, we excuse the Christian Scientist because we believe that, given his religious upbringing, he could not be expected to know or believe that medical treatment is efficacious and because he really believes that his act does his child no harm. However, I do not think that either Brandt or Hospers would be inclined to excuse the Christian Scientist if they supposed him to be ignorant that it is morally wrong to harm one's child or to believe that it is morally all right to refuse to save the life of one's child even when this can be done without the use of medical treatment. But now granted that ignorance of a basic moral principle does not excuse, why is this so?

One answer—that given by Brandt and Hospers (and by Aristotle as well)—is that ignorance of such principles is necessarily a reflection of a bad character. However, as we have seen, this leaves us with the problem of explaining how a bad character can prevent one from grasping the truth of a basic moral principle, rather than merely disinclining one to avoid the acts which this principle specifies to be wrong. But, as I suggested earlier, there is another reply. This is that ignorance of a basic moral principle could not possibly be an excusing condition because a person could not possibly be ignorant of a basic moral principle of the form, "Acts of kind A are wrong," unless he were ignorant either of what it is for an act to be an act of kind A or of what it is for an act to be morally wrong. And in the latter case he would be afflicted with a much more fundamental kind of ignorance. It may be correct to say that a very small child who is incapable of understanding the concept of moral wrongness (and who, therefore, literally does not know the difference between moral right and wrong) is also morally ignorant. But *this* kind of ignorance seems to be excusing. (Moreover, such a person could not have any false moral beliefs, since he could have no moral beliefs.) Thus, ignorance of basic moral principles must be distinguished from this moral fundamental kind of ignorance.[10] Surely, Brandt and Hospers do not suppose that the person they condemn is ignorant of what it is for an act to be morally wrong (let alone that he is ignorant of

---

[10] I shall discuss this kind of moral ignorance in Chapter Three.

what an act of killing is); rather, they suppose that, knowing this, he is ignorant that killing people is morally wrong.
It is the possibility of this kind of ignorance that I now wish
to question.

Let us now consider precisely what ignorance of a basic
moral principle must come to. Whatever one takes to be a
(or the) basic moral principle, one must hold (if one is a
cognitivist) either that the truth of such a principle is known
by intuition—i.e., by an immediate or noninferential grasping of a necessary connection between two distinct characteristics (between, say, causing harm and being morally
wrong)—or else one must hold that its truth is known
simply by knowing the linguistic conventions that determine the meanings of the terms in which the principle is
expressed.[11] I do not believe that any cognitivist today is
inclined to accept the first of these alternatives. It faces a
number of well-known epistemological and semantical difficulties that need not be rehearsed here.[12] But the second
of these alternatives—that adopted by those called definists
or naturalists—has also been much criticized.[13]

Most definists have claimed that there is only one basic
moral principle. For Bentham it is that an act is right (i.e.,
not wrong) if and only if it maximizes the general happiness.[14] More recent philosophers are inclined to propose

[11] Some intuitionists (e.g., Ross) hold that one directly knows general
moral principles through an immediate grasping of the connection between general moral characteristics, such as wrongness, and certain nonmoral characteristics, such as harm. Others, such as Prichard, hold that
what one grasps immediately is the presence of a moral characteristic in
some particular act in particular circumstances. One then arrives at general
moral principles by inductive generalization.

[12] For a survey of some of these difficulties see Brandt, *Ethical Theory*,
pp. 189-201.

[13] The chief criticism of this view is that it commits "the naturalistic
fallacy." I shall attempt to defend cognitivism against this charge in Chapter Seven.

[14] For an interpretation of Bentham's principle as analytic in character,

more sophisticated accounts of what moral rightness or wrongness consists in. For example: "An action is right if and only if it would not be prohibited by the moral code ideal for the society in which it occurs, where a moral code is taken to be 'ideal' if and only if its currency would produce at least as much good per person as the currency of any other moral code," or "[An act is right if and only if it] is required, or not forbidden to be done, by principles which would be accepted by rational contractors in an original position of equal liberty and in the absence of any particular knowledge of their own desires, nature, or circumstances, as ultimate standards governing their conduct toward other persons within their common institutions and apart from them, provided that these principles were to be publicly known and generally acted on."[15] Insofar as such principles are taken, not as principles that tell us which acts are morally right and wrong, but as principles telling us what it is for an act to be morally right or wrong, then we are assuming that to know such a principle is to know what moral rightness and wrongness consist in.

However, I am inclined to think that the common man's knowledge of what moral wrongness consists in is more primitive. His knowledge seems to consist in knowing such things as that the fact that an act causes suffering is a reason for judging it to be morally wrong. Principles such as those specifying that killing, causing pain, and deceiving are morally wrong define, for him, what "morally wrong" means. If so, then the more abstract principles proposed

---

i.e., as telling us what it means to say that an act is right or wrong, see my "Bentham's Principle," *Ethics* (vol. 84, 1974), pp. 128-39.

[15] The first principle is suggested by Brandt in his "Some Merits of One Form of Rule-Utilitarianism," *University of Colorado Studies*, Series in Philosophy, No. 3, 1967, pp. 39-65. Brandt, however, proposes this principle as a normative ethical principle telling us which acts are wrong. The second principle is proposed by D.A.J. Richards in *A Theory of Reasons for Action* (Oxford: Clarendon Press, 1971), p. 228. Richards does propose this as a definition of "morally right" and "morally wrong."

by philosophers may be viewed as philosophical definitions of moral wrongness, which attempt to explain the
rationale that underlies the commonly recognized criteria
of moral wrongness. Alternatively, one may view these
abstract principles as purporting to tell us what moral
wrongness consists in, and then view the commonly recognized principles as telling us what kinds of act have the
characteristic of moral wrongness. In the case ignorance of
such principles would be reducible to ignorance of matters
of fact—namely, that such and such acts have this characteristic. But then such ignorance would seem to be no
less (or no more) excusing than any other kind of factual
ignorance.

It has been argued, however, that insofar as we take
basic moral principles to be analytic or true by definition,
we deprive them of their normative or action-guiding character. Jonathan Harrison has argued that insofar as we
interpret any moral principle as analytic we render it utterly
uninformative and useless as an action-guide:

> Moral judgments such as that murder is wrong or
> that stealing is wrong never tell you what is right or
> wrong to do in any particular circumstances with which
> you may be faced. They only tell you that unless what
> you are contemplating doing is wrong, it is not steal-
> ing, or that unless what you are doing is wrong it is
> not murder. They do not tell you that what you are
> contemplating doing is wrong; and that, after all, is
> what you wanted to know.[16]

There are two points that I should like to make in re-
sponse to this argument. First, the moral principles which
seem to me to be, in some sense, analytic are not so because
the predicate-term "morally wrong" is, as it were, contained in the subject-term. That such acts as injuring, killing, causing pain, and deceiving are morally wrong is true,

[16] *Our Knowledge of Right and Wrong* (London: George Allen & Unwin,
Ltd., 1971), p. 71.

not in virtue of the definitions of "injuring," "killing," "pain," and "deceiving," but rather in virtue of the meaning of "morally wrong" (and the key term here is the adverb "morally"). Thus, it would be more appropriate to say in these cases that the subject-terms are, as it were, contained in the predicate-term. In this respect such principles are more like "three is an odd number" than "bachelors are unmarried." Hence, such principles cannot be said to be uninformative on the ground that to know that an act is an act of these sorts one must already have determined that it is morally wrong.

It is true, however, that insofar as these principles are interpreted as analytic they do not tell us what acts are wrong; rather, they tell us something about what it is for an act to be morally wrong (or what it means to say that an act is morally wrong). And this brings us to the second point that I wish to make in responding to Harrison's argument. Although such principles do not tell us how to tell when an act is morally wrong, they do tell us something about what kinds of acts are morally wrong in the same sense that "all bachelors are unmarried" tells us something about what sort of men are bachelors and "red is a color" tells us something about what characteristics of things are colors. But Harrison argues that the sorts of principles that I have mentioned are not analytic.

> Even if "Stealing is wrong" is analytic, "Taking what is not one's own is wrong" is not analytic; even if "Murder is wrong" is analytic, "Killing other people is wrong" is synthetic. . . . And though a contradiction would be involved in denying the analytic judgments, no contradiction is involved in denying the synthetic ones.[17]

Now, of course, if one interprets the proposition that killing is morally wrong as the proposition that all acts of killing are morally wrong, then it is true that no contra-

[17] *Ibid.*

45

diction is involved in denying it. For some acts of killing are not morally wrong—e.g., killing in self-defense. But can one deny that killing another human being is *prima facie* morally wrong? Can one deny that the fact that an act is a case of killing a human being is one of the criteria (though not the only one) of moral wrongness? Can one deny that the fact that an act is a case of killing another person is at least *a* reason—though not a conclusive reason—for judging it to be morally wrong? Can one, without self-contradiction, claim that the fact that an act is a case of killing someone is *irrelevant* to the question of whether it is morally wrong? It is not obvious to me that one can. Indeed, if someone were to claim that he fails to see what the fact that doing X would be a case of killing someone has to do with the question of whether or not X is morally wrong, it seems to me that we would have very good reason to doubt that he knows what it is for an act to be morally wrong.

Thus, I am inclined to agree with Brandt and Hospers that it would be absurd to excuse someone on the ground that he had no idea that there was anything wrong about killing (or hurting or deceiving) others. But the reason for this is not the one which they cite—namely, that ignorance of this sort is not possible unless one has a bad character. Rather, I suggest, the reason is that such ignorance is not possible given that one knows what moral wrongness is. And this means that perverse wickedness as the cognitivist conceives of it—i.e., as wrongdoing due to ignorance of basic moral principles—is not really possible.

But why should this concern the cognitivist? He will still be able to conceive of wickedness as *preferential* in character—i.e., as consisting in the agent's doing something that he knows to be morally wrong because he prefers the pursuit of his own good, or some particular desired end of his, to the avoidance of morally wrong acts. Moreover, it will now be easy for the cognitivist to explain how having such a preference reflects a bad character. For, a person who prefers the pursuit of his own good to the avoidance of moral wrongdoing will be correctly described as selfish; and a person who prefers the realization of some desired end even when this involves killing (or hurting or deceiving) others also exhibits an appalling lack of concern for the interests of others.

4. Perverse Moral Principles

At this point a noncognitivist might charge that all I have done so far is to point out the inadequacies of any cognitivist account of moral beliefs. But this is not quite right. Although one who adopts the noncognitivist version of perverse wickedness does not view wickedness as due to ignorance of basic moral principles, he does view the agents of such acts as failing to believe that what they do is morally wrong. He is no less committed than the advocate of the cognitivist version to the view that in cases of wickedness the agent does not himself believe that what he does is wrong. Thus, if one thinks (as I do) that there is something paradoxical about supposing that a person who knows what it means to say that an act is morally wrong could fail to understand that, say, hurting others is the sort of act that is morally wrong, then this will tell against the noncognitivist version as well.

As we have seen, both versions of perverse wickedness also assume that the agent of a wicked act believes that what he does is morally right. But this assumption is given greater emphasis by the noncognitivist version; for the noncognitivist argues that, given his preferences, the agent of a wicked act *must* be described as believing that he (morally) ought to act as he does. For noncognitivists like Nowell-Smith and Hare it is preferential wickedness that is impossible. This is because they identify a person's *moral* beliefs with his dominant (or overriding) and universalizable pro-attitudes (or prescriptions)—dominance (or overridingness) being the distinguishing feature of a person's moral principles. This sort of view makes it impossible for a person to prefer to promote his own advantage even at the cost of doing something that he himself believes to be morally wrong.[18] It implies, as Nowell-Smith (with some hemming and hawing) admits, that if a person has a dominant and universalizable pro-attitude toward the pursuit of his own interests—no matter what the cost in terms of suffering or harm to others—then he must be described as believing that one (morally) ought to pursue one's own interests regardless of the consequences for others.

> . . . If a man regularly decides that he ought (in the verdict-giving sense of "ought") to do whatever brings him pleasures or profits, his dominant pro-attitude is toward his own pleasure or profit. Whether or not we choose to call selfishness a moral principle with him, depends on the criterion we are using for the phrase "moral principle." If he behaves selfishly without acknowledging his wickedness and without feeling remorse, we could say that selfishness was one of his moral principles; and we hesitate to say this partly because he almost certainly does not address himself in the language of "ought" (in the self-hortatory sense) and partly because we are reluctant to believe that he really is what he makes himself out to be.[19]

Now this strikes me as paradoxical and absurd. We do not hesitate to say that he believes that this is how one morally ought to act because we think that only a madman

[18] To say that a person *prefers* to pursue his own advantage rather than avoid morally wrong acts is to say either (a) that he desires the former more strongly (i.e., that he has a dominant pro-attitude toward it) or (b) that he believes it is *better*, or that one *ought*, to pursue one's own good (in which case he has a dominant and universalizable pro-attitude toward promoting his own good). But, according to the view we are considering, if one believes a certain kind of act to be wrong, one's dominant and universalizable pro-attitude must be toward avoiding *it*.

[19] See his *Ethics*, p. 310.

could have such a dominant pro-attitude—say, a Harean fanatic who is so devoted to the ideal of "every man for himself" that he prefers its realization even at the cost of great harm or death to himself. Rather, we hesitate to say this because it is absurd to suppose that anyone could believe that this is how one is *morally* required to act. Does it even make sense to suppose that someone could (without incoherence among his beliefs) believe that such behavior is morally permissible? For that matter, does it even make sense to suppose that someone who understands what "morally wrong" means could fail to believe that this is morally wrong?

Insofar as we try to make any sense at all of the supposition that someone believes that what each person *morally* ought to do is to act so as to promote his own advantage, regardless of the consequences for others, we must suppose him to believe that everyone is better off if everyone acts in this way. Perhaps he rejects the Hobbesian notion that this would lead to a disastrous state of affairs for everyone and believes instead that this will make everyone more self-reliant, more self-sufficient, and hence stronger. But in this case we do not really suppose him to believe that one morally ought to pursue one's own advantage *no matter what the consequences for others*. For suppose that one's own advantage can be promoted by saving someone else from serious injury or risk of death (because, say, one needs his services as a slave and one is somehow able to make him one's slave). If one really believes that to rescue him is to harm him, by making him less self-reliant, then must one not also believe that it would be morally wrong to rescue him, even though this would promote one's own advantage? Thus, such a person must be said to have a perverse view, not ultimately about how one morally ought to act, but rather about what constitutes human harm and well-being. Perhaps, for example, he believes that to deprive a person of the uniquely valuable

49

experience of struggling for his life to the very end is to cause him a loss (harm) greater than death.

It seems even more absurd to suppose that someone believes that what one is morally required to do is to cause as much pain or suffering to others as possible—that it is morally wrong to fail to maximize misery and unhappiness. Yet, if a person is a sado-masochist, and thus has a dominant and universalizable pro-attitude toward maximizing human suffering (or is willing to accept a universalizable and overriding prescription requiring this), this is precisely what we must say about him, according to the kind of noncognitivist analysis of moral beliefs espoused by philosophers like Nowell-Smith and Hare. Now we might be able to make some sense of such a perverse moral belief by attributing other bizarre beliefs to such a person. For example, we might suppose that he believes that experiencing pain and suffering is a good thing and, indeed, vital to a person's well-being, because strength and wisdom come only through suffering. Such a person might think, then, that to cause pain and suffering to others is to benefit them, and therefore that one (morally) ought to cause pain and suffering to others. But in this case, once again, he has a perverse belief about what harms or benefits human beings and not a perverse basic moral belief, for his basic moral belief is that one ought to act so as to benefit rather than harm others.

Someone might also believe that all human beings are sinful and deserve to be punished, and, moreover, that God has commanded us to punish ourselves and others by creating as much misery and suffering as possible. In this way one might be able to make sense of the belief that one ought, all things considered, to create as much misery as possible. But can we also make sense of the belief that there is nothing at all wrong about causing pain or suffering to others—i.e., that this would not be morally wrong even if it were not necessary to make human beings wiser and stronger or to mete out divine justice? Does it make sense

to suppose that someone might believe that there is absolutely nothing wrong about causing pain and suffering
to others, even when this is harmful to them and benefits
neither them nor anyone else in any way? Can we make
sense of *this* perverse moral belief?

Thus, perverse moral beliefs are possible, but only insofar as they are derived from non-perverse moral principles together with perverse nonmoral beliefs.[20] For example, some people have suggested that Hitler believed that
it was his duty to kill Jews. But unless we suppose him to
have been guilty of rationalization (or otherwise factually
mistaken) or of inconsistency among his moral beliefs, it
is not so easy to make sense of this belief. Perhaps he
believed that Jews were a menace to all other human beings
and hence had to be destroyed in order to save civilization.
If he really believed this, or managed to convince himself
of this in order to justify his dislike of Jews, then it makes
sense to suppose that he believed that he was morally
required to kill Jews. Notice, however, that we do not suppose that he believed that there is nothing wrong about
killing other human beings; nor do we suppose that he
believed that it would not be wrong to kill Jews even if
they did not pose any threat to other human beings. If he
believed that it is (*prima facie*) wrong to kill other human
beings except when they are Jews, then his moral beliefs
were inconsistent—unless, of course, he believed that there
is something peculiar about Jews that accounts for its being
(*prima facie*) wrong to kill other human beings but not them.
In the latter case either he was simply factually mistaken
or else he perversely believed that the fact that one's victim

---

[20] By a perverse belief I mean one that seems obviously false to any
normal person (or, if one likes, to most people). I am assuming here that
beliefs about what is beneficial or harmful for human beings are not
themselves *moral* beliefs, although they are necessarily relevant to the
truth or falsity of moral beliefs. This is controversial. I shall say more
about this when I discuss criteria for distinguishing between moral and
nonmoral beliefs in Chapter Seven.

is of a certain racial origin makes it all right to kill him (this being, like the case where one's victim is unjustly trying to kill oneself, a legitimate exception to the general moral proscription against killing human beings). But could he really have believed that a person's having a certain racial origin was in itself a sufficient moral justification for killing him? One can understand the appeal to self-defense (or the defense of other human beings who are being unjustly attacked) and perhaps even the appeal to the need to punish by death those who are guilty of certain wrongs; for here one is appealing to considerations that we all recognize to be *moral* considerations. But why would (or how could) anyone think that the mere fact that a person had a certain racial origin (or skin of a certain color) make it morally permissible to kill him? Suppose that we ask him why he thinks this makes it permissible and he replies that it just does. Does this make sense? Can his thinking that it is right make it right? Can his being prepared to accept and universally apply a principle permitting this (even in the hypothetical case where he himself is a Jew) entitle him to think that it is right?

The kind of noncognitivist analysis of moral beliefs that allows that a person can believe anything whatsoever to be morally right or wrong, so long as he has certain pro- or con-attitudes (or is prepared to accept certain prescriptions) has other bizarre consequences as well. It implies, for example, that someone might be perfectly justified—given his particular pro-attitudes or preferences—in believing that those who avoid harming others when they could thereby promote their own advantage (or who make small sacrifices of their own interests in order to help others) act *immorally*—at least insofar as their acts reflect such character-traits as kindness and concern for others. Proponents of this way of defining moral (as opposed to nonmoral) beliefs and principles are also committed to holding that a person who has a dominant and universalizable pro-attitude toward not stepping on the lines of a pavement must be described as believing that stepping on the lines of a pavement is (in and of itself) *morally* wrong. And, according to Hare, if a person is, like the emperor Heliogabalus, disposed to have people slaughtered because he thinks that red blood on green grass is beautiful and is prepared to prescribe universally that such beauty be brought about at all costs—even at the cost of human lives—then such a person must be described as believing that the creation of such beauty is *morally* required. In this case aesthetic preference becomes a moral principle.[21] But is this not obviously just an example of putting aesthetic pulchritude before moral rectitude? Is it not paradoxical to suppose that Heliogabalus—or anyone—could believe that this is how one is *morally* required to act?

5. *Perverse versus Preferential Wickedness*

If one finds these sorts of consequences unpalatable, one can, of course, reject the notion of perverse wickedness and, instead, conceive of wickedness as preferential wickedness. It should be recognized, however, that one man's paradox is often another man's paradigm. Whereas philosophers like Hare and Nowell-Smith find it paradoxical to suppose that someone might judge it to be morally wrong to act in a certain way and yet prefer acting in that way nonetheless, I find such cases to be paradigms of wickedness. Whereas I find it paradoxical to suppose that someone might judge it to be morally wrong to fail to slaughter an innocent human being when this will produce the aesthetically pleasing effect of red (blood) on green (grass), they find this to be a paradigm of someone's having a perverse moral principle (assuming that he is prepared

[21] *Freedom and Reason* (Oxford: Clarendon Press, 1963), pp. 161, 168-69. The previous example of accepting a principle prescribing not stepping on the lines of a pavement as a moral principle is suggested by Jonathan Harrison in "When Is a Principle a Moral Principle?" *Proceedings of the Aristotelian Society*, suppl. vol. 28, 1954, pp. 111-34.

to prescribe it universally and accept it as overriding). Thus, arguments that appeal to alleged paradoxical or counter-intuitive consequences are apt to be less than conclusive. Moreover, it may seem that, when all is said and done, preferential wickedness and perverse wickedness (as the noncognitivist describes it) come to much the same thing. In both cases the agent of a morally wrong act does it because he has a perverse preference: he prefers promoting some desired end of his (e.g., beauty, his own welfare, or a purely Aryan society) to respecting the interests and welfare of others. To act on such a preference without having any qualms about it is the essence of what we should all agree to be wickedness. Thus, it may seem that there is little to choose between these two conceptions of wickedness.

There is more to our conception of wickedness than this, however. When we describe behavior as wicked, we imply that it is a particularly repugnant and odious form of immoral behavior. Wickedness is thought to be more evil than moral weakness because it is thought to be a kind of "saving grace" of the agent of a morally weak act that he acts contrary to his own resolves and is therefore inclined to feel remorse and to repent, whereas this redeeming feature is not found in cases of wickedness. If we interpret wickedness as perverse wickedness, however, the agent of a wicked act has a redeeming feature as well. For on this model of wickedness the agent fails to believe that what he does is wrong and "sincerely" believes that it is morally right. Indeed, he may even believe that it is his moral duty to act in this way, in which case he has at least the "saving grace" of conscientiousness. Moreover, insofar as we suppose that his wrongdoing is due to lack of conviction, we seem to be allowing that he does, at least, desire to avoid moral wrongdoing—that he would avoid doing what he does if he believed it to be wrong. And this makes his behavior seem not quite so reprehensible. If we interpret wickedness as preferential wickedness, however, no such redeeming feature is to be found. Unlike the agent of a morally weak act, the agent of a preferentially wicked act does not really prefer the avoidance of moral wrongdoing to advancing the end he pursues; hence he is not apt to feel remorse. But, unlike the agent of a perversely wicked act, he cannot be thought to have the "saving grace" of conscientiousness either; we cannot say that he might have avoided doing what he did if only he believed it to be wrong, for he does in fact believe it to be wrong. Thus, it is only when we conceive of wickedness as preferential wickedness that we come upon "true" wickedness. And this is why it seems better to describe the agent of a "truly" wicked act as knowing full well that what he does is wrong but choosing to do it nonetheless.

As we have seen, however, philosophers have claimed that the notion of preferential wickedness has paradoxical consequences of its own. They find it absurd to suppose that someone might believe that it is morally wrong to do something and yet believe that one ought, all things considered, to do it. Rather, they argue, moral considerations must be, for the person who accepts them, the most important kind of considerations. It has also been argued that, since moral requirements are categorical requirements, anyone who believes that he is morally required not to do something but has reason to do it nevertheless must be conceptually confused. Until we have considered these issues, the case for conceiving of wickedness as preferential wickedness will remain incomplete. These issues will be taken up in Chapter Seven.

T H R E E

* * * * *

AMORALITY

Sometimes when one describes a person or his behavior as amoral one is deliberately employing the term "amoral" rather than "immoral" because one thinks that the person or his behavior is somehow removed from the moral realm—not an appropriate object either of moral condemnation or commendation. In such contexts "amoral" has the same meaning as "nonmoral." In other cases—so I shall argue—we use the term "amoral" not to exclude the label "immoral" but rather to indicate a certain type of immorality.

In cases of what we commonly refer to as amoral wrongdoing, the agent is either unaware of or, at least, indifferent to the wrongness of what he does. Here the wrongdoing is due neither to weakness of will nor to bad values (at least, not bad *moral* values), but rather to a lack of concern about whether one's acts are morally right or wrong. The problem with the amoral agent, it seems, is not that he has bad moral principles, nor that he fails to live up to his good principles, but rather that he has no moral principles at all—at least, none pertaining to acts of the sort he performs.

One way of understanding the notion of amoral wrongdoing is to construe it as wrongdoing due to lack of moral convictions. But the notion of amorality seems to be broader than this. To say that a person is amoral is to say that moral considerations play no role in his practical deliberations and that moral beliefs form no part of his motivation for acting as he does. This may be so either because (1) he simply has no moral convictions, or (2) although he has moral convictions, these play no motivational role for him. This suggests that there are two kinds of amoral wrong-doing. In one kind of case the agent does not believe that what he does is wrong, but neither does he believe that it is right. This is because he has formed no moral convictions at all that pertain to acts of this sort. In the other kind of case the agent believes that what he does is wrong but is unmoved by this. He does it nevertheless because (a) doing this promotes some desired end of his and (b) he has no con-attitude toward acts insofar as he believes them to be morally wrong. Thus, although the term "amoral" is commonly applied to both of these kinds of wrongdoing, they are quite different.[1] For this reason I have chosen to restrict the term "amoral" to amoral wrongdoing of the first type and to refer to the other type of amoral wrongdoing as *morally indifferent* wrongdoing.

In this chapter I shall be concerned only with amoral wrongdoing in my restricted sense—i.e., wrongdoing due to lack of moral convictions. Can amoral wrongdoing of this sort also be a case of immoral behavior—i.e., can it be considered blameworthy or morally bad—or must it rather be considered a kind of nonmoral behavior that is neither morally good nor morally bad? What I am calling morally indifferent wrongdoing raises a different question. Here there is no reason to deny that it is immoral; for the agent knows (or, at least, believes) that what he does is wrong, but does not care. The chief question raised here is whether such behavior is (logically) possible. For it is a widespread conviction among moral philosophers that having some con-attitude toward a certain kind of act is a necessary

---

[1] Later I shall offer an explanation of why the term "amoral" is commonly applied to both kinds of behavior.

condition of believing that acts of that sort are wrong. I shall take up this issue in Chapter Six.

The kind of behavior that I am here interested in consists in a person's doing something that is morally wrong, but without either believing that such acts are morally wrong or believing that such acts are not morally wrong; he simply has no moral beliefs whatsoever about the rightness or wrongness of such acts. This might be so because he lacks the concept of moral wrongness—i.e., because he does not know what it is for an act to be morally wrong (or, if one is a noncognitivist, because he does not know what it means to say that an act is morally wrong). Such a person quite literally does not know the difference between right and wrong (in the moral sense). But it might be supposed that a person could also fail either to believe that a certain kind of act is morally wrong or believe that it is not morally wrong because, although he knows what it means to say that an act is morally wrong, he himself has formed no moral beliefs about acts of this kind. He may have other moral beliefs, or he may simply have no moral beliefs at all concerning which acts are morally wrong and which are not. This suggests that we should recognize the possibility of two different forms of amoral behavior (as I have defined it). The first consists in morally wrong acts done by an agent who lacks the concept of moral wrongness. The second consists in morally wrong acts done by an agent who has this concept but has no moral convictions about such acts. Both cases are problematic—but for different reasons. In the first case one might wonder whether morally wrong acts done by an agent who does not even possess the concept of moral wrongness could ever be said to be blameworthy—in which case amoral acts of this sort could not be a form of immoral behavior. It may seem that wrongdoing of this sort must be considered to be nonmoral in character. In the second case the agent does not seem so innocent, since he at least understands the difference between right and wrong. Moreover, if he refrains from making moral judgments because he does not care whether his acts are (morally) right or wrong, being concerned only with what furthers his own interests, his wrongdoing would seem to be immoral as well as amoral. But if one adopts a noncognitivist analysis of moral beliefs, this lack of moral concern will seem puzzling, since such analyses make having a con-attitude toward X a necessary condition of believing that X is wrong. If, on the other hand, one adopts a cognitivist account, then, as I shall explain later, it may seem rather puzzling how someone could understand what it means to say that an act is morally wrong and yet fail to believe that such acts as injuring others or deceiving them are (at least, *prima facie*) wrong. And it will seem even more paradoxical to suppose that someone understands the difference between right and wrong but has no moral beliefs at all.

1. Not Knowing the Difference between Right and Wrong

Let us first consider the case of an agent who does what is morally wrong but does not possess the concept of moral wrongness. Does one's admitting that he lacks this concept preclude one from judging that his act is blameworthy? In some cases this seems to be true. Suppose that a very small child sticks a pin into baby brother, causing him to shriek in pain. Now perhaps this child has so far learned what "wrong" behavior is only in the sense of "acts that mommy or daddy say not to do." I do not believe that we should say that such a child has yet acquired the concept of *moral* wrongness. We call such a child amoral, and in calling his behavior amoral we mean to imply that it is not blameworthy—not immoral.

But now suppose that the same sort of act—sticking a pin into a baby so as to cause it pain—is done by an adult who, for some reason or other, has not been taught what it means to say that an act is morally wrong. Let us suppose that this adult is rational and intelligent and, in other respects, normal. Let us suppose that he is able to appreciate the consequences of his acts for others—for example, he understands as well as any of us can in this case what his act does to the infant. Shall we say now that the mere fact that he fails to possess the concept of moral wrongness precludes us from judging his behavior to be blameworthy or immoral? It is not at all clear to me that the agent can, *on this ground alone*, escape a justified charge of immorality. Unless there is some other ground for excusing him—e.g., he suffers from an uncontrollable or irresistible desire to inflict pain or observe suffering—I do not see why his behavior, given that it *is* morally wrong, should not be considered immoral. If he knowingly and willingly inflicts intense pain on another human being merely for the sake of the pleasure he experiences in observing the suffering of this other person, then, unless some other excusing condition obtains, he acts immorally—whether or not he understands what it means to say that an act is morally wrong. Such a person may be said to be amoral, but he is not nonmoral. Unlike the young child who is not able to understand what he does and how it affects others, this person does have the capacities requisite for moral responsibility. Indeed, I am inclined to think that even in the case of a very small child who has not yet acquired (or fully acquired) the concept of moral wrongness, if such a child has learned to appreciate the consequences of his acts for others (if, e.g., he is able to understand what sticking the pin into baby does to baby), then the mere lack of the concept of moral wrongness on his part does not preclude his being blameworthy—although other things, such as his not yet having acquired adequate capacities of rational self-control, may.

One sort of person who is often described as being amoral is the psychopath. The label "amoral" is chosen in preference to "immoral" because it is thought to be at least questionable whether such a person thinks in terms of moral categories at all.[2] The psychopath has been described as seeing nothing wrong with his behavior and as lacking a moral sense. But it is not entirely clear, from the accounts of psychopathy given by psychologists, whether we should describe the psychopath as lacking the concept of moral wrongdoing or as simply being indifferent to matters of right and wrong. It is also not clear why (if) he should be excused rather than blamed.[3] Perhaps the most distinguishing characteristic of the psychopath is that he is entirely egocentric, without any concern whatsoever for the needs and interests of others. But as Antony Duff asks: "Why should this render him disordered, rather than just more callous or wicked than others?"[4] Why not call his behavior immoral rather than, or as well as, amoral?

The answer given by some is that the psychopath is not just selfish and indifferent to the welfare of others; he does not really understand the difference between moral right and wrong. He is not just an "immoralist," who understands but rejects conventional moral values; he cannot even understand these values.[5] He may have learned certain descriptive criteria for applying moral terms. He may know, for example, that the fact that an act causes someone to feel pain is a reason

[2] This label is attached to the psychopath by Norman Williams in *Introduction to Moral Education*, by Wilson, Williams, and Sugarman (Baltimore: Penguin Books, 1967), p. 272, and by Derek Wright in *The Psychology of Moral Behavior* (Baltimore: Penguin Books, 1971), pp. 208 ff. For the classic descriptions of the psychopath see H. Cleckley, *The Mask of Sanity* (St. Louis: C. V. Mosby, 1964), and W. McCord and J. McCord, *The Psychopath: An Essay on the Criminal Mind* (Princeton, N.J.: Van Nostrand, 1964).

[3] For a discussion of this issue see Vinit Haksar, "Aristotle and the Punishment of Psychopaths," *Philosophy*, vol. 39, 1964, pp. 323-40, and "The Responsibility of Psychopaths," *Philosophical Quarterly*, vol. 15, 1965, pp. 135-45.

[4] Antony Duff, "Psychopathy and Moral Understanding," *American Philosophical Quarterly*, vol. 14, 1977, p. 194.

[5] This sort of view is defended by Duff (*ibid.*). A more extreme version of this view is defended by M. S. Pritchard in his "Responsibility, Understanding, and Psychopathology," *The Monist*, vol. 58, 1974.

for judging it to be "wrong." He may know that others disapprove of acts of this sort, and that in calling them "wrong"
they are expressing their disapproval of such acts. But he
cannot understand why people disapprove of such acts, as
opposed to merely disapproving of acts that cause pain to
themselves. Hence, he cannot understand what it is to have
a reason to avoid an act simply on the ground that it causes
pain to someone else. Neither can he understand what it is
to have a reason to avoid an act on the ground that it involves
harming someone, or deceiving someone, etc. Thus, he is
unable to understand what it is for an act to be *morally* wrong.

This sort of view seems to me to exaggerate the psychopath's lack of understanding and to rest on some very questionable assumptions. I am not convinced, for example, that
judging an act to be morally wrong entails acknowledging
that one has a reason not to do it. But, even if this is granted,
I do not see why the psychopath cannot understand what it
is to have a reason to avoid an act simply on the ground
that it causes pain to another. Given that he himself is incapable of being moved by the pain of another, he himself
cannot have a good reason to avoid doing something on this
ground alone. But surely he can understand that most people
are affected by the pain or suffering of others and that, given
this, *they* have some reason to avoid doing things that cause
pain to others (just as he can understand that he has reason
not to touch things that are very hot, given his aversion to
his own pain). If one holds, as noncognitivists do, that having
some con-attitude toward a certain kind of act, or acknowledging that one has a reason not to do such acts, is a necessary condition of believing such acts to be wrong, then one
will deny that the psychopath himself believes that it is wrong
to cause pain to others. But this does not mean that the
psychopath cannot understand what others mean when they
claim that such acts are morally wrong.

In any case, it is not necessary to hold that the psychopath
fails to understand the difference between right and wrong
in order to explain why we consider him to be mentally

disordered rather than just wicked or to explain why we consider his responsibility for his behavior to be diminished. The reason for this may be that he suffers from a serious emotional impairment—he is unable to feel any genuine love or affection for others. Perhaps he has been so deprived of love and affection in childhood, so emotionally undernourished, that he has been rendered completely cold and unsympathetic, no longer capable of being moved by the prospects of pain or harm to others. Psychologists have also pointed out that the typical psychopath suffers from a diminished ability to control his own impulses. In this respect he is rather like the small child whom we excuse on the ground of not yet having developed adequate capacities of self-control. But if so, then it is these things—emotional impairment and lack of self-control—that justify us in excusing or withholding blame from the psychopath.

Thus, even if we were to admit that the psychopath does not understand what it means to say that an act is morally wrong, this would not be what excuses him (if indeed, his behavior is excusable). However, I am inclined to think that the amorality of the psychopath consists, not in a lack of moral understanding, but rather in his indifference to the rightness or wrongness of what he does. This indifference may manifest itself in either of two ways. It may manifest itself in the fact that he is not moved to act by whatever moral judgments he does make, but it may also manifest itself in his simply not bothering to make moral judgments at all. He may only be concerned to judge how his acts promote, or fail to promote, his own interests. Such a person may also be called "amoral."

2. Lack of Moral Convictions

This brings us now to the second type of amoral wrongdoing—i.e., wrongdoing by an agent who knows what it means to say that an act is wrong (and in this sense, knows the difference between right and wrong) but who does not himself believe either that such acts are morally wrong or that they are not wrong. It may be that he does not have any general moral beliefs at all, or it may be that he has simply not formed any general moral beliefs about acts of this kind. How one accounts for this sort of convictionless amorality will depend on what sort of analysis of moral beliefs one adopts. If one adopts a cognitivist account of the nature of moral beliefs, it may seem paradoxical to suppose that someone understands what "morally wrong" means and yet fails to believe, say, that it is wrong to hurt others—fails to see, that is, how the fact that an act hurts another is even relevant to the question of its wrongness. It is also difficult, on such accounts, to explain how a person who understands what "morally wrong" means could be completely lacking in moral beliefs.

On a definist (or naturalist or descriptivist) account to say (or believe) that an act is morally wrong is to say (or believe) that it possesses a certain characteristic—such as, for example, failing to maximize happiness and/or minimize unhappiness, or failing to conform to those basic rules of conduct that would be agreed to by all rational contractors in a certain hypothetical position. On this kind of view one could not know what "morally wrong" means without believing that acts of this sort are wrong. Of course, believing that if an act possesses this characteristic then it is wrong, one might still fail to have any general beliefs about which acts (e.g., lying, killing, etc.) possess this characteristic. In this case one's lack of substantive moral beliefs could be due to the fact that one does not care whether or not one's acts possess this characteristic, and hence does not even bother to consider which acts are morally wrong.

Could one in this way account for the fact that someone fails to believe, say, that it is wrong to inflict pain on others? We must remember here that at least part of the plausibility of such definist accounts of the meaning of "morally wrong" rests on the fact that they help us to explain why virtually everyone believes certain kinds of acts (hurting, killing, deceiving, etc.) to be wrong. Hence, on such an account the failure to believe (on the part of someone who knows what "morally wrong" means) that it is wrong to hurt others would have to be due to incredible ignorance. Such a person would have to be grossly ignorant about the nature of such acts (not fully realizing what hurting someone involves or does to that person) or the nature of human beings (not realizing, for example, that others dislike being hurt too). Thus, on any plausible definist account, if a person knows what is involved in hurting someone and knows how people feel about being hurt, then failure to believe that it is morally wrong to hurt others should count as at least strong evidence that he does not know what it is for an act to be morally wrong (what "morally wrong" means).

Complete lack of moral beliefs, or lack of certain basic moral beliefs, is also hard to square with intuitionist accounts of moral beliefs. On these accounts, certain key moral terms stand for indefinable characteristics, and most intuitionists hold that these characteristics are consequential, or supervenient—i.e., they are not grasped in isolation but only insofar as they attach, say, to particular acts or kinds of facts. Thus, if moral wrongness is such a characteristic, it is difficult to see how one can come to understand what "morally wrong" means without coming to believe that certain kinds of acts are wrong. Perhaps one could fail to believe that certain kinds of acts (e.g., deceiving others) are wrong so long as one believes that certain other acts (e.g., injuring others) are wrong. One might grasp this characteristic insofar as it attaches to the latter kind of act but not to the former. But how could a person fail to believe of any acts at all that they are wrong? If moral wrongness is a consequential characteristic that is not grasped in isolation, how is this possible?

According to certain noncognitivist accounts of the meaning of "morally wrong," however, this seems perfectly possible. According to Hare, for example, to understand the meaning of "morally wrong" is to understand that to say that an act is morally wrong is to universally prescribe that such acts not be done and to prescribe this principle as an overriding one. Now it certainly seems possible for a person to understand this, and thus to know what others mean when they say that certain acts are morally wrong, even though he himself makes no universal and overriding prescriptions—or, at least, none requiring or forbidding acts of certain kinds. Indeed, this is precisely how Hare defines the amoral person.

> He either refrains altogether from making moral judgments or makes none except judgments of indifference (that is to say, he either observes a complete moral silence, or says, "Nothing matters morally"; either of these two positions might be called a sort of amoralism. . . . [6]

It should be noted that Hare here recognizes two quite different forms of amorality. The first type, which we might refer to as *silent amorality*, consists in a person's not having any moral beliefs at all—i.e., for any given act (or kind of act), such a person neither believes that it is morally wrong nor that it is not morally wrong. The second type of amorality, which we may refer to as *indifferent amorality*, consists in believing that everything is morally permissible. Such a person believes, for any given act, that neither doing it nor not doing it is morally wrong. To believe that it is morally indifferent, say, whether or not one harms others is, according to Hare, to believe that it is neither the case that one ought not nor that one ought to harm others.[7] The

---

[6] R. M. Hare, *Freedom and Reason* (Oxford: Clarendon Press , 1963), p. 101.

[7] It is important not to confuse what I am here calling *indifferent amorality* with what I earlier called moral indifference. The morally indifferent person lacks a con-attitude toward acts insofar as he believes them to be morally wrong. He is indifferent to (or does not care about) the wrongness of his acts. He does not fail to believe that what he does is wrong (when it is wrong); he is simply unmoved by this. The indifferent-amoral person,

difference between these two kinds of amorality can be explained as follows. Both the silent-amoral person and the indifferent-amoral person are moral unbelievers—i.e., neither believes that any acts are morally wrong. But the indifferent-amoral person is also a moral disbeliever—i.e., he believes that no acts are morally wrong. He is the moral counterpart of the atheist, whereas the silent-amoral person is a kind of moral agnostic. The silent-amoral person does not believe that no acts are morally wrong; he merely fails to believe, of any acts, that they are morally wrong.

Hare suggests that each of these two amoral positions can be adopted either in general—i.e., with respect to all acts—or with respect to some particular act, such as imprisoning one's debtors when they refuse to pay. Thus, with respect to the question of whether or not to imprison one's debtors, Hare claims that there are four possible positions that one might adopt: (1) One might judge that one ought not to imprison one's debtors (we may call this the moral, or morally good, position). (2) One might judge that one ought to imprison one's debtors (we may call this the immoral, or morally bad, position). (3) One might judge that it is neither the case that one ought nor that one ought not to imprison one's debtors (this is the indifferent-amoral position). (4) One might refrain from making any judgment at all (the silent-amoral position).[8] Hare wishes to contrast both the third and fourth positions (the amoral positions) with the second (immoral) position. Wrongdoing due to the fact that the agent has adopted the third or fourth position would be described by Hare as amoral, whereas wrongdoing due to the fact that the agent has adopted the second position would be described by him (I believe) as *wicked*. Thus, for Hare, the "truly immoral" (or wicked) agent actually believes that he ought to act as he does—

---

however, does not believe that what he does is wrong. He believes that it is morally indifferent whether or not he acts as he does.

[8] See *Freedom and Reason*, pp. 100 ff.

e.g., to imprison his debtors or to exterminate Jews. The morally weak agent, on the other hand, believes that he ought not to act as he does. In contrast to each of these, the amoral agent neither believes that he ought to act as he does nor does he believe that he ought not to act as he does.

It seems to me, however, that the indifferent-amoral agent has much more in common with the wicked (immoral) agent than with the silent-amoral agent. Consider, for example a person who harms another—say, he kills him in order to relieve him of his wallet—and who believes that such acts are morally permissible. If he also believes (as he no doubt would) that refraining from such acts is morally permissible, then he has adopted the indifferent-amoral position with respect to such acts. Shall we describe his act as amoral or wicked? Such a person is not, strictly speaking, lacking in moral convictions; indeed, he is convinced that what he does is morally all right. And it may well be that if he did judge it to be morally wrong, he would not do it (this may be true of the wicked agent as well). Thus, it cannot be said that moral considerations play no role at all in his decisions about what to do. In this sense, he is not amoral; rather, he fails to avoid doing something that is morally wrong because he has a false (or bad) moral belief— namely, that it is morally all right to kill someone in order to obtain his money. In this respect he is like the wicked agent. Now perhaps it is more perverse to believe that one *ought* to act in this way, but, surely, both are perverse moral beliefs. Thus, I am inclined to classify together Hare's fanatically wicked agent (who kills another for his money because he believes that one morally ought to act in this way) and his indifferent-amoral agent (who kills another for his money and believes that such acts are not wrong) as being two kinds of perversely wicked agents. Whereas both are like the agent who acts amorally in killing others— in that neither believes that such acts are morally wrong, both are also unlike the agent who acts amorally—in that

68

they believe that killing others for personal gain is morally right.[9]

Thus, it is only the agent who has adopted the silent-amoral position who can be said to act in a truly amoral manner. Such a person, if he does what is wrong, neither believes that it is wrong nor believes that it is right. The truly amoral agent must be characterized, not as *believing* that what he does is *neither* morally wrong (something that one ought not to do) *nor* morally wrong not to do (something that one ought to do), but rather as *neither believing* that it is morally wrong *nor believing* that it is not morally wrong.

3. The Refusal To Make Moral Judgments

Let us turn now to a consideration of this kind of amorality. It will be instructive at this point to consider what Hare says about this sort of convictionless amorality. For it shall be my contention that Hare misconstrues the nature of amorality, and that taking note of this will lead us to the correct characterization.

Hare suggests that a person who knows what it means to say that an act is morally wrong might consider the question of whether or not killing others for personal gain

---

[9] It is true that they differ in one significant respect; in the one case the agent believes that acts of this sort are morally required and acts directly on this belief (out of a perverse sense of duty); whereas in the other case the agent acts for some other reason (such as personal gain) and merely believes that such acts are not morally forbidden. However, as I shall later point out, this difference is mitigated by Hare when he argues that, *unless one is a fanatic*, one will be not only unwilling to universally prescribe that such acts be *required*, but also unwilling to prescribe that such acts be *permitted*. See his *Freedom and Reason*, pp. 102 and 196, and *Essays on the Moral Concepts* (London: Macmillan and Co., 1972), p. 101. Thus, both are really "fanatics," according to Hare. Hare himself recognizes their kinship—their common perversity—which consists in their both being willing to universally prescribe that such acts as killing or harming others be, at least, permitted.

is morally wrong and then refrain from making any moral judgment at all about this matter. Indeed, Hare thinks that one way to escape from the conclusion that would otherwise be forced on one by a "golden-rule" argument—a way of escape open even to the non-fanatic, who is unwilling to universally prescribe that such acts of killing be required (or even permitted)—is to adopt this silent-amoral position. On closer inspection, however, it appears that Hare is mistaken about this. It is possible for a non-fanatic who has considered this question to refuse to *say* whether or not such acts are morally wrong, but, I shall argue, it is no longer possible for him to refuse to *believe* that such acts are morally wrong.

Hare thinks that one may escape the force of golden-rule arguments by adopting either the indifferent-amoral position or the silent-amoral position. In fact—as I shall now try to show—neither of these positions is open to the non-fanatic *once he has considered the question*. To see this, let us consider what is involved, according to Hare, in considering whether some act that one proposes to do is morally wrong. To consider this question is to address oneself to a golden-rule type of argument—i.e., to consider whether one is willing to universally prescribe that such acts be done. Now it must be pointed out that Hare confuses matters by having the moral deliberator ask what seems to me to be the wrong question. Hare has the moral deliberator ask himself what he ought to do and construes this as asking oneself whether one is morally required to do the act in question or whether one is morally required not to do the act.[10] But, who but a Harean fanatic would even be tempted to think that one is morally required, say, to imprison one's debtors? Surely the question that any normal person would ask is: "Is such an act morally permissible?"[11]

---

[10] See his *Freedom and Reason*, p. 91.

[11] This was first pointed out by D. P. Gauthier in his "Hare's Debtors," *Mind*, vol. 77, 1968, pp. 400-05.

Thus, the question to be considered is not, "Am I willing to universally prescribe that such acts be *required*?" but, "Am I willing to prescribe that such acts be *permitted*?" Unless a person is a fanatic, he will be unable to universally prescribe that such acts be permitted, since he will be unwilling to have others imprison him in the hypothetical situation where he is someone's debtor.[12] In that case, it seems, he must reject the judgment that it is all right (permissible) to imprison one's debtors; he must conclude that it is not the case that this is all right and, hence, that it would be morally wrong to do so. Hare fails to see this because he views the moral deliberator as asking himself whether he is willing to prescribe that imprisoning one's debtors be *required*. Thus, Hare says that if he is unwilling to universally prescribe *this*, he is only forced to conclude that it is not the case that one ought to imprison one's debtors. He is not thereby forced to conclude that one ought not to imprison ones debtors (i.e,. that it would be wrong to do so).[13] But suppose one finds oneself unwilling

[12] Gauthier (see previous note) also points out that there are difficulties with interpreting Hare's prescriptivism in such a way as to apply both to judgments of moral requiredness and to judgments of moral permissibility. In particular, he questions the inference from "It is all right for C to imprison me" to "C may imprison me"—where the latter is understood in such a way that assenting to it involves consenting to C's being allowed to imprison oneself. And H. J. Gensler and S. B. Torrance have each argued that the analysis of "all right" in terms of a universalizable permission is inconsistent with Hare's analysis of "ought" in terms of a universalizable prescription. See H. J. Gensler, "The Prescriptivism Incompleteness Theorem," *Mind*, vol. 85, 1976, pp. 589-96, and S. B. Torrance, "Prescriptivism and Incompleteness," *Mind*, vol. 90, 1981, pp. 580-85. I am not at all sure that Hare can successfully answer these objections. However, I shall, for the sake of argument, allow the validity of the above inference. What I am concerned to show here is that insofar as Hare's golden-rule argument *can* be applied to judgments of moral permissibility, then neither of the two amoral escape-routes is really open to the non-fanatic.

[13] " . . . That argument only forced him to *reject* the moral judgment 'I ought to imprison A for debt.' It did not force him to assent to any

even to prescribe that such acts be *permitted*? As Hare himself later admits, it is as unlikely that anyone but a fanatic would be willing to prescribe that such acts be permitted as it is that he would be willing to prescribe that they be required.[14] But if a person finds himself unable to prescribe that such acts be permitted, then he will be forced to reject not only the judgment that such acts ought to be done, but also the judgment that such acts are all right. Hence, it will not be open to him to adopt the indifferent-amoral position, for this position is open only to the fanatic, who is willing to prescribe either that such acts be required or, at least, that they be permitted.

If the escape-route of adopting the indifferent-amoral position is not really open to the nonfanatic, then what about the silent-amoral position? I shall now argue that adopting this position is not really possible either—given Hare's assumptions. Hare fails to see this because he does not clearly distinguish between what it is to *say* that an act is morally wrong (a linguistic performance) and what it is to *believe* that an act is morally wrong (a mental state). To *say* that an act is morally wrong is, according to Hare's theory, to universally prescribe that such acts not be done. But now what is it to *believe* that an act is morally wrong? Surely, one can believe that an act is wrong without saying so. Thus, believing that an act is wrong cannot consist in prescribing that such acts not be done. Or, does Hare suppose that believing an act to be wrong consists in saying to oneself that such acts are wrong—and thus prescribing

judgment; in particular, he remained free to assent, either to the judgment that he ought not to imprison A for debt (which is the one we want him to accept) or to the judgment that it is neither the case that he ought, nor the case that he ought not (that it is, in short, indifferent); and he remained free, also, to say 'I am just not making any moral judgments at all about the case.' " (*Freedom and Reason*, p. 100.) In his most recent book Hare reaffirms the existence of this moral escape route. See *Moral Thinking* (Oxford: Clarendon Press, 1981), p. 183.

[14] "It is as unlikely that he will *permit* C to put him (B) into prison as that he will *prescribe* it." (*Freedom and Reason*, p. 102. See also p. 196.)

to oneself that such acts not be done? But the notion of prescribing to oneself (like the notion of commanding oneself) is problematic.

I suggest, then, that Hare must identify *believing* that an act is morally wrong with *being willing* to prescribe universally that such acts not be done—i.e., that not doing such acts be required. Thus, whereas Hare can give a *prescriptivist* analysis of what it means to *say* that an act is morally wrong, he must give a *volitional* analysis of *believing* that an act is morally wrong. It is perhaps not so clear, however, what volitional state believing that an act is *not wrong* is to be identified with. It is clear that we cannot identify it with being willing to universally prescribe that such acts be required, for this would be to believe that *not doing* such acts is wrong (i.e., that such acts ought to be done). I suggest, then, that to believe that an act is not wrong is, for Hare, to be willing to universally prescribe that such acts *may* be done—i.e., that such acts be permitted.

But if one is not a fanatic—and thus cannot prescribe this—must one not come to believe that such acts are morally wrong? Hare thinks that one need not, because he thinks that one can simply refrain from making "any *universal* prescriptions, prohibitions, or permissions for circumstances just like this."[15] But this is only to hold that he need not *say* whether or not such acts are wrong. If he is unwilling to universally prescribe that such acts be permitted, he must be said to *believe*—at least, if he is consistent—that such acts are morally wrong. For, if a person is unwilling to prescribe that such acts be permitted, then he must—if he is consistent in his volitions—be willing to universally prescribe that not doing such acts be required.[16]

---

[15] *Essays on the Moral Concepts*, p. 101.

[16] Actually, it seems more natural to me to identify "*A*'s believing that X is wrong" with "*A*'s being *unwilling* to universally prescribe that X be permitted" rather than "*A*'s being *willing* to universally prescribe that not-X be required" (as Hare seems to suggest). If so, then the further move that I discuss here is unnecessary.

And this is to believe that such acts are morally wrong (ought not to be done). Now perhaps Hare thinks that, although such a person is unwilling to universally prescribe that such acts be permitted (since he is unwilling to permit others to imprison him if he is a debtor and refuses to pay), he is also unwilling to universally prescribe that not doing such acts be required (since he wished to imprison *his* debtors). But in this case—as Kant pointed out—he will be guilty of a contradiction of the will.

The only alternative open to Hare is to suppose that such a person simply refuses to even consider whether he is willing or unwilling to universally prescribe that such acts be permitted (or, perhaps, even required). Since he has not even considered the question of what he is willing to universally prescribe, we can only say that it is not the case that he believes such acts to be wrong (i.e., that he is willing to universally prescribe that they not be done), and it is not the case that he believes that such acts are not wrong (i.e., that he is willing to universally prescribe that such acts may be done). But in this case he does not *first* consider whether his proposed act is right or wrong and then refuse to make a judgment; he does not first listen to a "golden-rule" argument and then choose to stand mute. Rather, he does not even listen to (or consider) such arguments. He is not merely silent on moral matters; he turns a deaf ear to moral arguments. He is, thus, not so much *morally mute* as he is (willfully) *morally deaf*.

4. *Lack of Moral Concern*

What shall we say, then, about the person who simply refuses to even consider whether or not his acts are morally wrong—the "morally deaf" person? Perhaps he is the true amoralist we have been searching for. But why does he refuse to even consider whether or not his acts are morally wrong? Perhaps the explanation of his refusing to even consider the moral question is that he is solely concerned to pursue his own good and is indifferent about whether or not his acts are morally wrong. This sort of explanation might be proposed by those who adopt cognitivist analyses of the nature of moral beliefs. On such views one might believe that certain of one's acts have the (definable or indefinable) characteristic of moral wrongness, but simply not care that this is so. Thus, on a cognitivist account of moral beliefs, what I have called "morally indifferent" behavior is possible. The agent's indifference to the rightness or wrongness of what he does can reveal itself in the fact that he is not motivated by the belief that what he does is morally wrong. And, as we have seen, his indifference to whether or not his acts have the (definable or indefinable) characteristic of wrongness can also manifest itself in his simply not bothering to consider the question of the rightness or wrongness of what he does—in refusing to make any moral judgments at all. But it is not clear what it means, on a noncognitivist account of moral beliefs, to say that one does not care whether or not his acts are morally wrong. For on such accounts having some con-attitude toward a certain kind of act will be a necessary condition of believing that an act of this sort is wrong. What, then, can it mean, on an account like Hare's, to say that someone does not care whether what he does is morally wrong? We cannot say that this means that he does not care whether he is willing or unwilling to universally prescribe that such acts be permitted. For if we say this we shall be equating the moral wrongness of such acts with his being unwilling to universally prescribe that such acts be permitted, and this would commit us to a form of naturalism (or descriptivism) which is anathema for noncognitivists like Hare. The notion of moral indifference—of not caring whether one's acts (or someone else's) are right or wrong—simply makes no sense on a purely noncognitivist account of moral beliefs, because there is nothing about which one can be indifferent—i.e., there is no possible fact, consisting in a certain act's being morally wrong, that one could either care or not care about. For to believe that an act is wrong is not to accept as true some proposition to this effect; it is rather to have a universalizable and dominant con-attitude toward it (or, as Hare puts it, to accept a universal and overriding prescription prohibiting such acts).

But perhaps there is a kind of moral indifference that a theory like Hare's can recognize. This would consist in a person's not caring whether or not the acts he performs are *acts that he would come to believe to be morally wrong if he considered the question of their moral wrongness*. Thus, because he does not care about *this* (perhaps he cares only about what promotes his advantage), he never considers whether or not his acts are morally wrong and thus has no moral beliefs at all about them. So perhaps we can describe the person who does not care whether or not his acts are the kind which he would be willing to universally prescribe as permissible, if he were to consider this question, as, *in this sense*, morally indifferent. Thus, we have found one type of amoral behavior (other than that which involves lack of the concept or moral wrongness) that is consistent with Hare's theory. But it is not the kind of amorality that Hare has in mind when he speaks of the silent-amoral agent who, even *after considering* whether his proposed act would be right or wrong, chooses to stand mute and refrain from making any moral judgments at all.

We have, however, come some way toward understanding what amorality essentially consists in. For a lack of concern about whether or not one's acts are morally wrong—or about whether or not one would judge one's acts to be morally wrong if one considered this question—turns out (on any plausible cognitivist or noncognitivist account of moral judgments) to be a lack of concern for the interests or welfare of others. A person who does not care whether or not what he does is the sort of act he would be unwilling to universally prescribe as permissible if he considered this—i.e., if he considered the hypothetical circumstance where he is in someone else's shoes—shows an appalling lack of concern for the interests of others. Moreover, any plausible explanation from a cognitivist point of view, of why someone does not care whether or not his actions possess the characteristic of wrongness, would, I think, have to appeal to this same lack of concern.

If this is correct, then we seem to have no reason to deny that amoral wrongdoing can also be immoral. Insofar as we believe this lack of concern for the interests of others to be the result of the agent's having been psychologically damaged as a result of emotional deprivation in childhood (as many have said about the psychopath), we may be inclined to excuse it. But in such cases it is this, and not just the absence of moral belief or even the lack of moral concepts, that excuses. In other cases, however, we may have no good reason for excusing this lack of concern; hence, insofar as a person's lack of moral convictions is the result of his simply not having bothered to consider whether certain kinds of acts are morally right or wrong, lack of moral beliefs does not seem to be an excusing condition. Thus, amorality is one of the possible forms of immorality.

5. Amorality, Wickedness, and Moral Indifference

There are some important similarities between amorality, as I have conceived of it, and perverse wickedness—especially on the cognitivist interpretation of perverse wickedness. Indeed, it might be argued that what those who wish to conceive of wickedness in this way are really trying to get at is best described as a kind of amorality— i.e., wrongdoing due to the fact that the agent himself fails to believe that acts of this sort are wrong. Neither the amoral nor the perversely wicked agent believes that what he does is wrong; and, if one adopts a cognitivist perspective, both the amoral and the perversely wicked agent may be said to be ignorant that such acts are morally wrong.

Now I argued earlier that ignorance of the most basic moral principle according to which one's act is wrong is not really possible, since this would be incompatible with knowing what it means to say that an act is morally wrong. This is controversial, and the argument for this view will not even approach completeness until Chapter Six, where I shall attempt to deal with some of the criticisms that have been levelled at this kind of view. It is important to recognize, however, that this view allows that an agent can be ignorant of the most general *substantive* moral principle according to which his act is wrong.[17] Knowing that for an act to be morally wrong it must be such and such—i.e., knowing the analytic principle that defines what it means to say that an act is morally wrong—one may still fail to know which acts are such and such and therefore wrong. The amoral agent is ignorant of the basic substantive moral principle according to which his act is wrong, because he does not even bother to consider the question of which acts are morally wrong. He fails to make the effort required in order to determine whether acts of the sort he performs are morally right or wrong, because he does not really care whether they are morally right or wrong. Thus, we have here a kind of ignorance of moral principles that is not only possible; it is very close to the kind of ignorance that is supposed to characterize the agent of a perversely wicked act (on the cognitivist interpretation). For here the agent is not only ignorant of the most basic substantive moral principle according to which his act is wrong; his ignorance is nonexcusing and blameworthy, since it reflects a certain kind of character-fault—namely, a lack of moral concern.

Now, as we have seen, the agent of a perversely wicked act is not described, by those who conceive of wickedness in this way, as lacking in moral concern. This is not supposed to be the cause of his wrongdoing. Rather, it is suggested that if he himself believed that what he does is

---

[17] By a *substantive* moral principle I mean one that tells us which acts are right and wrong, as opposed to one that tells us what it is for an act to be right or wrong (or what it means to say that an act is right or wrong).

wrong he would be inclined not to do it. That is why he is also characterized as believing that such acts are right. But, as I argued earlier, if it is not allowed that the agent of a perversely wicked act is lacking in conscientiousness, then it is difficult to explain why he is ignorant of the moral principle according to which his act is wrong. If he is not lacking in moral concern, then why does he not make the effort required in order to determine whether such acts are wrong? Thus, whereas the ignorance attributed to the amoral agent is easily explained in terms of his indifference to matters of (moral) right and wrong, the ignorance attributed to the agent of a perversely wicked act is difficult, if not impossible, to explain.

The amoral agent fails to avoid wrongdoing because he does not care whether or not what he does is wrong. But such a lack of moral concern seems to make no sense, given a purely noncognitivist account of moral beliefs. For, on such accounts a person's moral principles are simply the expression of his own pro- or con-attitudes. Moreover, since noncognitivist analyses of moral beliefs make having some con-attitude toward X a necessary condition of believing that X is wrong, it makes no sense on such views to suppose that someone might believe that an act is wrong but not care whether or not he avoids doing it. Thus, what I have called morally indifferent behavior is not logically possible, given such analyses. The amoral agent does not both believe that what he does is wrong and yet not care that it is wrong. Rather, he is so unconcerned about wrongdoing that he does not even bother to consider whether his acts are right or wrong. Hence, he has no moral beliefs at all about what he does. His lack of moral concern manifests itself in a refusal to make any moral judgments in the first place. This kind of moral indifference makes no sense either from a noncognitivist perspective. For on this view there is for the judger no possible fact, existing independently of his con-attitudes and constituting the moral wrongness of his act, that he can either care or not care about. Earlier,

I suggested that perhaps a noncognitivist like Hare could construe lack of moral concern as an indifference to whether or not one would judge one's actions to be morally wrong if one considered this question. But since whatever moral judgments one were to make would simply be an expression of one's own pro- or con-attitudes, this construal of moral indifference makes it seem paradoxical.

I said earlier that the term "amoral" is commonly applied both to what I am calling amoral behavior and to what I have called morally indifferent behavior—even though these are quite different. I should like to conclude by offering an explanation of this. Amoral and morally indifferent wrongdoing are different in that in the former case the agent neither believes that what he does is wrong nor believes that it is not wrong, whereas in the latter case the agent believes that what he does is wrong but does not care that it is wrong. Nevertheless, amoral wrongdoing (when it is blameworthy) and morally indifferent wrongdoing are similar in that they reflect the same basic moral defect on the part of the agent—namely, an insensitivity or indifference to the feelings and interests of others. The morally indifferent agent is indifferent to the moral wrongness of his act because he lacks a concern for the welfare of others or, at least, lacks an equal concern for the good of everyone alike. This same lack of concern is exhibited by the kind of amoral agent who turns a deaf ear to moral arguments and refuses to even consider whether what he does is morally wrong. If one is a cognitivist, one may say that this is because he does not care whether his acts benefit or harm others. If one is a noncognitivist, one may say that this is because he does not care whether or not he would be willing to universally prescribe that acts of this sort be permitted—i.e., he does not care whether or not he could assent to a prescription permitting such acts in the hypothetical situation where he is in the other person's shoes. This is also to exhibit an indifference to the welfare of others. Even in the case of amoral wrongdoing by an agent who lacks the concept of moral wrongness, such an agent may (as we have seen) still be blameworthy if his behavior manifests an utter disregard for the interests of others and there are no excusing conditions—such as lack of self-control or emotional impairment.

Morally indifferent behavior is conscious wrongdoing, whereas amoral behavior is not. In both cases, however, one's behavior manifests a lack of concern about whether or not one's behavior has the kind of features that one believes (or would come to believe) make one's behavior wrong.[18] And on the most plausible analyses—either cognitivist or noncognitivist—of what it means to say, or believe, that an act is morally wrong, this translates into a lack of concern for the interests or welfare of others. This lack of concern (or adequate concern) for others may plausibly be taken to constitute the essence of immorality in general. When, however, it causes the lack of moral belief, immorality takes on the form of amorality.

[18] In the case of the amoral agent who lacks the concept of moral wrongness we can still say that he is indifferent about whether his acts possess certain characteristics. These will be characteristics like hurting or deceiving others—characteristics which others (but not he himself) know to be wrong-making.

F O U R

* * * *

MORAL NEGLIGENCE

In cases of moral negligence the agent is ignorant that what he does is in violation of his own moral principles, and hence he mistakenly believes (assumes) that what he does is right—either that it is morally permissible or perhaps even that it is morally required.[1] Ignorance of this sort is sometimes excusing and sometimes not. Aristotle suggests that it is not excusing when it is due to carelessness or negligence.

> Indeed, we punish a man for his very ignorance, if he is thought to be responsible for the ignorance, as when penalties are doubled in the case of drunkenness; for the moving principle is in the man himself,

[1] In those cases of moral negligence where the agent fails to advert (or advert properly) to the features of the act that make it wrong he, of course, fails to believe that it is wrong. But it may be questioned whether he also believes that it is right. It is not as though he has considered the question and then concluded that what he does is not wrong. However, having no reason (given his inadvertence) to suspect that what he does is wrong, he acts on the assumption that it is right. In this sense he does believe that what he does is right (morally permissible). After all, he is not, like the agent of an amoral act, lacking in moral concern. In certain other cases of moral negligence, such as those involving self-deception, the agent may even have convinced himself that what he does is morally required.

82

since he had the power of not getting drunk and his getting drunk was the cause of his ignorance. And we punish those who are ignorant of anything in the laws that they ought to know and that is not difficult, and so too in the case of anything else that they are thought to be ignorant of through carelessness; we assume that it is in their power not to be ignorant, since they have the power of taking care.[2]

The general view suggested by Aristotle is that ignorance of (or error about) matters of fact is excusing, provided it is not due to negligence. I shall argue that if negligence is understood in a broad enough sense this view is correct. In all of those cases where one's ignorance fails to excuse, this could have been avoided by taking certain precautions that it was reasonable to expect one to have taken; and "negligence" in the most general sense may be defined as the failure to take those reasonable precautions necessary to avoid wrongdoing. More will need to be said later about the nature of these precautions and about the distinction between reasonable and unreasonable precautions. But for the time being, it is sufficient to define "moral negligence" as any case of wrongdoing due to culpable ignorance of the fact that one's act violates one's own moral principles. It is this kind of wrongdoing that is the subject of the present chapter.

1. The Nature of Moral Negligence

It is important to distinguish what I mean by "moral negligence" from what is often called "negligence" in legal contexts. Jurists often use this term to refer to a particular kind of wrong act—namely, conduct that involves an unreasonable risk of causing harm or damage: "negligence is unreasonably dangerous conduct—i.e., conduct abnormally likely to cause harm," or "negligence is conduct which

---

[2] *Nicomachean Ethics*, 1113b30-1114a3.

involves an unreasonably great risk of causing damage."[3] As I am using the term "moral negligence," however, it refers to any kind of morally wrong act due to a particular kind of shortcoming on the part of the agent—namely, a culpable failure to take those precautions necessary to assure oneself, before acting, that what one proposes to do is not in violation of one's moral principles. Conduct due to such a shortcoming may take various forms, including not only conduct that involves an unreasonable risk of harm but also conduct that is undoubtedly harmful, as well as conduct that involves breaking a promise or deceiving someone.

Someone might fail to keep a promise because he fails to remember that he has promised not to do what he is doing. If his failure to remember is culpable, he has acted in a morally negligent manner. Again, if a person says something that is, in the circumstances, highly misleading (so that those who hear this are deceived and led to act on false information), and if he could and should have realized this, he is guilty of moral negligence. And, as we have already seen, a person may deeply hurt and humiliate someone because he fails to think about how a certain remark he makes will affect this person. Thus, moral negligence includes all wrong behavior that results from the fact that the agent is ignorant that his act is wrong because he failed to take reasonable precautions to avoid such ignorance.

Some jurists do construe negligence in a manner closely analogous to the notion of moral negligence that I am here employing. H.L.A. Hart, for example, defines negligence as "a failure to take reasonable precautions against harm,

---

[3] The first of these definitions is from Henry W. Edgerton, "Negligence, Inadvertence, and Indifference: The Relation of Mental States to Negligence," *Harvard Law Review*, vol. 39, 1926. The second comes from Henry T. Terry, "Negligence," *Harvard Law Review*, vol. 29, 1915. Both are reprinted, in part, in Herbert Morris, ed., *Freedom and Responsibility* (Stanford, Calif: Stanford University Press, 1961). See pp. 243 and 247.

unaccompanied by intention or appreciation of the risk of harm."[4] If we also construe the notion of harm in a broad enough sense, so that deceiving someone or breaking a promise counts as harming, then this notion of negligence is very close to my notion of moral negligence.

Moral negligence may be seen as involving the violation of a kind of second-order moral duty. Given that it is morally wrong (or that we have a duty) not to do certain kinds of acts, it follows that we also have a duty to make sure that what we propose to do is not an act of one of these kinds (e.g., deceiving or promise breaking) or, if it is, that this consideration is outweighed by other morally relevant considerations. This duty to ascertain—before acting— whether one's proposed act is in conformity with or violates one's moral principles must be distinguished from the various duties we have not to do the various acts that are forbidden by our moral principles. For even after we have fulfilled our duty to determine whether or not a certain act is in violation of our moral principles and have decided that, all things considered, it does violate these principles, we may still fail to avoid this act. We may fail to avoid doing something that we have judged to be morally wrong because we simply do not care if what we do is morally wrong (morally indifferent wrongdoing), or because we prefer the pursuit of some other end to the avoidance of moral wrongdoing (preferential wickedness), or because we do not take the measures necessary to resist or control some contrary desire or emotion (one kind of moral weakness).

On the other hand it may be that we would have avoided

---

[4] See his "Negligence, *Mens Rea* and Criminal Responsibility," in *Punishment and Responsibility* (New York: Oxford University Press, 1968), p. 137. This definition is meant to apply only to inadvertent negligence and does not include willful negligence (or recklessness), where the agent has "an appreciation of the risk of harm." As I will explain later, I shall construe moral negligence in such a way as to include a kind of willful moral negligence—what I shall call moral recklessness.

the act had we judged it to be wrong, but that we did not judge it to be wrong. Some have suggested that this may be due to the fact that we are ignorant of, or mistaken about, some basic moral principle (in which case we would have an instance of perverse wickedness). It may also be the case that, although we desire to avoid moral wrong-doing and have correct (or good) basic moral principles, we nevertheless fail to realize that this act violates those principles; and if our failure to realize this is culpable, then this will be a case of moral negligence. But when is igno-rance of this sort culpable? I have suggested that it is cul-pable when it could have been avoided by taking certain precautionary measures and when it is reasonable to expect the agent to have taken such precautions. This raises two questions: (1) How might such ignorance be avoided? (2) What sorts of precautions against making errors in one's moral judgments is it reasonable to expect one to take?

The first thing one must do is to advert to, or think about, what one is doing. One must consider what sort of act it is, what the circumstances are, what the consequences are apt to be, etc. Sometimes one acts impulsively, without thinking at all about what one is doing. At other times one does think about what one is doing but is rather careless about this. One may consider certain aspects of what one does (e.g., how it amuses others) but fail to consider certain other aspects of it (e.g., how it humiliates someone). And in many cases where one fails to consider the morally rel-evant features of one's act—or, at least, fails to consider all of them—one will be open to reproach. It might be said, for example, that one ought to have considered how one's act would affect Smith's interests or whether one was showing favoritism to Jones, that one ought to have re-membered that one promised to help someone else or that Smith was sick.

But how could one help not having realized, considered, remembered, etc.? Perhaps we should ask: Why did one fail to realize, consider, remember, etc.? It may be that one did not realize that one's remark would hurt Smith's feelings because one was so intent on amusing one's friends. One did not realize that Smith was in trouble because one was so preoccupied with one's own problems. One failed to consider the interests of Smith because one's own ambitions prevented one from thinking of anything other than how one's own goals were affected. One did not realize that one was showing favoritism to Jones because one was so smitten by her beauty that one thought only about how to please her. One did not remember that one promised to give this piece of furniture to one's sister because an antique dealer offered one a very high price for it. One forgot that Jones was ill and should not be disturbed because one was so angry with him when one discovered what he had done.

Thus, we need to take care not to be blinded or distracted by anger, greed, lust, ambition, sorrow, disappointment, the desire to impress others, etc. Such feelings and desires not only cause us to do things that we believe to be morally wrong; sometimes they prevent us from seeing that what we do is wrong. In order to prevent them from doing this it is often necessary for us to take certain precautions and to adopt certain countermeasures. We must learn how to control our desires and feelings, and this involves learning what measures or steps we can take to prevent them from unduly influencing or obscuring our judgments about what we ought (or ought not) to do. We learn, for example, to anticipate the sorts of circumstances that generate strong feelings and desires and to be on our guard, so that when we do respond with the typical feelings or desires we can moderate their influence by deliberately focusing on those features of our action that these desires and feelings tend to obscure. If we know that we are inclined to be selfish or greedy or partial to those whom we like, at least in certain circumstances, here again we can learn how to remind ourselves of what we might otherwise ignore and to take certain countermeasures (bending over backwards, as we say, to be unselfish or fair). These are all ways of exercising rational control over one's feelings and desires, and we hold people responsible for exercising certain capacities of self-control that we (correctly or incorrectly) assume normal human beings to possess. Indeed, we hold people responsible not only for exercising such capacities of self-control; we hold them responsible for acquiring them, so that lack of such capacities does not always excuse.[5]

This brings us to the second question we raised about culpability for ignorance and mistakes: What sorts of precautions is it *reasonable* to expect a person to take in order to avoid ignorance and mistakes? An issue has been raised by jurists in connection with criminal negligence that must also be raised in connection with moral negligence. This is the issue of whether negligence should be judged according to so-called "objective" or "subjective" standards. According to H.L.A. Hart, a person is said to be judged negligent according to an *objective* standard if the fault attributed to him consists in a failure "to take those precautions which any reasonable man with normal capacities would in the circumstances have taken."[6] However, as Hart points out, the difficulty with employing such a standard is that it leads "to an individual being treated for purposes of conviction and punishment as if he possessed capacities for control of his conduct which he did not possess, but which an ordinary or reasonable man possesses and would have exercised."[7] Thus, it has been suggested that, from a moral point of view, a *subjective* standard is preferable—one that makes the ascription of negligence depend on an affirmative answer to the question: "Could the accused, given his mental and physical capacities, have taken these precautions?"[8]

[5] This is pointed out by Gary Watson in "Skepticism About Weakness of Will," *The Philosophical Review*, vol. 86, 1977, pp. 316-39. See pp. 331-32.

[6] H.L.A. Hart, *Punishment and Responsibility*, p. 154.

[7] *Ibid.*, p. 153.

[8] *Ibid.*, p. 154.

It may seem obvious that we ought to employ such a subjective standard in judging moral negligence, especially since the reasons given for employing an objective standard for criminal negligence have to do with considerations of the practical efficacy of applying the law—considerations which do not seem relevant to judgments of moral negligence.[9] But perhaps the use of an objective standard can be justified even in judgments of moral negligence; for even though the agent at present lacks those capacities for thinking about and controlling his conduct that we attribute to the normal reasonable man, it may be that we judge that he could have acquired or developed these capacities. Often such capacities can be acquired only if we are willing to sacrifice the time and effort required to develop certain kinds of habits and skills. Jurists have also pointed out that sometimes lack of normal capacities, instead of excusing one, may simply mean that one is obligated to take special precautions: "It is obvious that blind men take different precautions than those taken by men who can see and that conduct which would be careful in one who can see is negligent in one who cannot."[10] Thus, if a person is terribly forgetful or absent-minded, we expect him to take extra precautions to compensate for this. This holds true also for other kinds of defects, such as quick-temperedness, so long as the agent is aware that he has them.

So far we have been discussing only what might be called "inadvertent moral negligence." However, as I am construing the notion of moral negligence, it includes all cases of wrongdoing due to culpable ignorance or mistake about some morally relevant fact, such that one does not realize that one's act is the sort of act that one believes to be morally wrong. Sometimes this is due to carelessness—i.e., to one's having failed to advert to those features of one's act that make it wrong, when one could and should have. But, as

[9] See *ibid.*, p. 155.

[10] Warren A. Seavey, "Negligence—Subjective or Objective?" *Harvard Law Review*, vol. 41, 1927. Reprinted in Morris, ed., *Freedom and Responsibility*. See p. 260.

I shall explain more fully below, there may be other causes of this as well, and some of these may also be such that we hold the agent responsible for his ignorance. For example, the agent may fail to realize that his act is the sort of act that he believes to be morally wrong because he is guilty of self-deception. He may have deliberately ignored those features of his act that make his act wrong, or he may have indulged in rationalization in order to persuade himself that it is nevertheless justified, all things considered (even though he "knows in his heart" that it does not really conform to his moral principles). In other cases the agent may realize that his act has a certain feature or features that might make it wrong, depending on other features or circumstances of the act. Perhaps it involves deception or infringing on someone's right to something. But the agent may do it anyway, assuming that it is probably all right, or hoping that it is, but not deliberating further to make sure that it is not wrong. I shall refer to such cases as cases of *moral recklessness*. In both of these cases—moral recklessness and self-deceptive moral wrongdoing—the agent is not entirely unaware of his own wrongdoing, nor is the wrongdoing clearly unintentional. In these respects they differ significantly from cases of inadvertent moral negligence. Nevertheless, as I shall explain when I discuss them below, there are good reasons for classifying them both as types of moral negligence.

2. Negligence and Weakness of Will

Moral negligence and moral weakness are different. In cases of moral negligence the agent fails to believe that his act is wrong when he could and should have realized this. In cases of moral weakness the agent believes that his act is wrong but does it nevertheless. Yet, in other respects they are quite similar. In both cases the agent fails to act in accordance with his own moral principles. (This distinguishes both from cases of perverse wickedness and amorality.) In both cases the agent desires to avoid wrongdoing and prefers this to the realization of whatever end happens to be the object of his action. Thus, in both cases the agent is inclined to feel remorse afterwards when he reflects on the wrongness of his act (in the case of the morally weak agent) or is made to realize the wrongness of his act (in the case of moral negligence). In these respects both differ from cases of moral indifference and preferential wickedness.

Indeed, I shall argue that, although they are in one respect quite different, moral negligence and moral weakness are in fact close cousins. Their kinship consists in the fact that they exhibit the same basic fault on the part of the agent—namely, a failure to take those measures and precautions necessary to ensure that one's actions are in conformity with one's moral principles. Moreover, in both cases this involves a failure to exercise certain capacities of rational self-control.

In order to see how this is so, it will be useful to consider Aristotle's account of incontinence (*akrasia*). This will involve a brief excursion into Aristotelian exegesis but one which, I hope, will prove enlightening. For it shall be my contention that, for Aristotle, the notion of incontinence includes both moral negligence and moral weakness, but that Aristotle does not clearly distinguish between them. This is because he is more concerned with what they have in common—namely, both are cases where the agent fails to act in accordance with his own moral principles because he fails to exercise certain capacities of rational self-control.

Aristotle begins his account by characterizing the agent of an incontinent act as knowing that what he does is wrong but doing it nevertheless as a result of desire or emotion. "The incontinent man, knowing that what he does is bad, does it as a result of passion, while the continent man, knowing that his appetites are bad, refuses on account of his rational principle to follow them."[11] Now this certainly sounds like a description of weakness of will rather than

---

[11] *Nicomachean Ethics*, 1145b10-15. (W. D. Ross translation.)

negligence. But we must remember that even the morally negligent agent knows (or believes) that what he does is wrong in the sense that he knows (or believes) that acts of this sort are wrong; he simply fails to realize that his act is an act of this sort and hence wrong. Now, strangely enough, this is precisely what Aristotle seems to say about the incontinent agent when he comes to consider why, if the incontinent agent knows that what he does is wrong, he allows himself to be led by desire or emotion to do it.

Aristotle points out that in order for a person's conduct to be governed by a correct practical principle he must not only know the general principle, he must also, on the proper occasion, recognize that his particular action falls under this principle:

> . . . Since there are two kinds of premises, there is nothing to prevent a man's having both premises and acting against his knowledge, provided that he is using only the universal premises and not the particular; for it is particular acts that have to be done. And there are also two kinds of universal terms; one is predicable of the agent, the other of the object; e.g., "dry food is good for every man," and "I am a man," or "such and such food is dry"; but *whether "this food is such and such," of this the incontinent man either has not or is not exercising the knowledge.*[12]

In order to fully understand this account we must understand Aristotle's distinction between having and exercising knowledge, and we must also understand Aristotle's account (given later) of what causes this kind of ignorance.

The distinction between having and exercising knowledge is employed elsewhere by Aristotle in a number of contexts, but the closest parallel to the way in which this distinction is employed here occurs in the *Prior Analytics*, where Aristotle is discussing knowledge and error with

[12] *Ibid.*, 1146b35-1147a10. Emphasis added.

respect to sensible, particular things. We can have knowledge (or be ignorant or make mistakes) with respect to
particular things in three different senses, he suggests: "For
to know is used in three senses: it may mean either to *have
knowledge* of the universal or to *have knowledge* proper to
the matter at hand or to exercise such knowledge: conse-
quently three kinds of error are also possible."[13]

Aristotle gives examples to illustrate this. If a person
knows that *all* triangles have angles equal to two right
angles, then there is a sense in which he knows this to be
true of this figure inscribed in the semicircle—since it is a
triangle. This is to have knowledge of the universal with
respect to this triangle. But a person can know that every
triangle has angles equal to two right angles and yet fail
to recognize that this particular figure is a triangle. In this
case he has knowledge of the universal, but he does not
have "knowledge proper to the matter in hand" (i.e.,
knowledge of the particular as such). Suppose that he does
recognize this figure to be a triangle. In this case he has
knowledge both of the universal and knowledge proper to
the matter at hand. But suppose that, although he knows
that every triangle has angles equal to two right angles and
that this figure is a triangle, he nevertheless fails to draw
the conclusion that this figure has angles equal to two right
angles. This is certainly possible, according to Aristotle:

> Nothing prevents a man who knows both that A
> belongs to the whole of B and that B again belongs to
> C, thinking that A does not belong to C, e.g., knowing
> that every mule is sterile and that this is a mule, and
> thinking that this animal is with foal: for he does not
> know that A belongs to C, unless he considers the two
> propositions together. . . . For when he thinks that the
> mule is with foal he has not the knowledge in the sense
> of its actual exercise. . . .[14]

[13] *Prior Analytics*, 67a1-10 (translated by A. J. Jenkinson).
[14] *Ibid.*, 67a30-67b35.

In this case he *has knowledge* that this particular figure is a triangle (or that this particular animal is a mule) *but without exercising it*—since he does not use it, together with the knowledge he has that all triangles have angles equal to two right angles (or that all mules are sterile), to draw the conclusion that this figure has angles equal to two right angles (or that this animal is sterile).

If we now draw the relevant analogies to the case discussed in the *Nicomachean Ethics*, we get the following results. The agent knows that dry food is good for one, but he fails to know that the piece of food before him is good for him (so he chooses to eat something not as good for him). Why? Aristotle suggests that this is because, although he knows that such and such food (e.g., chicken) is dry, he either does not have the knowledge that *this* food is dry or else he has it but is not exercising it. Thus, his ignorance that this food is good for him is due either to the fact that he does not recognize this food to be such and such (does not even *have* this knowledge) or else it is due to the fact that, although he does recognize this food to be such and such (e.g., chicken), he does not conjoin this information with that contained in the other premises in order to infer that this food is good for him—i.e., he does not *exercise* his knowledge that this food is such and such.[15] In either case he does not really know that this food is good for him and this explains why he does not choose to eat it.

But what explains why he either fails to realize that this food is such and such or fails to use this knowledge to infer that this food is good for him? Aristotle says that it is because "incontinent people must be said to be in a similar condition to men asleep, mad, or drunk." "For outbursts of anger and sexual appetite and some other passions, it

---

[15] He may, however, exercise the knowledge he has of the two universal premises, since he may conjoin them and conclude that such and such food is good for one.

is evident, actually alter our bodily constitution, and in some men even produce fits of madness."[16]

The suggestion seems to be that, like people who are asleep, mad, or drunk, the incontinent agent is temporarily incapacitated—in this case by some desire or emotion that he has allowed to get out of control. The result is that he is either so blinded by appetite or passion that he does not see that his act is an instance of a kind he believes to be wrong, or else he sees that it is an act of that sort but forgets for the moment that such acts are wrong. Perhaps, for example, sexual appetite blinds him—at least for the moment—to the adulterous nature of his act and allows him to see it only as something immensely pleasurable. Or, perhaps, although he realizes that what he is doing is beating his wife, his rage prevents him from reminding himself how terribly wrong it is to do such a thing. Later, when the appetite has been satisfied or the passion has spent itself and he realizes what he has done (awakens, comes to his senses, is in a more sober frame of mind), he is inclined to feel remorse and regret what he has done. He is, nevertheless, responsible for his ignorance, and hence blameworthy, because he should and could have controlled his appetite or passion.[17]

What is interesting about this account is how it attributes to the incontinent agent elements of both negligence and weakness of will. Insofar as it attributes to him a lack of rational self-control over his desires and emotions (if he had properly managed them, they would not have incapacitated him—blinded him or made him forget), it suggests that the fault is weakness of will. But insofar as it claims that he does not fully realize that his particular act is wrong, it suggests that the act is due to culpable ignorance. Had he taken the proper steps and precautions nec-

---

[16] *Nicomachean Ethics*, 1147a10-20.

[17] Aristotle claims that the incontinent agent is defeated by desires and emotions that most people are able to master. See *Nicomachean Ethics*, 1150a10-15 and 1150b10-15.

essary to manage his desires and emotions, he would have realized that his act was wrong. This makes it seem like a case of moral negligence.

Indeed some scholars have accused Aristotle of not being willing to recognize any genuine cases of moral weakness at all—i.e., cases where the agent fully realizes that his act is wrong, but does it anyway, due to the influence of desire or emotion. Thus, it has been said that Aristotle was blind to the phenomenon of moral struggle.[18] But what we need to realize is that moral struggle can occur on two different levels; and this is what Aristotle failed to make clear.

The morally weak agent realizes full well that his particular act is wrong (he is not blinded by desire or passion). Whether or not Aristotle elsewhere recognizes the possibility of such behavior or agrees with Socrates that it is impossible is still a matter of controversy among scholars.[19] It is clear, however, that in the central passages designed to explain incontinence that we have been looking at here, what Aristotle is describing is not a case of moral weakness but rather a case of moral negligence. A person who chooses to make a certain remark because he believes that he will thereby amuse or impress his friends may be so consumed with the desire to amuse or impress that he fails to see that his remark may also insult and hurt the feelings of one of them. But if his act is blameworthy, it is a case of moral negligence—not a case of moral weakness.

Yet, as I pointed out earlier, there is a certain kinship between moral negligence and moral weakness. In both cases there is a failure to exercise certain capacities of rational self-control over one's desires and emotions so as to ensure that one's actions are in conformity with one's moral principles.[20] The difference is that in cases of moral neg-

[18] See, for example, W. D. Ross, *Aristotle* (New York: Meridian Books, Inc., 1959), pp. 217-18.

[19] For a good discussion of this controversy see W.F.R. Hardie, *Aristotle's Ethical Theory* (Oxford: Clarendon Press, 1968), pp. 258-92.

[20] H.L.A. Hart points out that negligence involves a fault consisting

ligence desire or passion prevents the agent from judging that his act is wrong in the first place, whereas in cases of moral weakness desire or passion prevents one from acting on one's judgment. This shows that one's desires and emotions need to be controlled on two different levels, and hence that lack of self-control (or incontinence, in Aristotle's sense) can also occur on two different levels.

3. Moral Recklessness

Jurists commonly distinguish between negligence proper (or inadvertent negligence) and recklessness (or willful negligence). "Recklessness" refers to the conscious choice of a course of action that involves an unreasonable risk of damage or harm. Whereas in cases of negligence proper the agent fails to realize that his conduct is unreasonably dangerous, in cases of recklessness he is aware of this but chooses to take the risk of doing damage or harm rather than alter his behavior. It should also be pointed out that in cases of recklessness, although the agent is aware of the risk, he does not really believe that damage or harm will ensue, but mistakenly thinks, or hopes, that it will probably be averted in this case.[21] Thus, he cannot be said to intentionally act so as to cause damage or harm, although he does intentionally run the risk of doing damage or harm.

Let us now consider whether an analogous distinction might be drawn between moral negligence proper (or inadvertent moral negligence) and something that might be called moral recklessness. I have said that moral negligence

---

essentially in the failure to exercise "the capacities and powers of normal persons to think about and control their conduct." *Punishment and Responsibility*, p. 140.

[21] "The party runs a risk of which he is conscious; but he thinks (for a reason which he examines insufficiently) that the mischief will probably be averted in the given instance." John Austin, *Lectures on Jurisprudence* (London: John Murray, 1873); in Morris, ed., *Freedom and Responsibility*, p. 240.

involves a violation of a second-order duty of due care—namely, a duty to take those precautions necessary to assure oneself, before acting, that one's actions are not in violation of one's moral principles. One violates this duty when one fails to adequately advert to the morally relevant features of one's act, and one also violates this duty when, having adverted to the morally relevant features of one's act, one fails to deliberate adequately in order to assure oneself that one's act is not, all things considered, wrong. In the former case we have inadvertent moral negligence; in the latter case we have what I shall call moral recklessness. For example, someone might act impulsively, failing to advert properly (when he can and should) to those features of his act that make it wrong. This would be a case of inadvertent moral negligence. On the other hand, a person might be aware that the act has some feature or features that might, depending on other circumstances, make it wrong; but he does it anyway, assuming or hoping that it is probably all right, but without deliberating further (when he could and should) to make sure that it is. This is what I am calling moral recklessness.

Moral recklessness must be distinguished from acting recklessly in the legal sense. It is, of course, morally wrong not only to deliberately kill or injure others; it is also wrong to act in such a way as to knowingly create an unreasonable risk of death or injury to others. But this is not what I mean by "moral recklessness." Needlessly exposing others to danger (say, by reckless driving) is a morally wrong act in the same sense as deceiving others or actually injuring them—i.e., it is a violation of a first-order moral duty. But, as we have seen, morally wrong acts of each of these kinds can be done for a variety of reasons and hence can be instances of different forms of immoral behavior. It may be, for example, that one simply prefers to promote one's own advantage rather than avoid risking death or injury to someone, in which case one's reckless behavior will be an instance of preferential wickedness. Or it may be that one is simply unmoved by the wrongness that consists in exposing someone to danger, in which case we have an instance of moral indifference. Or it may be that one acts recklessly because one has failed to adequately control one's rage, in which case it is an instance of moral weakness.

Some philosophers might even suggest that a person might unreasonably expose another to danger because he believes such acts to be right (at least, perhaps, when one can profit from this). If so, we have a case of perverse wickedness. A person might also needlessly expose another to harm because (although believing this to be wrong) he fails to realize (when he could and should) that his act does pose a danger to others. In this case we do not have a reckless act, however, since in cases of recklessness the agent is aware of the danger. This last case is, rather, a paradigm of (inadvertent) negligence in the legal sense.

But it is also possible that someone might unjustifiably risk injuring another—or, for that matter, do something that involves deceiving or even killing someone—because, although he is aware that his act has such a wrong-making feature and might therefore very well be wrong, he falsely assumes without further deliberation that, in light of certain other features, it is, all things considered, all right. *This* is moral recklessness.

Cases of moral recklessness are not always easy to distinguish from certain cases of amorality. If, realizing that performing the act runs the risk of moral wrongdoing, he fails to deliberate further to try to determine whether or not it really would be wrong, all things considered, because he does not really care whether what he does is right or wrong, then we have a case of amorality. Here the fault lies in a lack of moral concern rather than in a failure to exercise certain capacities of rational self-control, such as moral deliberation. However, it may also be the case that the agent who fails to deliberate *is* morally concerned— though perhaps he is not concerned enough. Perhaps he fails to deliberate further, not because he lacks the desire to avoid moral wrongdoing, but because what he proposes to do is very important to him and he does not want to have to be bothered by moral scruples. He realizes that if he were actually to conclude that it is wrong he would not be able to do it. Perhaps he is a young business executive who is desperate to increase his company's profits. He realizes that the advertisement that he is proposing has certain deceptive elements in it, so that, if he were to consider the matter further, he might conclude that it is a case of false advertising and therefore wrong. However, not wanting to lose the greater profits (and the consequent promotion) that a successful advertisement would make possible, he avoids further deliberation and rests on his present belief that the deceptive elements of the advertisement are (probably) not so serious as to make it wrong.[22] This seems more like a case of willful negligence rather than of amorality, since the agent is not exactly lacking in moral concern (although perhaps he does not care *enough* to do his very best to avoid moral wrongdoing); rather, he fails to exercise the kind of self-control necessary to keep his other desires and concerns (such as his desire for a promotion or his fear of losing his job) in check, so that they do not interfere with his concern to avoid moral wrongdoing.[23]

In cases of moral recklessness the agent may be said to be taking an unreasonable risk of moral wrongdoing. In-

[22] As I shall point out in the next section, instead of simply refusing to deliberate further, he might deliberate, but in a self-deceptive manner— i.e., he might rationalize by inventing a story that justifies what he does. In both cases we have a kind of willful moral blindness.

[23] The following is another example of moral recklessness. A military commander realizes that a certain maneuver will involve the deaths of a number of innocent civilians and that, even though it is necessary in order to avoid other losses, this might make the action wrong, all things considered. Fearing that this might be so but hoping that it is not, and wanting desperately to gain a victory and avoid further losses to his own men, he refuses to think about the matter further (when he has time to do so) and simply acts.

deed, one might say that whereas recklessness in the legal sense consists in the conscious choice of an action involving an unreasonable risk of causing harm, moral recklessness consists in the conscious choice of a course of action involving an unreasonable risk of moral wrongdoing. But this analogy is apt to be misleading, since the criteria for determining what constitutes a reasonable (or unreasonable) risk are quite different in each case. In the context of the law the reasonableness of the risk is determined by the magnitude and likelihood of the harm being risked when weighed against the importance and likelihood of the benefits to be gained by taking the risk, together with the necessity of taking the risk for this purpose.[24] Thus, it would be unreasonable to pass another vehicle on a blind curve just in order to get to a dinner party on time, even if the road was lightly travelled and oncoming traffic was not very likely (whereas if one was transporting a seriously injured person to the hospital and it was known that people die of such injuries unless treated within thirty minutes, then taking the risk might not be unreasonable). In this case what makes the risk unreasonable (unwarranted) is the relative unimportance of the benefit to be gained when weighed against the magnitude of the harm (loss of life) being risked. Here the fault on the part of the agent consists, not in a failure to adequately assess the risk before acting in order to determine if it is warranted, but rather in choosing to act on a risk that is unwarranted.

I have suggested a quite different criterion for assessing the reasonableness of the risk of moral wrongdoing. Here the reasonableness of the risk depends on whether the agent has made an honest and adequate attempt, before acting, to resolve his doubts about the moral propriety of his act. If he suspects that the act might be wrong and yet makes no adequate attempt to confirm or disconfirm his

[24] Here I follow Henry T. Terry. See his "Negligence," in Morris, ed., *Freedom and Responsibility*, p. 244.

suspicion (as in the case of the young business executive who refuses to deliberate further about the deceptive elements of his advertisement for fear that he might conclude that it is a case of false advertising), then the risk of wrongdoing is unreasonable. If, on the other hand, he has made an honest attempt to determine the rightness or wrongness of his act and has concluded that, all things considered, it appears to be morally permissible, then he cannot be accused of moral recklessness.

But suppose that, after due moral deliberation, he remains uncertain about the moral permissibility of his act. It might be suggested that anyone who does something about whose rightness he has a reasonable doubt is guilty of taking an unreasonable risk of wrongdoing, and hence, acts in a morally reckless manner. However, this would be to adopt a quite different notion of moral risk-taking (and hence of moral recklessness) than the one I am employing. Moreover, this view adopts much too strict a requirement regarding the precautions we must take in order to avoid moral wrongdoing.

There are two kinds of cases where a person might be said to have a reasonable doubt about the moral permissibility of what he does: (1) In the one kind of case he is aware that the act has some wrong-making feature, but is uncertain about how to weigh this against other morally relevant features of the act.[25] He may be inclined to think that it is, all things considered, all right; but he may not be certain of this. For example, he may realize that the act involves killing another human being but wonder whether it is wrong, all things considered, since the "victim" has suffered severe and irreversible brain damage and exists

[25] Or, he may be uncertain about whether the moral principle that would make it wrong, if it is wrong, is really applicable to cases like this. For example, it may be a case of killing someone that is also a case of euthanasia. And he may wonder whether the moral proscription against killing others applies to cases where the killing benefits, rather than harms, the "victim" and is done at the "victim's" request.

only in a permanent comatose state, and since another person's life can be saved if the first person's heart is used for a transplant.

In cases like this it is, of course, morally incumbent on the agent to make some attempt to resolve his doubt through further moral deliberation (insofar as this is possible). If, however, the agent has fulfilled this duty, and, after due deliberation, remains uncertain but is inclined to think that the act is, all things considered, probably all right, then he cannot be accused of moral recklessness if he performs the act. If, *after due and honest deliberation*, he remains unconvinced that the act is wrong, then, it seems to me, he may consider his act innocent (right) until proven guilty (wrong).

(2) In the other kind of case where someone might be said to have a reasonable doubt about the rightness of what he does, the person may believe that if a certain wrong-making feature obtains the act is wrong, but he may be uncertain about whether this wrong-making feature really exists. For example, someone may be convinced that if the fetus at this stage of development does indeed have a soul (or the capacity to suffer, or self-consciousness) then it is wrong to kill it; but he may not know whether the antecedent is true. This kind of case is quite different. Here what one is uncertain about is whether some morally relevant fact obtains. One is convinced, however, that if this fact does obtain it will outweigh all other relevant moral considerations, such as the effect of the pregnancy on the rights and interests of the pregnant woman.

Now it might be argued that if, given these circumstances, the agent proceeds to kill the fetus, he can be accused of taking an unreasonable risk of wrongdoing. Indeed, according to Roger Wertheimer, this sort of view lies behind one Catholic argument against abortion:

> . . . The official church position (not the one believed by most of the the laity or used against the liberals, but the official position) is that precisely be-

cause ensoulment is an unverifiable occurrence, we can't locate it with certainty, and hence abortion at any stage involves the *risk* of destroying a human life.[26]

However, as Wertheimer points out, it is not obvious that taking this kind of risk will always be unwarranted: "Is it morally indefensible to fire a pistol into an uninspected barrel? After all, a child *might* be hiding in it."[27] If it is wrong to perform the act in cases like this, it will be because it is a case of acting recklessly in the legal sense—i.e., it will be a case of choosing to do something that involves an unreasonable (i.e., unwarranted) risk of harming someone. And, as we have seen, whether or not taking this kind of risk is warranted depends on weighing the magnitude and likelihood of the harm risked against the benefits to be gained by taking the risk.

One may be convinced that if killing the fetus were indeed a case of killing a human organism with the feature in question (say, having a soul, or having the capacity to suffer), then it would be wrong to kill it, since this consideration would outweigh all other moral considerations— such as the fact that the abortion is necessary to save the pregnant woman from economic hardship or necessary to preserve important educational or career opportunities. But, of course, one is not certain that the fetus does have this characteristic. One may think that the closer the fetus is to birth the more likely it is that it has this characteristic, and the closer it is to conception the less likely it is that it has it. Because of this it is not obvious that killing the fetus in a very early stage of pregnancy involves taking an unreasonable risk—especially since the benefits to be gained might be very important. (This holds true even if we grant the

---

[26] Roger Wertheimer, "Understanding the Abortion Argument," *Philosophy and Public Affairs*, vol. 1, 1971. Reprinted (in a shortened version) in Joel Feinberg, ed., *The Problem of Abortion* (Belmont, Calif.: Wadsworth Publishing Co., 1973). See p. 38.

[27] *Ibid.*

questionable assumption that the fact that one is killing a human organism having the feature in question would— if it obtained—outweigh all other moral considerations.)

In any case, insofar as taking such a risk can be said to be warranted, the agent cannot be said to act wrongly if he does the act. He cannot be accused of recklessness in the legal sense; and, so long as he has made an honest attempt to assess the probability that this fact obtains and to weigh this against the benefits of taking the risk, it cannot be a case of moral recklessness either. He can be accused of acting wrongly (recklessly, in the legal sense) only if the risk of harm is unjustified, given the relative unimportance of the benefits to be gained. In this case he does not merely take an unreasonable *risk* of wrongdoing; he chooses to actually engage in wrongdoing. He chooses to take an unreasonable risk of harming another human being; and this is in itself a case of wrongdoing. His act is wrong for the same reason that it is wrong to drive an automobile in a reckless manner.

Whether or not he is also guilty of moral recklessness will depend on why he chooses to take such an unwarranted risk. If it is because he does not care whether or not he harms another (and hence acts wrongly), it will be a case of morally indifferent behavior. If it is because he prefers to promote his own advantage rather than avoid risking harm to others, it will be a case of preferential wickedness. If it is because, hoping that the risk is warranted but suspecting that it is not, he nevertheless fails to deliberate further and instead acts on his hope, then it will be a case of moral recklessness.

Thus, as I am construing the notion of moral recklessness, it consists not merely in doing something that one suspects might be wrong (indeed, as we have seen, *this* is not always wrong), but rather in doing something that one is inclined to think is right but suspects might be wrong— *without deliberating further (when one can) to resolve one's doubt*. One is guilty of moral recklessness only if, in addition to performing some wrong act—such as deceiving someone or needlessly exposing someone to harm—one does this because one is also guilty of violating a second-order moral requirement. This is the duty to try to resolve, before acting, any doubts one might have about the moral rightness of one's act. Once this duty has been fulfilled, one cannot be accused of moral recklessness. Of course, having fulfilled this duty and concluded that the act (whatever it is— deceiving someone or exposing others to harm) is unjustified or wrong, one might still do it, perhaps because one's will (resolve) is weak. In that case one will act wrongly, but it will be a case of moral weakness rather than of moral recklessness.

4. Self-Deception

Self-deception is certainly one important source of immorality; indeed, it may be a much more frequent cause of wrongdoing than most of us suspect.[28] I am inclined to treat self-deceptive wrongdoing as a kind of moral negligence rather than as a kind of moral weakness, as is more commonly done. This is because moral negligence, as I conceive of it, covers all those cases where wrongdoing is due to the agent's failure to believe that his act is morally wrong (when he could and should), and where the agent's failure to realize this is not due to his failing to believe the basic moral principle according to which his act is morally wrong. Self-deceptive wrongdoing fits this description, since

[28] Bertrand Russell was well aware of the importance of self-deception as a source of immoral behavior: "Very few people deliberately do what, at the moment, they believe to be wrong; usually they first argue themselves into a belief that what they wish to do is right. They decide that it is their duty to teach so-and-so a lesson, that their rights have been so grossly infringed that if they take no revenge there will be an encouragement to injustice, that without a moderate indulgence in pleasure a character cannot develop in the best way, and so on and so on." From "The Elements of Ethics," in Sellars and Hospers, eds., *Readings in Ethical Theory* (New York: Appleton-Century-Crofts, Inc., 1952), p. 15.

the self-deceiving wrongdoer has convinced himself that what he does is not wrong. But self-deceptive wrongdoing is not a clear-cut case of unconscious wrongdoing. The self-deceiving wrongdoer has persuaded himself that what he does is all right; still, he "knows in his heart" that it is wrong—he is not completely unaware that what he is doing is wrong.

Thus, it has been suggested that the self-deceiving wrongdoer both believes that what he does is wrong and believes that it is right (not wrong).[29] In this respect he is the exact opposite of the amoral wrongdoer, who neither believes that what he does is wrong nor believes that it is right. However, this description of self-deceptive wrongdoing makes it appear much more paradoxical than it actually is. Even though there may be some sense in which the self-deceiver believes that his act is wrong, there is also a more important sense in which he fails to realize that what he does is wrong—at least, he fails to acknowledge or admit to himself that it is wrong. Moreover, his dominant belief—and the one that is operative—is that his act is not wrong.

In order to see this, let us consider a typical case of self-deceptive wrongdoing. A person has certain ambitions which he can fulfill only by doing something that he believes to be morally wrong. He does not want to do anything that is morally wrong; he desires to avoid wrongdoing. Yet he does not want to give up his ambitions either. So he is faced with a dilemma. There appear to be three main options.[30] (1) He could forgo the pursuit of his ambitions, or at least modify them, so that wrongdoing is no longer necessary to fulfill them. But he is unwilling to give up or

[29] See Raphael Demos, "Lying to Oneself," *Journal of Philosophy*, vol. 57, 1960, pp. 558-95.

[30] I am indebted to Herbert Fingarette for this way of putting it. See his *Self-Deception* (London: Routledge & Kegan Paul, 1969), pp. 138-39. Fingarette's masterful treatment of this topic has greatly influenced my own thinking about it.

modify his ambitions. (2) He could pursue his ambitions in spite of the fact that he acknowledges this to require wrongdoing—a clearly immoral course of action. But he finds this equally unacceptable. He is, after all, a moral person—or so he tells himself. Moreover, this course of action would involve an intolerable burden of guilt. (3) He could pursue his ambitions, but without acknowledging the wrongdoing that this requires. This is the course of action adopted by the self-deceiver.

A nice trick. How does he do it? Well, for one thing, he completely ignores, insofar as he can, those features of his behavior that make it wrong. For example, he chooses not to think about how what he does might harm someone or deceive someone. Another thing he might do is to try to think of (or manufacture) reasons that would justify his behavior—i.e., he might engage in rationalization. For example, in order to justify his deception of a rival who stands in his way, he might construct a story that attributes certain motives and intentions to his rival (and he may imagine that he finds clues of these motives and intentions in various things his rival says and does). Attributing these motives and intentions to his rival allows him to see his own behavior as a case of justified self-defense—for his rival is out to ruin him in any way he can, and if he tells his rival the truth he will only be making himself vulnerable to a malicious antagonist. In this way he persuades himself that his behavior is morally all right.

Now insofar as the self-deceiver succeeds in this endeavor he will have rendered himself incapable of recognizing the moral wrongness of his behavior. He has general moral principles according to which behavior of this sort is wrong, but he fails to realize, when he could and should, that his act violates these principles. Thus, his behavior is an instance of what I am calling moral negligence. But it is interesting to note that there are some significant differences between this form of moral negligence and the two species of inadvertent negligence discussed earlier. Like the agent whose wrongdoing is due to impulsiveness or carelessness, the self-deceiver may also fail to notice those features of his behavior that make it wrong.[31] But the impulsive and the careless wrongdoer fail to notice them simply because they (unintentionally) fail to pay attention to what they do—or to certain aspects of this. The self-deceiver, on the other hand, fails to notice them because he *deliberately ignores* them. Although all three of them may be ignorant of and blind to the morally relevant features of their behavior, it is only the self-deceiver who can be said to be willfully ignorant and willfully blind.

It is this kind of *moral ignorance* and *moral blindness* that, I believe, those who wish to conceive of wickedness as perverse wickedness have in mind. For here we have a kind of moral ignorance that *is* a reflection of perverse values or preferences—e.g., putting the pursuit of one's own self-interest, or the requirements of the Third Reich, above not harming others. However, those who conceive of wickedness as perverse wickedness view the agent of a wicked act as being ignorant of the moral principles according to which his act is wrong. I have tried to show that ignorance of *basic* moral principles is not possible, given that one knows what it is for an act to be morally wrong. I have admitted, however, that ignorance of derivative moral principles is possible, because such ignorance may be the result of ignorance of matters of fact.

Now it is interesting to note that the self-deceiver's deception can take the form of deceiving himself about the truth of derivative moral principles. For example, although he believes that it is (*prima facie*) wrong to kill people and (*prima facie*) wrong to deceive them, he concludes that it is not wrong to kill *Jews*, or not wrong to deceive *one's rivals*. Why does he believe that it is all right to kill Jews, or all

---

[31] Or, he may notice them but convince himself that these moral considerations are nevertheless overridden by others that he imagines to obtain.

right to deceive one's rivals? Well, perhaps he believes that Jews are a menace to the human race—a corrupting influence that will ruin the whole human race unless they are wiped out. Perhaps he believes that "all's fair in love and war," and that people who view you as their rival cannot be trusted to act morally toward you; so that you must simply do what you can to protect yourself from such unprincipled people.

These are "crazy" or perverse factual beliefs. If a person has such beliefs because he is incredibly stupid or gullible, has been brainwashed, suffers from paranoid delusions, etc., we should be inclined to excuse him. Moreover, insofar as his ignorance of the wrongness of killing Jews, or deceiving one's rivals, is based on such excusable ignorance of matters of fact, it is not the sort of ignorance that could make one wicked; it is not the kind of ignorance that is supposed to characterize the agent of a perversely wicked act.

But ignorance of derivative moral principles might be culpable. This would be so if it were due to self-deception. Suppose, for example, that someone simply, for whatever reason, finds himself hating Jews. He does not think that it is all right to kill people merely because you dislike them, yet he wishes to kill Jews. So he manufactures a story to persuade himself that there is something peculiar about Jews that makes killing them morally permissible. Suppose, to take another example, that someone is the sort of person who despises those who stand in his way. He does not think it right to deceive people merely in order to promote one's own interest at the expense of their's. So he concocts a (almost) paranoid tale about the "true" nature of rivals. If this is so, then his ignorance is not excusing, for he is himself responsible for his mistaken factual beliefs and his consequent moral blindness and false (derivative) moral principles.

What we have here is something rather close to what perverse wickedness is supposed to be (at least, on the cognitivist interpretation of it). But it is not quite the same, for the agent of a perversely wicked act is supposed to be ignorant of basic moral principles. Moreover, he is supposed to be ignorant of moral principles which are such that to be ignorant of such principles is *never* excusing, since it is proof of a bad moral character. As we have seen, the ignorance that characterizes the self-deceiver is such that it can (when caused by paranoid delusions, for example) be excusing.

Of course, someone might wish to question whether the self-deceiving wrongdoer really is blameworthy. Perhaps his ignorance is excusing. After all, he has been deceived, if only by himself. Perhaps he is sick and cannot help himself. Well, perhaps he is. This could be so; there are some cases where self-deception is symptomatic of some genuine mental pathology. And in such cases the self-deceiver's ignorance is excusing, even though he brings it on himself. For in such cases (e.g., paranoia and schizophrenia) the compulsion to construct stories is probably too great to expect anyone to overcome it. But self-deception is not always symptomatic of such pathologies. And when it is not, there may be no good reason to excuse it.

Our tendency to blame the self-deceiver can be tempered, however, by the realization that the self-deceiver does have moral concern. He could not act as he does if he allowed himself to believe it to be wrong. If he did not care whether what he does is right or wrong, there would be no need for self-deception. Herbert Fingarette suggests that the self-deceiver's fault consists not in a lack of concern to avoid moral wrongdoing, but rather in a lack of spiritual or moral courage—which I would interpret as the courage to stand one's ground with respect to maintaining one's moral convictions against the onslaught of contrary desires and emotions.[32] This suggests, however, that the self-de-

[32] See, *Self-Deception*, pp. 139 and 143.

ceiver is guilty of a kind of weakness. Indeed, should we not characterize him as having a weak will?

As I mentioned earlier, some philosophers are inclined to treat self-deceptive wrongdoing as a species of weakness of will.[33] But in genuine cases of weakness of will the fault lies in a failure to ensure that one's act conforms to one's practical judgment. Thus, in cases where the fault consists in a failure to judge that one's act is wrong, even though it violates one's moral principles, what we have is not moral weakness but moral negligence. As we noted earlier, however, self-deceptive wrongdoing is not a clear-cut case of unconscious wrongdoing; for there is a sense in which the self-deceiver realizes that what he does is wrong—even though he refuses to acknowledge this. If we describe the self-deceiver as being unable to admit the truth to himself, we imply that he in some sense does know the truth. It suggests that he has made a prior assessment of his proposed act and judged it to be wrong; and, as Fingarette points out, the consequent act of self-deception involves a "coverup" not only of the fact that the behavior is wrong, but also of the fact that one has judged it to be wrong.[34]

Now insofar as the self-deceiver does initially judge his act to be wrong, and then allows some desire or emotion to interfere with his acting on the judgment, it looks as though his behavior is a case of moral weakness; for the fault seems to consist in a failure to ensure that his behavior conforms to his practical judgment. However, insofar as his self-deceptive maneuvers lead him to actually revise his judgment (i.e., insofar as he succeeds in convincing himself that, contrary to appearances, the act is not wrong), then it looks as though the fault lies in failing to judge that his

[33] Hare, for example, views it as a kind of "purposive backsliding." See *Freedom and Reason* (Oxford: Clarendon Press, 1963), pp. 82-83. Also see Stephen Lukes, "Moral Weakness," in G. W. Mortimore, ed., *Weakness of Will* (London: Macmillan and Co., 1971), p. 154 (first published in *Philosophical Quarterly*, vol. 15, 1965, pp. 104-14.

[34] See *Self-Deception*, pp. 48-49.

act is wrong—in allowing his desires and emotions to cloud or interfere with his making the correct practical judgment. Moreover, inasmuch as he does not, at the time of action, act contrary to his revised judgment, his behavior cannot be described as a case of moral weakness. Thus, all things considered, I am still inclined to classify self-deceptive wrongdoing as a type of moral negligence.

One might also be inclined to treat the self-deceiving wrongdoer as a kind of moral hypocrite. As we have seen, we speak of the self-deceiver as "knowing in his heart" that what he does is wrong, because this seems necessary to explain why he adopts (and perhaps continues to employ) certain self-deceptive maneuvers. But it does not follow that he is insincere when he tells others that what he does is not wrong, for, if his self-deception has been successful, he really does believe what he says. He tells others just what he tells himself. Yet, as Fingarette points out, when "we come to see that the story he is telling both himself and us is not unintentionally wrong but purposely wrong," we are inclined to "ascribe to him a peculiar, 'deeper' insincerity."[35] Nevertheless, this is not the sort of cynical, self-conscious insincerity that we usually have in mind when we call someone a hypocrite (although the self-deceptive kind of insincerity may actually be much more common).

5. Types of Moral Negligence

In cases of moral negligence the agent fails to realize, when he should and could, that his act violates his own moral principles. I have argued that what makes his ignorance culpable is the fact that it could have been avoided by taking certain reasonable precautions, and that his failing to take such precautions is a case of failing to exercise certain capacities of rational self-control with respect to his desires and emotions. I have also indicated that there are four main

[35] *Ibid.*, p. 53.

types of moral negligence. Two of them (*impulsive* and *careless* moral negligence) are types of *inadvertent* moral negligence, and the other two (*moral recklessness* and *self-deceptive wrongdoing*) are cases of *willfull* moral negligence.

(1) Impulsiveness: In cases of what might be called impulsive (or thoughtless) moral negligence the agent simply acts without thinking at all about the circumstances and consequences of his act that make it either right or wrong. The act may be a direct attempt to satisfy some desire or the manifestation of an immediate emotional reaction.

(2) Carelessness: In other cases the agent pays some attention to what he is doing but is careless about this. He takes note of certain features or aspects of what he does (he sees, for example, how it amuses his friends), but he fails to advert to other morally relevant features of it (for example, how it humiliates someone).

(3) Recklessness: In cases of moral recklessness the agent is aware that his act has certain features that might, depending on other features of it, make it wrong; but he deliberately disregards this. Although he hopes that what he does is all right, he suspects that if he deliberated further he might conclude that it is wrong.

(4) Self-deception: In cases of self-deceptive wrongdoing the agent "knows in his heart" that what he does is wrong, but he has managed to convince himself that it is not wrong. Either he deliberately ignores those features of it that make it wrong, or else he manufactures a story according to which these features are overriden by other morally relevant features.

F I V E

* * * *

MORAL WEAKNESS

Aristotle likens the agent of a morally weak act to a city that has good laws but fails to apply them. As we have seen, this analogy applies equally well to the agent of a morally negligent act. In both cases the agent fails to make his behavior conform to his own moral principles. However, the agent of a morally negligent act fails to realize that his act violates his own moral principles. He is thus not (fully) conscious of the wrongness of what he does. Now, in spite of what Aristotle seems to suggest, the agent of a morally weak act is fully conscious of the wrongness of what he does. The explanation of his doing it lies not in his being ignorant of this, but elsewhere. To determine just what the correct explanation is, is the aim of this chapter.

Insofar as moral weakness is a kind of conscious wrongdoing, it is similar to moral indifference and preferential wickedness. In all of these cases the agent believes his act to be morally wrong and yet chooses to do it when he could have chosen not to do it. Morally weak behavior may be distinguished from morally indifferent behavior by the fact that the person who acts in a morally weak manner not only believes his act to be morally wrong, he desires to avoid doing it in virtue of its being morally wrong; whereas the agent of a morally indifferent act has no con-attitude toward his act in virtue of its being wrong. Thus, the question of whether morally indifferent behavior is possible reduces to the question of whether it is possible for a person to believe that his act is morally wrong without having some con-attitude toward it. In cases of preferential wickedness the agent has some concern to avoid his act in virtue of its moral wrongness, but he prefers the realization of some other desired end to the avoidance of moral wrongdoing. He believes that it is better, all things considered, to realize this end than to avoid moral wrongdoing. The agent of a morally weak act, on the other hand, prefers to avoid moral wrongdoing rather than do what he does. Although his desire to do what he does is stronger than his desire to avoid wrongdoing (at least, at the time he does it), he nevertheless judges that it is better (and in this sense prefers) to avoid wrongdoing. This is what makes the morally weak agent's behavior seem paradoxical or puzzling. Since the agent of a preferentially wicked act acts in accordance with his practical judgment or evaluative preference, his behavior is not puzzling in this respect. Whether acts of preferential wickedness are possible turns on the question of whether it is logically possible for a person to believe or judge that it is morally wrong to do some act and yet prefer—in the sense of believing that it is better, all things considered—to do this act.

Thus, questions about the possibility of moral indifference and preferential wickedness both turn on questions about the correct analysis of moral beliefs—about what it is to believe or judge that an act is morally wrong. If it is a necessary condition of believing or judging that an act is morally *wrong* that one have some con-attitude toward it, then moral indifference is not logically possible. And if it is a necessary condition of believing that an act is *morally* wrong that one have an overriding or dominant con-attitude toward not doing it (i.e., that one prefers, or thinks it better, to avoid it rather than pursue some other end), then preferential wickedness is not logically possible either.

Now it is important to observe that the possibility of moral weakness does not turn on such considerations. For it has been suggested that moral weakness will seem problematic only if one adopts a noncognitivist or prescriptivist account of moral beliefs. That this is not so can be seen once one realizes that even if one denies that having an overriding or dominant con-attitude toward an act is a necessary condition of believing it to be morally wrong, one must still hold that the agent of a morally weak act has both a con-attitude toward his act and prefers to avoid doing it, simply because this is necessary to distinguish morally weak from morally indifferent and preferentially wicked behavior. That is, even if having such a con-attitude and such a preference is not a necessary condition of *believing an act to be morally wrong*, it is still a necessary condition of *acting in a morally weak manner*. Thus, moral weakness is problematic just because it involves weakness of will—i.e., acting contrary to one's preference or practical judgment concerning what it is better for one to do. As we shall see, some philosophers have argued that in such cases it is psychologically impossible for the agent to do anything other than what he does. This raises a question about whether the agent can be considered blameworthy in cases of weakness of will, and, hence, about whether moral weakness can be a species of immoral behavior. I shall consider this issue shortly. But first I should like to consider the phenomenon of moral weakness in some detail.

1. Varieties of Moral Weakness

I have described cases of moral weakness as cases where the agent does something that is morally wrong, even though he desires to avoid doing what is morally wrong and believes not only that what he does is wrong, but that it is better to avoid moral wrongdoing than to act as he does. It is important to notice that this description applies to quite a large variety of behavior, for some people have tended to equate morally weak behavior with only one kind of behavior that fits this description—namely, yielding to temptation. This is what most discussions of moral weakness have tended to focus on. In such cases the agent is said to be overcome by desire or appetite; that is why, for example, he continues smoking or commits adultery. It must be noticed, however, that not all cases of being overcome by desire or emotion are correctly described as cases of succumbing to temptation. In some cases what we have is irascibility—or failure to control one's temper. For example, a mother who thinks that it is wrong to beat one's children might nevertheless become so annoyed and so angry because of her child's misbehavior that she beats and injures her child. This could be described as a case where one loses control and succumbs to emotion, but it could not be described as succumbing to temptation.[1] The latter suggests succumbing to a desire or appetite for something. In other cases one might be overcome by some other emotion, such as revulsion or fear. Consider, for example, a person who fails to come to the aid of some poor beggar who has been injured, because this person finds the beggar so repulsive (perhaps the beggar is filthy and grossly deformed) that he finds himself unable to look at the beggar. Here again we have a case of being overwhelmed by an emotion that is not a case of yielding to temptation.

All of the cases that we have so far considered can, however, be described as succumbing to some desire or emotion

---

[1] Gwynneth Mathews claims that "it would seem odd to suggest that failure to control one's temper was a form of weakness of will." See "Weakness of Will," in G. W. Mortimore, ed., *Weakness of Will* (London: Macmillan and Co., 1971), pp. 164-65 (first published in *Mind*, vol. 75, 1966, pp. 405-19). However, my example clearly shows that failure to control one's temper *can* be a case of weakness of will. If we suppose that the mother wills (i.e., has resolved) not to beat her children because she believes this to be wrong, then in this case her will is overcome by her anger. Although I disagree with Mathews on this point, in other respects I have found her discussion of the varieties of weakness of will to be quite helpful, and my own thinking has been much influenced by it.

that one has failed to adequately control. In these cases moral weakness takes the form of *intemperance*. But there are some cases of moral weakness that do not fit even this broader description. Sometimes moral weakness takes the form of *irresolution* rather than intemperance.[2] There are a number of ways in which an agent might exhibit lack or resolve (or strength of purpose). One might simply procrastinate. For example, a person thinks it wrong not to visit his aged mother, who lives some distance away, but he keeps putting it off—and then she dies. Here he does not succumb to any particular desire or emotion; rather, he simply has a lot of other things to do and, at any given time, cannot be bothered—i.e., he finds himself too busy or finds it too inconvenient to visit his mother. There is also the possibility of backsliding—i.e., of a weakening or erosion of one's resolve to do something one believes one ought to do. For example, a person might resolve to send a hundred dollars a month to his mother, who is poor and in need of help. Perhaps he does so for a year or so, but then his resolve weakens—he skips a month now and then and, finally, no longer sends anything. In these cases it is not so much that one has allowed some particular desire or emotion to get out of control; rather, there is a more general breakdown of one's capacity of self-control and self-governance. In both kinds of cases the agent exhibits a lack of willpower; but whereas in the one sort of case (intemperance) the agent does not quite make the effort required to resist or manage some particularly strong

[2] I am here using the term "intemperance" to refer to any failure to keep in check some desire or emotion that prompts us to do something that we believe is wrong and prefer not to do. The term "irresolution" usually refers to vacillation or indecisiveness. However, I am using it to refer not only to this, but also to cases of procrastination and to backsliding—where one makes a resolution and then allows the strength of one's resolve to become gradually eroded (making an exception here and there) over time. In all of these cases we have a lack of strength of purpose or resolve.

desire or emotion, in the other sort of case (irresolution) he fails to make the effort required in order to preserve the strength of his resolve.

In still other cases irresolution may take the form of indecisiveness or vacillation. Suppose that a person believes that one of his co-workers has been unjustly treated by their employer and that he ought to speak out and lodge a protest with his employer. But suppose that, having reached this conclusion, he is beset by a general feeling of insecurity or by fear of retaliation, so that instead of acting he is led to re-examine his decision and to consider whether his employer's action was perhaps justified after all. Let us suppose that he does not really believe that the employer's action was justified, but he continually looks for reasons that might justify it and hence fails to ever act in the way he really believes he ought to act. Cases like this bring us close to the borderline between moral weakness and moral negligence. Depending on how we fill in the details, some cases like this might be described as cases of rationalization or self-deception. If he really comes to doubt his belief that his employer acted unjustly (and hence that he ought to protest) or if he vacillates between this belief and its contradictory, then what we have is not so much a case of one's desires or emotions leading one to act in a manner contrary to one's moral beliefs (or to fail to act on these beliefs); rather, it is a case of one's desires or emotions clouding or altering one's beliefs. And culpable failure to prevent one's desires and emotions from doing *this* is moral negligence.

Some cases of moral weakness also appear to be at the borderline with moral indifference. Consider those cases where a person fails to do something that he believes he ought to do because he finds it inconvenient and does not want to be bothered, or because he finds that it requires much more effort than he had anticipated. In such cases we may often wonder whether to attribute the agent's failure to act as he believes he ought to act to lack of willpower or to lack of concern. Suppose, for example, that a person fails to stop and render assistance to another motorist whose vehicle has become disabled in a remote area. Let us suppose that this person believes it to be morally wrong not to stop in a case like this. Why, then, does he fail to stop? Perhaps he is not completely unmoved by the wrongness of not stopping—or by those features of not stopping that make it wrong. Still, he thinks it would be a bother and a nuisance to stop, although he does not think that this justifies his not stopping. Is his failure due to lack of willpower (strength of resolve), or is it due to lack of (sufficient) concern to avoid morally wrong acts? If, after failing to stop, he later feels remorse and blames himself, then this is evidence for having some concern (however weak) to avoid moral wrongdoing, but not having the willpower to overcome the stronger desire to avoid being inconvenienced. But perhaps strength of will (resolve) is simply a function of the strength of one's desire to avoid morally wrong acts. I have been using the label "moral indifference" to refer to morally wrong behavior that is due to the lack of any (however weak) desire to avoid moral wrongdoing. But perhaps we should also apply this term to cases where the desire exists but is too weak to play any motivational role.

This brings up one of the problems in connection with moral weakness that we shall have to explore later. Perhaps it is true in all cases of moral weakness that the agent's will is weak just because he does not care enough. Perhaps if the agent really cared enough he would be able to resist the temptation, control his anger, or overcome his revulsion; perhaps he would not procrastinate or vacillate and would take the trouble or make the effort. I shall return to this problem later in this chapter.

First, however, I should like to conclude the discussion of the nature and variety of moral weakness. We have seen that we cannot classify all cases where a person has good moral principles but fails to act on them as cases of moral weakness, for this description also fits cases of moral indifference and preferential wickedness—as well as cases of moral negligence. What distinguishes moral weakness from these other kinds of immorality is that the agent of a morally weak act not only (1) believes that his particular act is wrong (which distinguishes him from the agent of a morally negligent act); he also both (2) wants to avoid doing what is morally wrong (which distinguishes him from the agent of a morally indifferent act) and (3) prefers to avoid doing what is morally wrong to doing what he does (which distinguishes him from the agent of a preferentially wicked act).

Are these three features jointly sufficient for correctly characterizing a case of wrongdoing as a case of moral weakness, or should we perhaps add that the agent afterwards feels remorse or blames himself? I do not think that we should accept this last condition as a necessary condition of moral weakness. That the agent afterwards feels remorse or blames himself is significant, it seems to me, only insofar as this counts as evidence that the first three conditions obtain. Perhaps a certain person has concluded that such self-accusations and feelings of guilt really serve no good purpose and, in fact, are usually counterproductive; because of this he has trained himself not to "cry over spilt milk." Nevertheless, such a person could still have moral beliefs and could act in a morally weak manner.

We have seen, however, that cases of wrongdoing where these three conditions obtain are quite varied Certainly they do not all fit the description of yielding to temptation—nor even that of succumbing to some desire or emotion. Because of this Gwynneth Mathews suggests that "they are not all cases of lack of self-control or lack of self-restraint. These do not seem to be the generic concepts, but rather species of weakness of will."[3] I have suggested that there are two main species of moral weakness: intemperance and irresolution; and, although Mathews does not

[3] See the paper cited above, p. 165.

see cases of the latter as exhibiting lack of self-control, there is a sense in which both species of moral weakness betray a lack of self-control. We can fail to exercise self-control either by failing to make the effort required (i.e., failing to take the measures necessary) to resist some strong desire or emotion that prompts us to do what we believe to be wrong (in cases of intemperance) or by failing to take those precautions necessary to ensure that our resolve is not impeded by indecisiveness or eroded over time because we become preoccupied with other concerns and neglect to remind ourselves of what is most important (in cases of irresolution). Moreover, in both cases the fault lies in the agent's failure to control his desires and emotions; for even in cases of irresolution the agent vacillates because of, say, fear or feelings of insecurity, or he allows his resolve to weaken because he becomes too absorbed by other, less important concerns.

Weakness of will, then, consists essentially in the failure to exercise certain capacities of rational self-control over one's desires and emotions. I have already said something about what exercising these capacities of self-control amounts to in discussing moral negligence, which, I have argued, is due to the same kind of shortcoming on the part of the agent; and I shall say more about just what is involved in exercising what might be called *willpower* later in this chapter. First, however, let us see why the failure to exercise self-control in certain circumstances seems problematic.

2. Why Weakness of Will Is Problematic

In cases of weakness of will the agent acts contrary to his own preference or judgment concerning what it is better (or best) for one to do, when he could have chosen otherwise. Consider a typical case. Suppose, for example, that a person judges that, all things considered, it is better for him not to smoke than to smoke. Whatever reasons he has to smoke—that it gives him pleasure, that it alleviates feel-

ings of anxiety, that it satisifies a craving which, left un-
satisfied, interferes with his ability to concentrate and work—
he judges that the reasons he has not to smoke (reasons
in terms of the preservation of his life and health) are
weightier. Nevertheless, he chooses to smoke even though,
it seems, he could have chosen not to smoke. Why does
such behavior seem puzzling or impossible?

Donald Davidson has suggested that such behavior is
problematic because it seems impossible, given two principles about the connection between practical judgments,
motivation, and action that seem self-evident or, at least,
difficult to deny. The first (*P1*) is that "if an agent wants to
do X more than he wants to do Y and he believes himself
free to do either X or Y, then he will intentionally do X if
he does either X or Y intentionally"; and the second (*P2*)
is that "if an agent judges that it would be better to do X
than to do Y, then he wants to do X more than he wants
to do Y."[4] If these premises are true, then it is always false
to suppose that an agent could intentionally do Y even
though he judges that it would be better to do X and believes himself free to do either.

It has been suggested, however, that this way of explaining the problematic character of weakness of will rests
on an equivocation between two senses of the phrase "wants
to do X more than Y—an evaluational sense and a motivational sense.[5] In the evaluational sense, to say that a
person wants to do X more than he wants to do Y is to
say that he prefers to do X rather than Y, i.e., that he ranks

[4] "How Is Weakness of the Will Possible?" in Joel Feinberg, ed., *Moral
Concepts* (London: Oxford University Press, 1969), p. 95.

[5] This point has been made by each of the following: Gerasimos Santas,
"Plato's *Protagoras* and Explanations of Weakness," in G. W. Mortimore,
ed., *Weakness of Will*, p. 58. (This article was first published in *The Philosophical Review*, vol. 75, 1966, pp. 3-33.) Neil Cooper, "Oughts and Wants,"
also in *Weakness of Will*, p. 197 (first published in *Aristotelian Society*, suppl.
vol. 42, 1968, pp. 143-54); and Gary Watson, "Scepticism About Weakness
of Will," *The Philosophical Review*, vol. 86, 1977, p. 321.

doing X higher in his scale of values than doing Y. In the motivational sense, to say that a person wants to do X more than he wants to do Y is to say that he wants to do X more strongly than he wants to do Y—i.e., that he is more strongly motivated to do X than to do Y. The argument that seems to entail the impossibility of weakness of will equivocates because the first premise ($P1$) is plausible only if the key phrase, "wants to do X more than he wants to do Y," is taken in its motivational sense, whereas the second ($P2$) is plausible only if this phrase is taken in its evaluational sense.

Thus, one way of attempting to dispel the problematic character of weakness of will is to claim that although the agent prefers, for example, nonsmoking to smoking, he nevertheless chooses to smoke on a certain occasion because his desire to smoke on that occasion is motivationally stronger than his desire to preserve his health and life. The success of this maneuver designed to save the phenomenon of weakness of will depends, of course, on our having criteria for determining an agent's preferences or evaluative rankings that are independent of our criteria for determining the strength of his desires or motives. Now there does not appear to be any *a priori* reason for supposing that there is a necessary correlation between the agent's evaluative rankings of the alternatives before him and the strength of his desires for these alternatives. Moreover, we do employ criteria for determining an agent's evaluative preferences that are independent of our criteria for determining the strength of his desires. For example, that an agent feels regret or shame upon having smoked is taken to be an indication of his preferring not to smoke, although it is not an indication of his having (or having had) a stronger desire not to smoke.

Nevertheless, this way of accounting for the phenomenon of weakness of will does not avoid all the problems that have been raised about weakness of will. There is, first of all, the problem of what criteria we are to employ in determining that the agent's stronger desire is the desire to do the act which he in fact performs. If our only criteria for saying that this is the stronger desire is that it is the desire on which the agent acts (in which case, it would be logically impossible for the agent to act against his strongest desire), then the explanation in terms of strength of desires of why the agent acts contrary to his preference or practical judgment is empirically empty and trivial.[6]

Moreover, this raises the further question of in what sense the weak-willed agent could have done otherwise. (And if the morally weak agent could not have done otherwise, how can his act be said to constitute a species of *blameworthy* moral wrongdoing?) Even if we admit that it is *logically* possible for an agent to act against his stronger or strongest desire, can this be *psychologically* possible. It has been suggested that "the mark of a compulsive desire is its capacity to motivate the agent contrary to his or her practical judgment."[7] If so, how is weakness of will to be distinguished from psychological compulsion? If we suppose that the weak-willed agent, unlike the agent subject to psychological compulsion, is able to resist his stronger desire, how can we explain his failure to exercise his capacity to resist this desire? Since the weak-willed agent judges, for example, that it is better not to smoke, he must also judge that it is better to resist his desire to smoke. But if he judges that he ought to resist this desire and if he has the capacity to resist it, then how is it that he does not resist it? Is it because, although he has the capacity to resist it, he fails to make a sufficient effort to resist it? But then why does he not try hard enough? Given that he has sufficient reason not only to refrain from smoking but also to resist his desire to smoke and yet smokes, what grounds

[6] This is pointed out by Santas, "Plato's *Protagoras* and Explanations of Weakness," p. 56.

[7] Gary Watson, "Scepticism About Weakness of Will," p. 327.

have we for saying that he could have resisted—that his desire was not irresistible?[8]

Thus, even if we grant that, although he prefers not smoking to smoking, his desire to smoke is stronger, how can we explain his failure to resist this desire, assuming that he has the ability to resist it? Davidson suggests a solution which concedes that, in one sense, the agent prefers to continue smoking—i.e., there is a sense in which he believes that he ought to continue smoking (that it would be better to do so); and it is this judgment that is the operative one, according to Davidson.[9] The solution consists in drawing a distinction between conditional (or relativized) evaluative judgments and unconditional (or *simpliciter*) evaluative judgments. According to Davidson, the person who exhibits weakness of will acts contrary to his conditional judgment as to what it is better for him to do, but not contrary to his unconditional evaluative judgment. This is not inconsistent with his two principles, since the principle concerning evaluative judgments applies only to *unconditional* evaluative judgments.[10]

Davidson claims that the person who exhibits weakness of will believes that what he does is, in some respect, good or desirable to do, since he does it intentionally—i.e., for a reason. Thus he judges, for example, that (1) *given* the fact that X will maximize his pleasures, it is better to do X than not to do X. But he also judges that (2) *given* that X is morally wrong, it is better not to do X. And he judges that (3) *all things considered*, it is better not to do X. Each of

---

[8] This line of argument is suggested by Santas in "Plato's *Protagoras* and Explanations of Weakness," p. 61, and by John Benson in "Wants, Desires, and Deliberation," also in Mortimore, ed., *Weakness of Will*, pp. 213-14 (first published in *Aristotelian Society*, suppl. vol. 42, 1968, pp. 155-72). The argument is most fully developed by Watson in "Scepticism About Weakness of Will."

[9] See "How Is Weakness of the Will Possible?" pp. 108 ff.

[10] This is (P2): "If an agent judges that it would be better to do X than to do Y, then he wants to do X more than he wants to do Y."

these three judgments is a relativized or conditional judgment. Davidson's principles connecting evaluative judgments and action apply to none of them; each is equally insulated from action.[11] At the same time, the agent judges unconditionally that it is better to do X; and he acts in accordance with *this* judgment. Since, however, he acts contrary to his judgment of what is better, *all things considered*, his action is—although not impossible—irrational; for it is a principle of rationality that one "perform the action judged best on the basis of all available reasons."[12]

Unfortunately, Davidson's solution is unsatisfactory— for several reasons. First of all, the nature of the unconditional evaluative judgment to the effect that it is better to do X (the wrong act) is mysterious. What kind of judgment is this? If the judgment about what it is better to do, all things considered, does not constitute an unconditional evaluatve judgment, what does?[13] Secondly, Davidson admits that this unconditional judgment is, like the action it prescribes, irrational. Indeed, he suggests that the only judgments that are rational (ones for which the agent has reasons) are the conditional ones. But since his principles do not apply to these, they are, in a significant sense, not practical. Moreover, it seems that the agent has no reason at all to make the unconditional judgment that it is better to do X. Davidson suggests that *the reason why* he judges (unconditionally) that it is better to do X is the same as his reason for judging that it is better to do X, given that X maximizes his pleasures.[14] But surely the phrase "the reason why" must here refer to the psychological explanation of his judgment, not to its justification; a rationally justified

---

[11] As Davidson makes clear. See "How Is Weakness of the Will Possible?" p. 110.

[12] *Ibid.*, p. 112.

[13] This question is posed by Watson in "Scepticism About Weakness of Will," p. 319.

[14] See "How Is Weakness of the Will Possible?" p. 110.

unconditional judgment, it would seem, must correspond to the all-things-considered judgment.

Perhaps the point that Davidson is trying to make is simply this. If one thinks that in order to show how weakness of will is possible one must be able to explain what reason the agent has for choosing to do X (e.g., smoke) when he judges that it is better, all things considered, not to do X, or what reason he has not to (make the effort to) resist the stronger desire to do X, then one is mistaken. For, of course, he has no reason for *this*; acts of weakness of will are irrational.[15] The only reason he has to make the unconditional judgment that it is better to smoke is the same reason that he has to make the conditional judgment that, relative to maximizing his pleasures, it is better to smoke—which is, I suppose, that he finds smoking to be quite pleasurable. But this reason is not really sufficient to justify the unconditional judgment.

Nevertheless, we are still faced with the mysterious character of this unconditional judgment, which is connected to action but insulated—or so it seems—from rational justification (whereas the conditional, all-things-considered, judgment is rationally justified but insulated from action). Moreover, why must we suppose that the agent cannot judge *unconditionally* that it is better *not* to smoke? This is impossible, according to Davidson's principles. But, as Gary Watson has pointed out, "Is there not equally good reason to think that people act contrary to their unqualified or unconditional judgments, as there is to think that people act contrary to their all-things-considered judgments?"[16]

This leaves us with the problem with which we began. The skeptic about weakness of will holds that either the agent does, in some sense, prefer to smoke (or think it better to smoke) or else he is not really able to resist his

---

[15] This point is emphasized by Irving Thalberg in "Acting Against One's Better Judgment," in Mortimore, ed., *Weakness of Will*, pp. 232 ff., esp. p. 244. (This was first published in *Theoria*, vol. 21, 1965, pp. 242-54.)

[16] See "Scepticism About Weakness of Will," p. 319.

desire to smoke. If we rule out the possibility that the agent, in some sense, prefers or thinks it better to act as he does, then what explanation *can* we give for his failing to resist his desire to smoke? According to some, the only explanation that can be given is that it is psychologically impossible for the agent—at least at the time—to resist his desire to smoke. Let us now consider this position.

3. The Psychological Impossibility Thesis

The view that it is psychologically impossible for the agent to act otherwise was first proposed (so far as I know) by R. M. Hare.[17] Two main objectives were subsequently raised against this view. First, critics argued that it presupposes "a crude form of determinism."[18] Neil Cooper charges that it implies "that it is psychologically necessary to act in accordance with one's strongest desires or 'in the line of least resistance.' "; and he replies that, although there is certainly "a tendency to act in accordance with our strongest desire," it is possible to resist this. The morally weak agent "either does not struggle against this tendency on this occasion or does not struggle hard enough."[19] But this argument is once again faced with the retort: Why does he not struggle or struggle hard enough—if he can, wants to, and thinks he ought to?

The second objection is perhaps more serious. It holds that the view in question reduces moral weakness to cases of psychological compulsion, and that this precludes us from holding that the agent of a morally weak act can be

---

[17] See *Freedom and Reason* (Oxford: Clarendon Press, 1963), pp. 80-81. The thesis is also suggested by Santas in "Plato's *Protagoras* and Explanations of Weakness," and Benson in "Wants, Desires, and Deliberation," and it is given a full-scale defense by Watson in "Scepticism About Weakness of Will."

[18] See Stephen Lukes, "Moral Weakness," in Mortimore, ed., *Weakness of Will*, p. 152.

[19] See Cooper, "Oughts and Wants," p. 218.

blameworthy—an obviously unacceptable consequence. "If it is literally true that the agent was powerless, could not help himself, could not do anything else, then, however much he blames himself, we would be as little inclined to reproach or reprove as we would in a clear case of kleptomania."[20]

However, Gary Watson has shown that it is possible to defend a version of the psychological impossibility thesis that avoids both of these objections. Watson rejects the thesis of "epithumetic determinism," as it has been called,[21] because he holds that normal persons have a capacity of self-control, which "involves the capacity to counteract and resist the strength of desires which are contrary to what one has chosen or judged best to do."[22] And he also succeeds in distinguishing weakness of will from cases of psychological compulsion. There are some desires that cannot be resisted even by those who possess the normal capacity for self-control, he suggests. These are compulsive desires. In cases of psychological compulsion the agent gives in to desires that cannot be resisted even by exercising the normal capacity for self-control, but in cases of weakness of will the agent gives in to desires that could have been resisted by a person with the normal capacity for self-control. It is not that the latter's desire is too strong; rather, his will is too weak. His will is too weak because *he* does not have the normal capacity for self-control.

But if he is unable to resist because he lacks the normal capacity for self-control, why do we blame him? Should we not excuse him? We are justified in blaming him, according to Watson, because he should have and could have acquired this capacity for self-control. "There are capacities and skills of resistance which are generally acquired in the normal course of socialization and practice, and which we

[20] See Mathews, "Weakness of Will," p. 170.
[21] See Cooper, "Oughts and Wants," p. 219.
[22] See "Scepticism About Weakness of Will," p. 336.

hold one another responsible for acquiring and maintaining."[23] This is certainly a plausible view, and Watson argues quite persuasively for it. Nevertheless, I am not entirely convinced.

Is it really true that the weak-willed agent cannot resist—at least, at the time of action? What is the evidence for supposing this? Watson's argument is that, if we suppose that the agent has the capacity to resist, then we can give no good explanation of why he fails to resist. We must suppose that either he does not try to resist or else he does not try hard enough. But why? Given that he can resist, wants to resist, and thinks he ought to resist, his failure to resist is utterly mysterious. Hence, we are entitled to doubt that he could resist and to conclude instead that he was not able to resist.

But perhaps there is another explanation. Perhaps the agent simply does not *care enough* to make very much of an effort in order to resist. Granted that the agent wants to resist and thinks that he ought to resist, perhaps the desire to resist and the resolve to resist are only strong enough to produce some inadequate effort of resistance. Perhaps if the agent really cared enough about avoiding the act judged to be wrong, he would succeed in resisting the contrary desire—even if the contrary desire is still stronger than the desire to avoid doing what is wrong. It may be, as I mentioned earlier, that the strength of one's will (resolve) is simply a function of the strength of one's concern to avoid wrongdoing. If so, then it might be argued that the agent could have resisted if he had cared enough and that he is to be blamed for not caring enough.

It might also be argued that we sometimes have independent evidence that the agent could have resisted if he tried or tried hard enough. This evidence consists in the fact that the agent has in fact resisted similar desires in similar circumstances. For example, a person stops smok-

[23] *Ibid.*, pp. 331-32.

ing and successfully resists the desire to smoke for several weeks. But then—perhaps because he no longer keeps reminding himself of how important it is (and why) not to smoke—his resolve gradually weakens, so that he finally gives in, even though the desire to smoke may now actually be weaker than when he first stopped smoking. Another sort of example is this. A person has tried to stop smoking for years. Now he is told that there are indications of lung cancer. He stops smoking immediately. Is this not evidence that he could have resisted the desire to smoke earlier—if he had been concerned enough about it? Thus, it is not clear to me that psychological impossibility is the only—or even the most plausible—explanation of the agent's failure to successfully resist.

Watson holds that the weak-willed agent is unable to resist because he lacks the normal capacity of self-control—even though he could and should have acquired this. But what about normal persons who do have this capacity of self-control? Why cannot such a person fail on occasion to exercise this capacity? And if he does fail, is not this a case of weakness of will (granted that the other defining conditions obtain)? Watson speaks as though this capacity of self-control is unique—in the sense that the person who has it will necessarily exercise it when the occasion arises.[24] But once we question his assumption that the agent's being unable to resist is the only (plausible) explanation of his failure to resist successfully, this assumption about the uniqueness of the capacity of self-control also becomes questionable.

Watson's position also commits us to holding that weakness of will can be exhibited only by a weak-willed person—i.e., a person who lacks normal powers of self-control. Must the agent of an act of weakness be the sort of person who is never able to exercise self-control with respect to any desires or emotions? Why cannot people who

[24] *Ibid.*, p. 336.

are not weak-willed persons act in a weak-willed manner on some occasions (just as even a generous person may sometimes act selfishly)? For that matter, why cannot a weak-willed person at least sometimes exhibit strength of will? This implication of Watson's thesis gives us another reason for doubting it.

4. Willpower

How, then, shall we account for weakness of will? If it is not psychologically impossible for the weak-willed agent to resist, then why does he fail to exercise self-control over his desires or emotions? If we deny that he prefers to act as he does, what other explanation can we give? I have suggested that perhaps the answer is that the agent is simply not concerned *enough* to avoid doing that which he thinks he ought not to do. But suppose that one *is* concerned. How, then, does one resist or manage the desire or emotion that prompts one to refrain from acting as one judges that one should act? If the weak-willed agent does have the capacity to resist and control his desires and emotions, what does this capacity consist in?

Actually, it comprises a number of (mostly) acquired skills and abilities, which we may collectively refer to as *willpower*. What willpower is can best be understood if, instead of considering this question in the abstract, we ask ourselves what we do in concrete cases in an attempt to manage and moderate the influence of our desires and emotions. What we discover, when we do this, is that the exercising of willpower consists not in some mysterious and inexplicable effort of the will, but rather in our adopting a variety of rather familiar kinds of precautions and countermeasures.

Consider, for example, what we do when we wish to resist a desire to do something that we have judged to be undesirable—e.g., smoking or overeating. When we experience a desire to smoke, or to have a second helping, we remind ourselves of what it is about these things that makes them undesirable. We also remind ourselves of how we shall feel later if we do something that we have judged to be undesirable and foolish. We shall feel ashamed and blame ourselves. Conversely, we may think of how good we shall feel later if we successfully resist, and we try to think of all the positive benefits to be gained from this. Often we try to distract ourselves from the object of desire by concentrating on other things—perhaps also reminding ourselves that this desire shall soon pass. If one has trouble controlling one's anger one resolves to "count to ten." One tries to anticipate situations that might irk one before they occur. One reminds oneself of the futility of losing one's temper; and here again one reminds oneself of all of the bad consequences of giving in to it. Similar things can be said about how to overcome fear or revulsion. Here we also learn somehow to brace or steel ourselves.

In many cases anticipation and advance planning are important. If we know that we are likely to procrastinate, we can set a date and schedule our activities accordingly, so that we cannot appeal to the excuse that we are too busy: "I shall visit my mother on the 25th of this month, and I shall not schedule anything else for that date." Anticipation is especially important to prevent backsliding—i.e., the erosion of one's resolve over time. One must not let oneself forget why it is important to do (or not to do) it. Sometimes one must resolve not to make any exceptions to the rule one has adopted (e.g., to send one's mother a hundred dollars a month), and one must remind oneself that it is all too easy to find "excuses" for making exceptions. Similar things can be said about guarding against indecisiveness and vacillation. We must remind ourselves that of course human judgment is fallible, but we must *act* on occasion.

These are all ways of exercising rational self-control over our actions. Exercising such control involves a wide variety of familiar skills, abilities, and habits that we hold people responsible for both acquiring and exercising. Watson suggests that the weak-willed agent has failed to acquire these capacities for self-control and now is unable to resist his desires. But I have suggested that, although this may be where the fault lies in some cases, in other cases we fault the person for failing to exercise the capacities he *has* acquired. And the latter, I should contend, is far more common. For the capacities I have been discussing are quite ordinary; it would be most unusual for a person not to have acquired most of them. Thus, cases where the agent literally cannot exercise such capacities because he has failed to acquire them are rare. But weakness of will is quite common.

I noted earlier (in discussing moral negligence) that rational self-control, or willpower, can be exercised on two different levels, since desire or emotion can either prevent the agent from acting on his judgment or prevent the agent from judging that his act is wrong in the first place. Failing to prevent one's desires and emotions from interfering with one's implementing one's judgment results in moral weakness, whereas failing to prevent them from obscuring one's realization that one's act is wrong is the cause of moral negligence. If we now recall the earlier discussion of moral negligence, we will see that controlling our desires and emotions on either of these levels requires quite similar, and sometimes the same, sorts of skills and abilities. We saw how, in order to prevent ourselves from failing to advert to certain morally relevant features of our behavior, we must remind ourselves of such things as our strong desire to impress others or to be partial to those we like (desires that produce a kind of tunnel vision in us), so that we can anticipate and take appropriate countermeasures. Similarly, we can all learn to be on our guard against self-deception by learning how to be as good at questioning our own motives as we are at questioning those of others.

Willpower, then, should not be thought of as consisting in some mysterious "summoning up of all the means in our power" (to use Kant's phrase) or in the self's exerting some peculiar effort of the will in order to tip the scales in favor of what is right. It is much more ordinary and mundane than all that.

5. Weakness, Negligence, and Indifference

The general conclusion to which I am drawn is that there is nothing *peculiarly* problematic about moral weakness. For one thing, it is no more or no less problematic than moral negligence. In cases of moral negligence the agent also fails to exercise certain capacities of self-control when he wants to and thinks that he ought to. Of course, unlike the morally weak agent, he does not realize that what he does is wrong (and hence does not realize the need to resist the desire or emotion that prompts him to act as he does). But this is because he has already failed to exercise his capacities of rational self-control on a more fundamental level— that of preventing one's desires and emotions from obscuring one's judgment about what is right and wrong in the first place. Moreover, once we examine what such a lack of self-control involves (on either of these two levels), we find that it involves a failure to exercise rather familiar skills and abilities that virtually all of us possess. There is, thus, nothing very mysterious about what we need to do and can do in order to resist and manage our desires and emotions.

This is not to say, however, that there is *nothing* problematic about weakness of will—or about negligence. The basic question still remains: why does the agent fail to exercise these capacities of self-control when he both thinks he ought to and wants to? I have suggested that whether or not one chooses to exercise these capacities (whether or not one makes the effort to resist some desire, e.g., and how hard one tries) may depend on *how much* one is concerned to avoid doing what one thinks one ought not to do. (I am assuming here that there is no *necessary* connection between believing that one ought not to do something and one's having some con-attitude toward doing it—let alone, a dominant or overriding con-attitude toward doing it. I shall argue in behalf of this position in the next chapter.) Perhaps if the weak-willed smoker (or overeater) were concerned enough about his health, he would choose to exercise these capacities in a more than merely half-hearted manner. Unlike the agent of a morally indifferent act, the agent of a morally weak act is not completely lacking in moral concern. He may, therefore, make some inadequate effort to control the desire or emotion that prompts him to do the wrong act or to vacillate or procrastinate in implementing his decision not to do it. But, like the morally indifferent agent, he does not care enough to do all that is required. Similarly, the agent of a morally negligent act is concerned enough about avoiding wrongdoing to want to pay some attention to the question of whether what he does is morally right or wrong. In this respect he is to be contrasted with the amoral agent, who has no concern at all, and thus makes no attempt to determine the rightness or wrongness of what he does. Thus, although both the morally weak and the morally negligent agent do want to avoid doing that which they think they ought not to do (for the very reasons that lead them to think they ought not to do it), they do not want to avoid doing it enough to make more than a merely inadequate effort with respect to exercising these capacities of self-control.

But why are they not more concerned? Why do they not care enough to make a greater effort or try harder? Why do some people care more than others (and some people, the morally indifferent, care not at all)? Is this something in our control—something for which we can hold people morally responsible? Perhaps some people fail to care, or care enough, about avoiding moral wrongdoing because they have failed to develop in themselves a proper degree of sympathy for others and a sense of justice. Then why have they failed to foster these qualities in themselves?

Can anyone be held morally responsible for the ultimate determination of his behavior?

One can always raise these deeper questions about moral responsibility—and thus raise the old conundrum about the compatibility of free will and determinism. However, this does not show that there is anything peculiarly problematic about moral weakness. For these kinds of questions can be raised in connection with all the various forms of immorality. Why do morally indifferent and amoral agents not care at all whether what they do is morally right or wrong? Why does the agent of a wicked act prefer to pursue his own advantage to avoiding causing harm to others? Is it because none of them really care (or care enough) about the welfare of others? But why do they not care? Here again we can ask all the same questions, and our answers will be equally satisfactory or unsatisfactory.

I shall have something to say about these deeper issues of free will and moral responsibility in Chapter Eight. But my primary concern here is not with these deeper issues. We commonly assume that some people are blameworthy for their acts—so long as their acts are due to their own shortcomings (such as lack of self-control or lack of concern for others) instead of being due, say, to unavoidable ignorance or compulsion. I am not so much concerned with whether the commonly accepted criteria of blameworthiness are correct, or whether they are ever really satisfied. My concern here is with the question: granted the commonly recognized criteria of blameworthiness, what forms of blameworthy behavior are possible? It is the variety rather than the possibility of immorality that I am here interested in exploring. Thus, the question to which we now turn is this: is moral weakness the only possible form of blameworthy wrongdoing, given the assumption that the agent believes his act to be wrong, or are there other possible forms of conscious wrongdoing—in particular, are what I have called moral indifference and preferential wickedness possible?

S I X

* * *

MORAL INDIFFERENCE

The question of whether morally indifferent behavior is possible turns, as we have seen, on the question of whether it is possible for a person to believe that an act is morally wrong without having some con-attitude toward that act. That it is not possible is the central claim of all those who defend noncognitivist analyses of moral beliefs and judgments—i.e., those who claim that having a moral belief consists in having some kind of pro- or con-attitude rather than in accepting some proposition that can be assessed as true or false. The thesis that it is a necessary condition of believing an act to be morally wrong that one have some con-attitude toward that act is accepted both by those who adopt a purely noncognitivist account of moral beliefs— i.e., by those who deny that there is any proposition as such expressed by the judgment that an act is morally wrong—and by those who adopt a kind of "mixed" theory. The latter agree with the "pure" cognitivists that to believe that an act is morally wrong is to accept some (true or false) proposition to this effect, but they reject a purely propositional analysis of moral beliefs on the ground that no such theory can account for the fact that when one makes a moral judgment one is (necessarily) expressing a pro- or con-attitude.

For such a theory holds that an ethical judgment simply is an assertion of fact—that ethical judgments constitute merely an alternative vocabulary for reporting facts. It may be that they should be reinterpreted so that this is the case. In actual usage, however, this seems clearly not to be so. When we are making merely factual assertions we are not thereby taking any pro- or con-attitude toward what we are talking about; we are not recommending it, prescribing it, or anything of that sort. But when we make an ethical judgment we are not neutral in this way; it would seem paradoxical if one were to say "X is good" or "Y is right" but be absolutely indifferent to its being sought or done by himself or anyone else. If he were indifferent in this way, we would take him to mean that it is generally regarded as good or right, but that he did not so regard it himself. We may be making or implying factual assertions in some of our ethical judgments—when we say, "He was a good man," we do seem to imply that he was honest, kind, etc.—but this is not all we are doing.[1]

I shall refer to the thesis which holds that having some con-attitude toward an act is a necessary condition of believing it to be morally wrong as *the thesis of internalism*.[2] This thesis has important consequences for ethical theory. If it is true, then no purely cognitivist, or propositional, account of the meaning of moral judgments or the nature of moral beliefs can be adequate. Moreover, this thesis also

[1] William K. Frankena, *Ethics* (Englewood Cliffs, N.J.: Prentice-Hall, Inc., 1973), p. 100.

[2] This thesis is one species of what Frankena calls "internalism," since it implies that the motivating force of moral beliefs or judgments is logically internal to them. For Frankena's distinction between "externalism" and "internalism" as two different general viewpoints regarding the relationship between moral obligation and motivation see his "Obligation and Motivation in Recent Moral Philosophy," in A. I. Melden, ed., *Essays in Moral Philosophy* (Seattle: University of Washington Press, 1958), p. 40.

seems to imply that there is a logical gap between moral judgments and factual claims, since it is thought to be a defining characteristic of a merely factual claim that the acceptance of, or assent to, such claims does not depend on one's having any pro- or con-attitudes. This means— many have argued—that no mere factual claim can *in and of itself* entail, or even provide us with a reason or evidence for, moral judgments.

The thesis of internalism also implies that moral indifference is not logically possible. If it is true, then it can never be a possible explanation of wrongdoing that, although the agent believed his act to be morally wrong, he simply did not care that it was wrong. In this chapter I shall argue that moral indifference *is* possible and, hence, that the thesis of internalism is false. Many of those who accept this thesis consider it to be not so much a thesis to be argued for as a statement of a datum that needs to be explained or accounted for by an adequate ethical theory. Thus, it is said to be a criterion of adequacy of any theory of the meaning of moral judgments that it be able to account for their magnetism, or dynamic quality, or moving appeal.[3] Now, although I shall argue that the thesis of internalism is false, I do not wish to deny that it has a strong intuitive appeal. There does indeed appear to be *something* paradoxical about supposing that a person believes that some act is wrong and yet has no con-attitude whatsoever toward it. And this suggests that the burden of proof rests on those who deny the thesis of internalism. It is incumbent on one who wishes to deny this thesis to offer some other explanation—i.e., one that does not presuppose the truth of this thesis—of why it seems odd or paradoxical to suppose that someone believes X to be wrong and yet has no

[3] See, for example, C. L. Stevenson, "The Emotive Meaning of Ethical Terms," in Sellars and Hospers, eds., *Readings in Ethical Theory* (New York: Appleton-Century-Crofts, Inc., 1952), p. 417. This paper was first published in *Mind*, vol. 46, 1937.

con-attitude toward X. This is precisely what I now propose to do.

1. The Thesis of Internalism

It has been argued that it is absurd or paradoxical to suppose that a person could believe that it would be morally wrong for him to do something and yet fail to have a con-attitude toward doing it because, if a person said that a certain act was morally wrong but it was clear that he had no con-attitude toward it, we would have sufficient grounds for concluding either that he was being insincere, that he did not literally mean what he said, or that he was simply misusing language. This claim is usually supported by an appeal to what we are all supposed to recognize to be the criteria for the acceptance of (assent to), or agreement with, a moral judgment.

Thus, C. L. Stevenson argues that if we were trying to convince someone that something he did was wrong, and if he replies, "I agree that it was morally wrong, but I do not disapprove of what I did or feel ashamed of myself for having done it," we would be justified in concluding that he did not really agree with us or believe that it was wrong. We would be justified in concluding either that he was being insincere or that what he really meant to say was that, according to the standards accepted by most people, it would be considered morally wrong. But we could not say that *he* agreed with us or that *he himself* believed it to be morally wrong unless he shared our disapproval of his act—i.e., unless he agreed with us in attitude.[4]

Now it must be admitted that Stevenson is correct in claiming that we would not ordinarily say that someone accepts or agrees with what someone else says in saying, "X is wrong," unless he has an attitude of disapproval

[4] See *Ethics and Language* (New Haven: Yale University Press, 1944), pp. 16-17.

143

toward X. But, I shall argue, it does not follow that a person who fails to disapprove of X cannot be said to believe (himself) that X is morally wrong—as opposed to believing merely that other people believe that it is morally wrong. Stevenson's claims seem plausible because to say, "X is morally wrong," is a conventional means of expressing one's disapproval of X. To use a notion developed by H. P. Grice, saying "X is morally wrong," *conversationally implicates* that the speaker disapproves of X. This is because, as Grice points out, we expect the speaker to be observing certain maxims of appropriate conversation directing him to make his "conversational contribution such as is required by the accepted purpose or direction of the talk exchange."[5] Now, as Stevenson points out, if we are trying to convince someone that something he did was wrong, we are primarily concerned to persuade him to adopt an attitude of disapproval toward it. That is to say, we are primarily concerned about other people's moral beliefs insofar as these have a bearing on their attitudes and dispositions to act in certain ways. Thus, as M.B.E. Smith has pointed out, "were someone to tell us that he has a certain moral belief and then confess that he has no inclination to act upon it, his utterance would be puzzling to us. For he has at once told us that he has a certain belief and ensured that his information is irrelevant to our usual concern in discovering his moral conviction."[6] But, as Smith goes on to say, this does not show that he does not really hold the belief in question.

Stevenson's claims about our criteria of moral agreement seem plausible because, given that saying, "X is morally wrong," conversationally implicates that the speaker disapproves of X, we would not ordinarily say that a person agrees with someone who says this unless he shares that

[5] See his "Logic and Conversation," in Cole and Morgan, eds., *Syntax and Semantics, vol. 3, Speech Acts* (New York: Academic Press, 1975), p. 45.

[6] M.B.E. Smith, "Indifference and Moral Acceptance," *American Philosophical Quarterly,* vol. 9, 1972, pp. 89-90.

attitude of disapproval. Indeed, unless he shares that disfavor, it would be misleading for us to say that he believes X to be morally wrong. For it seems also to be a conversational implicature of saying, "Jones believes X to be morally wrong," that Jones disapproves of X. If so, this conversational implicature would seem to be parasitic on the primary implicature, which consists in the fact that Jones's saying, "X is morally wrong," conversationally implicates that Jones disapproves of X. But it does not follow that that Jones disapproves of X is entailed (or logically implied) by *what* we say in saying "Jones believes X to be morally wrong." As Grice points out, we must distinguish between what is implied by what we say and what is implied (conversationally implicated) by our saying it.[7] Thus, it does not follow that Jones's disapproving of X is a necessary condition of his believing X to be morally wrong. An air of paradox results not from our supposing (or believing) that Jones believes X to be morally wrong when it is clear that he does not disapprove of X, but from our *sayings* that he believes this when it is clear that he does not disapprove of X.

Moreover, nothing that has so far been admitted shows that Jones's believing X to be morally wrong cannot be identified with his accepting some proposition about X. For the fact that the utterance of a certain sentence is a conventional means of expressing disapproval does not preclude the fact that its utterance also counts as expressing a proposition. If so, one must consider the possibility that the person believes (i.e., accepts as true) the proposition

[7] See "Logic and Conversation," p. 58. Of course, a noncognitivist may wish to claim that Jones's having a con-attitude toward X is logically implied by what we say in saying, "Jones believes X to be wrong"—not just conversationally implicated by our saying this. My argument is that the evidence cited by Stevenson and others does not require this stronger hypothesis, but can just as well be explained by the weaker hypothesis of conversational implication. At the very least, the evidence cited does not decide between these two hypotheses.

expressed by the utterance but does not share the attitude expressed. To use an example suggested by M.B.E. Smith, the utterance of the sentence, "Jones eats like a pig," is a conventional way of expressing disgust. Now suppose someone believes that Jones habitually uses his sleeve to wipe his mouth, picks up his food with his fingers, and belches loudly; but suppose that he does not disapprove of Jones's behavior on this account. Such a person may correctly be described as *believing the proposition expressed by the utterance of "Jones eats like a pig,"* even though it might be misleading to describe him as *believing that Jones eats like a pig.* For to say the latter is to suggest (or conversationally implicate) that he shares the attitude conventionally expressed by uttering this sentence.

Now for all that has so far been admitted, it remains an open question whether one expresses some proposition in saying, "X is morally wrong." And, if so, a person can believe the proposition expressed by saying, "X is morally wrong," even though he does not share the attitude conventionally expressed by its utterance. Of course, whether we can identify believing or judging that X is wrong merely with accepting (as true) the proposition expressed by this utterance is another question. I shall later argue that we can. But so far I have been concerned only to point out that Stevenson's observations do not suffice by themselves to establish either the thesis of internalism or the necessity of a noncognitivist analysis of moral judgments.

Similar claims about our criteria for the acceptance of (or assent to) a moral judgment have been made by R. M. Hare. Hare claims that to judge that X is morally wrong is to commit oneself to the judgment, "I ought not to do X," when the circumstances are appropriate, and that this entails assenting to the prescription, "Let me not do X," and hence not doing X if it is within one's physical and psychological power not to do it.[8] The argument offered in

[8] See *The Language of Morals* (Oxford: Clarendon Press, 1952), pp. 168 ff.

behalf of this criterion of assent is that to say, "X is morally wrong" (or, "X ought not to be done") is to condemn X— i.e., that this utterance is a conventional means of performing the speech-act of condemnation. And one might add, by way of elaborating Hare's argument, that it is a sincerity condition of the speech-act of condemning X that the speaker have a con-attitude toward X—which, for Hare, amounts to his being prepared to assent to the imperative, "Let X not be done." One might draw an analogy here with promising. A person who utters the words, "I promise to do X" (under the commonly recognized circumstances in which this counts as making a promise) but does not intend to do X will be said to have made an insincere promise (and, in this sense, not to have meant what he said). Similarly, Hare suggests, a person who utters the words, "X is morally wrong" but does not have a con-attitude toward X (and hence is not prepared to assent to the prescription, "Let X not be done") will be said to be insincere. He does not really mean what he says and thus cannot be said to "sincerely" believe that X is wrong.

But this argument commits the same error as Stevenson's—namely, that of confusing what is implied by one's saying something (conversational implicature) with what is implied by what one says (logical implication), and thus confusing the necessary conditions of using language to perform a certain task (e.g., expressing disapproval or condemning) with the necessary conditions of being in a certain state of mind (such as believing X to be morally wrong). Noncognitivists like Hare habitually use the expression "moral judgment" to refer indiscriminately to moral utterances (linguistic entities) and to moral beliefs (states of mind, or mental entities)—apparently assuming that what holds true of the one also holds true of the other.

Now since saying that X is morally wrong conventionally counts as condemning X, and since having a con-attitude toward X is a sincerity condition of performing the speech-act of condemning X, a person who says this but fails to have a con-attitude toward X is being both insincere and misleading—unless, of course, he also utters a disclaimer to the effect that he lacks this attitude.[9] But it does not follow that he cannot mean or believe what he says. One can draw the further conclusion that he cannot really mean or believe what he says only if one assumes that the meaning of "X is morally wrong," is to be identified with its illocutionary force (or speech-act potential). But this commits us to a dubious and much criticized theory of meaning—the so-called "meaning as use" theory. According to this theory, if a word (e.g., the word "wrong") is conventionally used to perform a certain speech-act (such as condemning), then to point this out is to give (at least a partial) explication of the meaning of this word. The chief difficulty with this sort of speech-act analysis of the meaning of a word like "wrong" is, as John Searle has pointed out, that it fails to satisfy what seems to be a perfectly valid criterion of adequacy for any analysis of the meaning of a word— namely, that any "analysis of the meaning of a word (or morpheme) must be consistent with the fact that the same word (morpheme) can mean the same thing in all the grammatically different kinds of sentences in which it can occur."[10] Thus, if one claims that the meaning of the word "wrong" can be explained by saying that it is conventionally used to perform the speech-act of condemnation, one is faced with the objection that this does not seem to explain the meaning of this word as it occurs in such sentences as "Is X wrong?" "I wonder if X is wrong," and "If X is wrong, it ought to be made illegal." Moreover, it seems obvious that "wrong" has the same meaning in each of these sentences as it does in the simple present indicative, "X is wrong." It is interesting to note that even J. O. Urmson, who in some of his earlier writings seemed to be defending

---

[9] As Grice points out, it is possible to cancel a conversational implicature. (See "Logic and Conversation," p. 57.)

[10] See *Speech Acts* (London: Cambridge University Press, 1970), p. 139.

148

such speech-act analyses of words like "good" and "valid," now agrees with this line of criticism:

> In the study of ethical discourse, of the speech-acts which appear in discussions of moral issues, it is no doubt of importance to insist that many ethical utterances have to be construed as expressions of approval and commendation. . . . The insights, we may acknowledge, have been valuable; but their value has been diminished by treating them as insights into the meaning of ethical terms, which they are not, instead of the use we make of language in speech.[11]

If this criticism of the speech-act analysis of "X is wrong" is correct, then it remains an open question as to whether some purely propositional or cognitivist account of its meaning may yet turn out to be correct. Indeed, as D.A.J. Richards has suggested, if the word "wrong" has the same meaning in all of the grammatically different kinds of contexts in which it can occur, it seems plausible to explain this in terms of the fact that the same proposition is being expressed by one who utters the sentence with, in each case, a different illocutionary force.[12]

Whether there is some proposition expressed by one who utters the sentence, "X is morally wrong," and, if so, what it is, is, of course, another question. I shall not attempt to deal with this large and difficult question here. So far I have only been concerned to point out that this possibility is ruled out neither by the observation that the utterance of "X is morally wrong" conversationally implicates that the speaker has a con-attitude toward X nor by the observation that to say this is to condemn acts of this sort (together with the further observation that having some con-attitude toward X is a sincerity condition of condemning

[11] *The Emotive Theory of Ethics* (New York: Oxford University Press, 1971), p. 6.

[12] See *A Theory of Reasons for Action* (Oxford: Clarendon Press, 1971), p. 6.

X). And if it is true that the utterance of "X is morally wrong" does express a proposition about X, then a person who fails to have a con-attitude toward X may nevertheless accept this proposition as true and, in this sense at least, believe that X is morally wrong. Moreover, if one rejects both Stevenson's claim that the word "wrong" has an "emotive" meaning (which seems to equate meaning with perlocutionary force) and Hare's analysis of its meaning in terms of its illocutionary force, it seems that we no longer have any reason to deny that such a person can mean, and hence believe, what he says.[13]

At this point the internalist may reply that, even if all of this is admitted, we still have not shown that moral indifference is possible. For, in the first place, even if we admit that the utterance of "X is morally wrong" counts as asserting a proposition about X and that one can accept this proposition as true without having a con-attitude toward X or being prepared to condemn X, we cannot identify believing X to be morally wrong merely with accepting this proposition as true. Even if we admit that accepting a certain proposition is a necessary condition of believing X to be morally wrong, we may still insist that it is not a sufficient condition. This is because believing X to be morally wrong involves making (or having made) an *evaluative* judgment, and having some pro- or con-attitude is a necessary condition of making an evaluative judgment.

In the second place, the "pure" noncognitivist will simply deny that there is some particular proposition that is asserted by anyone who sincerely says that X is morally wrong (and which must be accepted by anyone who agrees with what is thus said). According to the noncognitivist,

[13] The term "perlocutionary force" refers to the effects that one brings about *by* making a certain utterance, rather than what one does *in* making a certain utterance (the illocutionary force). The terms "illocutionary" and "perlocutionary" were first introduced in order to make this distinction by J. L. Austin. See his *How To Do Things with Words* (Oxford: Clarendon Press, 1962), pp. 99 ff.

there is no such proposition. Hence, the distinction we have tried to draw between the proposition expressed by the utterance of "X is morally wrong" (its meaning, as some would say) and the speech-acts which its utterance is conventionally used to perform (its illocutionary force) is inapplicable in this case. Neither, then, can we distinguish, as we have tried to do, between a person's merely accepting the proposition expressed by the utterance of "X is morally wrong" and his having the con-attitude toward X that is typically expressed (or conversationally implicated) by its utterance.

Let us now consider each of these replies, beginning with the second, more forceful, reply to the effect that there is no proposition necessarily asserted by anyone who sincerely says that X is morally wrong. Why have some philosophers denied that there is such a proposition?

2. The Alleged Fallacies of Cognitivism

One charge that has been levelled against any attempt to analyze the meaning of "X is morally wrong" in terms of some proposition expressed by its utterance is that no such analysis can explain why it is a non-contingent fact that to say, "X is morally wrong," is to condemn or express disapproval of X. But, as we have seen, this charge can be met by pointing out that the utterance of "X is morally wrong" is also a conventional means of expressing disapproval of X or of performing the speech-act of condemning X.

There is, however, a more serious objection to any propositional analyses of "X is morally wrong." This is that any such analysis will involve us either in the mysteries associated with intuitionism or the fallacies entailed by naturalism. One who adopts a cognitivist, or propositional, account of the meaning of "X is morally wrong" may claim either (a) that the meaning of this proposition is *sui generis* and not susceptible to any definition or analysis—at least, not in terms of any merely descriptive predicates (the position of the intuitionist), or (b) that the meaning of this proposition can be explicated in terms of certain descriptive predicates (the position of the naturalist or descriptivist). When asked to specify just what this proposition is, one inevitably runs into this Scylla and Charybdis.

The intuitionist alternative holds that this proposition consists in predicating some unique, unanalyzable, nonnatural characteristic of X.[14] The trouble with this is that most philosophers find that they are not acquainted with any such mysterious characteristic and are, therefore, inclined to deny that it exists. Moreover, the intuitionist is committed to holding that basic (or nonderivative) moral propositions are both synthetic and *a priori*—another mystery. And, while admitting that this mysterious characteristic of wrongness is dependent on (or consequential to) certain other natural (or empirical) characteristics, intuitionists leave us with the further mystery of explaining *why* this should be so. Finally, intuitionists have been charged with making it seem utterly mysterious why anyone who believes that an act has this peculiar characteristic should be motivated not to do it.

These mysteries can be avoided, it seems, only if one embraces naturalism.[15] The naturalist holds that the most basic moral propositions are true by definition—in this way solving the problem of how we know them to be true without appealing to the mysterious notion of an intuitive grasp of a necessary and yet synthetic connection between distinct characteristics. For example, Bentham suggests that

[14] For examples of intuitionism see G. E. Moore, *Principia Ethica* (Cambridge: Cambridge University Press, 1903), and W. D. Ross, *The Right and the Good* (Oxford: Clarendon Press, 1930). Ross holds that both "right" and "good" are indefinable, whereas Moore only considers "good" to be unanalyzable.

[15] For defenses of naturalism see R. B. Perry, *Realms of Value* (Cambridge, Mass: Harvard University Press, 1954), and F. C. Sharp, *Ethics* (New York: The Century Co., 1928).

"X is the right thing to do" simply means "X maximizes the general happiness."[16] However, critics have argued that such naturalistic analyses of the meaning of ethical terms rest on a number of confusions (or fallacies).

In the first place, it has been argued that any such analysis confuses evaluation with description. The earlier, intuitionist critics claimed that such definitions confuse certain good-making (or right-making) characteristics with the characteristic of goodness (or rightness) itself.[17] Later critics, such as Hare, claimed that even the intuitionists failed to recognize just how radical the difference is between evaluative predicates and descriptive predicates. These later critics claimed that naturalistic definitions confuse the *criteria* for the application of terms like "good" and "right" with their *meaning*.[18] Both sets of critics agree, however, that the naturalist confuses certain good-making (or right-making) characteristics with the meaning of "good" (or "right").

For the intuitionist, the naturalist confuses certain characteristics designated by descriptive terms—namely, certain good-making or right-making characteristics—with the characteristics designated by evaluative terms like "good" and "right." To expose this error G. E. Moore suggested that we employ what came to be called "the open-question technique."[19] No matter what descriptive characteristic (or set of characteristics) the naturalist proposes to define the meaning of "good," it will always make sense, he claimed, to ask whether something that has this characteristic is good. This shows, Moore argued, that goodness is not identical with this characteristic. But this test for sameness of meaning has been much criticized. Critics have pointed

[16] See Jeremy Bentham, *An Introduction to the Principles of Morals and Legislation*, Chapter 1, paragraph X.

[17] This criticism is made by G. E. Moore in *Principia Ethica* and by W. D. Ross in *The Right and the Good*.

[18] This criticism is made by R. M. Hare in *The Language of Morals*.

[19] See *Principia Ethica*, pp. 15-16.

out that this technique does not succeed in showing that two terms are not synonymous in cases where they are only covertly synonymous—i.e., if they do not obviously have the same meaning and can be shown to have the same meaning only after further reflection.[20] Indeed, it is doubtful that any complex philosophical definition of terms like "true," "know," and "cause" could pass this test. Moreover, this technique for exposing what Moore called "the naturalistic fallacy" seems to involve a fallacy of its own. For it rests on the assumption that if two terms have the same meaning, then no one can believe that one of them applies while doubting that the other applies. And this, it has been pointed out, ignores the fact of referential opacity in contexts of believing and doubting.

For noncognitivist critics like Hare, the chief difficulty with naturalistic analyses is that they have the effect of robbing evaluative terms of their commendatory or prescriptive functions. In saying that something is good, we are commending things like this; and in saying that an act ought to be done, we are prescribing that acts like this be done. But one does not commend something merely by applying descriptive predicates to it. Thus, any theory which equates the meaning of an evaluative term like "good" or "ought" with the meaning of some descriptive term or expression has the effect of making it impossible to use these evaluative terms for the purposes of commending or prescribing. Thus, Hare contends that the difference between evaluative and descriptive terms is more radical than even the intuitionists would admit. They see the difference as consisting in the fact that they designate quite different sorts of characteristics, whereas the difference consists in the fact that evaluative terms are used to perform a wholly different sort of linguistic function from that of describing. Thus, the mistake made by the naturalist is not that of

[20] This criticism was first made by R. B. Brandt, *Ethical Theory* (Englewood Cliffs, N.J.: Prentice-Hall, Inc., 1959), pp. 163-66.

confounding an evaluative characteristic with some other kind of characteristic; it consists, rather, in confusing the meaning of evaluative terms with their conventionally recognized criteria of evaluation.

This mistake is simply made explicit by a naturalist who defines "good" as "meets the criteria or standards of assessment or evaluation."[21] For to say that something meets the conventionally recognized criteria or standards of evaluation appropriate to it is merely to describe it in a certain way, but to say that something is good is to commend it. Thus, the reason why it always remains an open question as to whether something that satisfies the appropriate criteria of evaluation is also good is that it is one thing to describe something in a certain way and quite another thing to commend it. Having admitted that it has certain characteristics, we always can either commend it or not (approve of it or disapprove of it).

The basic assumption behind Hare's version of the open-question test for sameness of meaning seems to be this: no two terms or expressions can be equivalent in meaning if the typical or primary use of one of them differs from that of the other. But critics have claimed that this test confuses the *meaning* of an expression with its *use* (or illocutionary force)—a point alluded to earlier—and one of them has argued that it is this test (and not naturalism) that rests on a fallacy. John Searle calls it "the speech-act fallacy" to infer from the fact that in calling something "good," for example, one is praising or commending it that one can therefore explain its meaning by saying that it is used for this purpose. Moreover, Searle argues that it is also a fallacy—what he calls "the naturalistic fallacy fallacy"—to infer from the fact that evaluative statements have a different illocutionary force from descriptive statements that they cannot be entailed by descriptive statements.[22] It is a mistake because

[21] See John Searle, *Speech Acts*, p. 152.
[22] *Ibid.*, pp. 132 and 139.

entailment depends on meaning, and meaning (i.e., sense and reference, for Searle) is different from illocutionary force (i.e., speech-act potential). Thus, even though the statement that X is a valid deductive argument is evaluative, whereas the statement that the premises of X entail its conclusion is descriptive, the latter nevertheless entails the former—because, Searle argues, the proposition expressed by the latter entails the proposition expressed by the former.[23]

I must confess that I find these arguments quite convincing. Nevertheless, there are some difficulties that one faces if one adopts Searle's position. According to Searle, the sentences "Jones is a Negro" and "Jones is a nigger" have the same meaning since they express the same proposition, even though their utterances have different characteristic illocutionary forces. It follows, then, that the former entails the latter. Now this is just what anti-naturalists like Hare object to. "Naturalists," Hare complains, "put forward arguments of the form that is typified by 'He's black; so he's a nigger; so he's inferior.' "

> If, he might argue, a man has curly hair and a black skin and thick lips, and is descended from people with similar features, then we cannot deny that he is a nigger. But "nigger" is a term of contempt. Therefore, if we have the word "nigger" in use, we are led ineluctably from factual propositions about his skin-color etc., to the indubitably evaluative proposition that he is a nigger. If one knows that he has black skin, etc., one cannot but (*logically* cannot but) despise him.[24]

Now, surely this argument *is* fallacious. However, it does not seem to me that Searle and other naturalists are committed to recognizing it as valid. The correct reply to this objection—as Hare himself recognizes—is to point out that one cannot be forced by acknowledging the premises of

[23] *Ibid.*, pp. 136 and 148.
[24] See *Freedom and Reason*, pp. 188 and 193.

this argument to judge blacks to be inferior or to despise them, since one can avoid this simply by refusing to use the word "nigger." Thus, Searle may reply, although one who accepts the proposition expressed by "Jones is a Negro" is logically committed to accepting the proposition expressed by "Jones is a nigger," he is not committed to expressing this proposition by *saying*, "Jones is a nigger."

Nevertheless, there are two further problems that face us if we accept Searle's account of this matter. First, there is the problem of what to say about beliefs (as opposed to utterances). What are we to say about the belief that Jones is a nigger? Is this belief different from the belief that Jones is a Negro? If so, then believing that Jones is a nigger cannot be identified with merely accepting the proposition expressed by the utterance of "Jones is a Negro." What, then, can it consist in except also being disposed to condemn or disapprove of Jones because one accepts this proposition as true? This suggests, similarly, that even if the utterance of "X is morally wrong" does express some proposition that can also be expressed by uttering some sentence employing merely descriptive terms, *believing X* to be morally wrong consists in something more than merely accepting this proposition as true. I shall return to this problem later in this chapter.

First, however, I should like to consider another difficulty that still faces us even if we accept what Searle says about the naturalistic fallacy fallacy. This problem arises when we consider what one is to do if one wishes to reject the claim that Jones is a nigger, or the unfavorable evaluation of Jones that is expressed by someone who says that Jones is a nigger. As Searle admits, it will not do to say that Jones is not a nigger, for the "utterance of 'He is not a nigger,' is just as improper as, 'He is a nigger'; the very utterance of that particular word is an indication of hostility, contempt, etc., for Negroes and is, therefore, taboo."[25] Now this is just the problem, according to Hare: "If a man

[25] See *Speech Acts*, p. 156.

wishes to reject the evaluations incapsulated in the word 'nigger,' he can do so by using another value-word—often a more general one; he may say, 'A man can be a negro, and be none the *worse* for that.' " Indeed, Hare argues, "We have these more general, primarily evaluative words just because we do not want to be the prisoners of our own conceptual apparatus."[26] The naturalist, however, wishes to tie certain descriptive criteria even to the most general evaluative terms.

3. Neutrality and Autonomy

This brings us now to what I take to be the most serious objection to naturalism: "The most fundamental objection against naturalism is that it makes moral questions depend on conceptual ones—whereas we feel that to accept a certain conceptual apparatus is one thing, and to adopt a certain system of moral principles another."[27] This objection involves two closely related charges. First, the naturalist is being charged with attempting to justify certain moral principles merely by appealing to the definitions of certain moral terms. When we examine his proposed definitions, we find that they are really substantive moral principles. Thus, the naturalist is accused of trying to smuggle in certain moral principles under the guise of merely defining terms, or (if he claims to be giving us a reformative rather than a reportive definition) attempting to establish the truth of certain moral principles through verbal legislation. Because of this the naturalist is accused of violating what might be called *the neutrality requirement* on metaethical theory—namely, that no analysis of the meaning of moral terms can be such that to accept it as correct one must also accept a substantive moral principle.

The second charge involved in this objection against nat-

[26] *Freedom and Reason*, pp. 189-90.
[27] *Ibid.*, p. 187.

uralism is that it attempts to deprive us of our freedom to form our own moral opinions. According to Hare, "One of the most important constituents of our freedom, as moral agents, is the freedom to form our own opinions about moral questions, even if that involved changing our language."[28] This charge has also been expressed by claiming that naturalism denies the autonomy of moral agents. To be fully free, and hence fully responsible for their behavior, moral agents must be autonomous or self-legislating—i.e., each must be free to decide or judge for himself how he ought to act. This suggests another requirement (or condition of adequacy) for any metaethical theory. Closely related to the neutrality requirement (and a logical consequence of this requirement) is what might be called *the autonomy requirement*. This is that no analysis of the nature of moral judgments can be correct if it implies that persons are not fully free to decide for themselves how they ought to act—and thus to either accept or reject any moral principle whatsoever.

Let us now consider each of these charges, beginning with the charge that the naturalist violates the neutrality requirement. Suppose that one claims (as I believe Bentham intended to be claiming) that to say that an act is morally wrong is to say that it fails to maximize the general happiness—i.e., that "X is morally wrong" means the same as "X fails to maximize the general happiness." Is this really to claim, in effect, that a certain *substantive* moral principle is true by definition? This depends on what one means by "a substantive moral principle" and on whether one takes the principle that *acts are morally right if and only if they maximize the general happiness* to be a substantive moral principle.

One way of understanding the notion of a substantive moral principle is to interpret a substantive principle as a *synthetic*—as opposed to an analytic—*proposition*. Thus

---

[28] *Ibid.*, p. 2.

understood, a substantive moral principle is one that tells us what kinds of things are good, or what kinds of acts are right; whereas an analytic moral principle tells us what it means to say that something is good, or that some act is right. Alternatively, we may view a synthetic moral principle as one that specifies certain good-making or right-making characteristics; whereas analytic moral principles specify what goodness (or rightness) itself consists in—i.e., they specify what it is for something to be good (or right). As G. E. Moore pointed out, we must distinguish the question, "What things are good?" from the question, "How is 'good' to be defined?"[29] But it does not seem to me that the naturalist *is* guilty of confusing these two questions. Indeed, this same distinction is pointed out and emphasized by R. B. Perry in his defense of naturalism.

> There are two questions: "What is morally good?" and "In what does moral goodness consist?" . . . The first question is answered when the predicate of . . . goodness, whatever it means, is assigned to a grammatical subject; the second question is answered when the predicate itself is analyzed or clarified. It is the second question and the discussions to which it gives rise that constitute the primary subject matter of moral theory.[30]

Thus, Perry not only recognizes this distinction; he makes it perfectly clear that he is only attempting to clarify or analyze the meaning of such predicates as "morally good" and "morally right" and is not making any claims about what sorts of persons are good or what sorts of acts are right. And it seems to me that Bentham can be interpreted as making a similar sort of claim. Insofar as he is understood as an ethical naturalist, his principle of utility (that acts are right if and only if they maximize the general happiness) is to be taken, not as a synthetic proposition telling us what sorts of acts are right and wrong, but as an analytic

[29] See *Principia Ethica*, p. 5.
[30] R. B. Perry, *Realms of Value*, p. 87.

proposition telling us what it means to say that an act is morally right or wrong (i.e., what it is for an act to be morally right or wrong). Thus understood, the principle of utility is not intended as a substantive moral principle.[31] Nor does accepting this principle commit us (in and of itself) to accepting any substantive moral principles. What sorts of acts are right and wrong is to be determined by what the facts are—i.e., by which acts do, and do not, maximize the general happiness.

Another way of understanding the notion of a substantive moral principle is to equate a substantive moral principle with a *normative* moral principle and to interpret a normative principle as one the acceptance of which commits one to acting in a certain way. On this interpretation the naturalist is being charged, not with illegitimately smuggling in *propositions* about what kinds of acts are right (or what kinds of things are good), but rather with attempting to smuggle in certain *prescriptions* about how we ought to act (or choose). This is the interpretation that would be preferred by noncognitivists, and it leads directly to the further charge that naturalism violates the autonomy requirement by robbing us of the freedom to decide for ourselves how we ought to act. Let us now consider this second charge.

It is of the essence of naturalism to hold that certain descriptive criteria must be employed by anyone who wishes to make moral judgments, since these criteria define what it means to say that an act is morally right or wrong. Thus, a utilitarian naturalist might claim that anyone who wishes to make moral judgments must employ the criterion of utility, because to say that an act is morally right is to say that it satisfies this criterion, whereas to say that it is morally wrong is to say that it violates this criterion. It follows,

[31] For an interpretation of Bentham's principle as analytic in character, i.e., as telling us what it is for an act to be (morally) right or wrong, see my "Bentham's Principle," *Ethics*, vol. 84, 1974, pp. 128-39.

moreover, that anyone who judges an act to be morally wrong is thereby committed to accepting some proposition as true—for example, that this act fails to maximize the general happiness (for one kind of act-utilitarian) or that it fails to conform with that set of rules whose observance by everyone would serve to maximize the general happiness (for one kind of rule-utilitarian).

As opposed to this, noncognitivists like Hare reject the view that to say, "X is morally wrong," is to assert some particular proposition about X. What proposition it expresses depends, for each speaker, on what descriptive criteria he happens to accept as governing his universalizable and overriding prescriptions. Thus, if he is prepared to prescribe universally that acts are not to be done if and only if they violate the criterion of utility, then in saying, "X is morally wrong," he will be asserting the proposition that X violates this criterion. But, Hare insists, no one is logically committed to employing this or any other criterion just in order to make judgments about what acts are morally wrong. Rather, one is free to employ any criterion (or set of criteria) whose implications for universally prescribing one is prepared to accept. To claim, as the naturalist does, that anyone who makes judgments about the moral rightness or wrongness of actions *must* employ a certain criterion is to deny his freedom to form his own opinions about which acts are right and which acts are wrong. Thus, to be fully autonomous a moral agent must be free to either accept or reject any criterion whatsoever.

I shall now argue that this charge rests on a number of confusions and is therefore misguided. What Hare is claiming in effect is this: if moral agents are to be free to form their own opinions about whether any given act is morally right or wrong, then there can be no objective criteria for deciding this question. This is a mistake. One might as well argue that in order for scientific investigators to be free to form their own opinions (say, about whether the earth is a sphere or whether there is life on Mars) there must be no objective criteria for determining whether something is a sphere or whether life exists. Hare considers this analogy and rejects it:

> It might be objected that moral questions are not pe-culiar in this respect—that we are free also to form our opinions about such matters as whether the world is round. In a sense this is true; but we are free to form our own moral opinions in a much stronger sense than this. For if we say that the world is flat, we can in principle be shown certain facts such that, once we have admitted them, we cannot go on saying that the world is flat without being guilty either of self-contra-diction or of a misuse of language. That nothing of this sort is possible in morals is a thesis which must have the support of all those who reject naturalism.

Thus, Hare concludes that "we are free to form our own moral opinions *in a much stronger sense* than we are free to form our own opinions as to what the facts are."[32]

It is important to recognize, however, as Hare himself admits, that the naturalist cannot be accused of denying that we are *just as free* to form our own moral opinions as we are to form our own scientific opinions. And the nat-uralist may claim that this is all that is necessary in order to recognize the autonomy of moral judgers. For surely Hare does not wish to hold that, because there are objective criteria for determining when life is present, we are not completely free to make up our minds about whether life exists on Mars. Similarly, the naturalist may contend, just because there are objective criteria for determining when an act is morally wrong, it does not follow that we are not completely free to make up our own minds about whether, say, abortion or capital punishment is wrong. Indeed, the kind of freedom that Hare seems to be insisting on is not merely the freedom to form our own opinions, but also the

---

[32] See *Freedom and Reason*, p. 2.

freedom to decide what is to count as evidence for these opinions.[33]

But now why does Hare think that to be fully autonomous we must be free to decide for ourselves even what counts as evidence for our moral judgments? It is because he thinks that, unlike factual judgments, moral judgments commit us to acting in certain ways—i.e., because he accepts the thesis of prescriptivism (one version of internalism). Thus, accepting a moral judgment has a quite different bearing on our freedom of action than does accepting any factual judgment. Believing that it is snowing outside commits me (in itself and apart from what my desires and interests happen to be) neither to going outside nor to staying indoors. But believing that it would be morally wrong to leave the house just now does commit me, in and of itself, to staying in the house (at least, so long as there are no overriding moral considerations). Thus, Hare thinks that to accept something—say, utility, as Bentham conceives of it—as a criterion of right and wrong is to restrict our freedom of action.

This consequence follows, however, only if one accepts the thesis of prescriptivism. And this is just what is at issue in this chapter. I am arguing that there is no good reason for anyone to accept this thesis. If this thesis is rejected, then the charge that naturalism compromises our freedom of action falls by the wayside. It is true, of course, that if we accept the naturalist's proposed definition (and with it a certain criterion for distinguishing between right and wrong acts), then, if we also accept certain factual claims, we shall be committing ourselves to certain substantive moral judgments about how we ought to act. Thus, anyone who accepts Bentham's definition of "morally right" and "morally wrong" must, if he also accepts certain generally accepted factual claims about stealing, also accept the moral principle

[33] This was pointed out by Philippa Foot in "Moral Arguments," *Mind*, vol. 67, 1958, pp. 502-13.

that stealing is wrong. But we need not suppose that accepting the latter commits one to any *prescription* directing one not to steal.

Following a suggestion made by G. H. Von Wright, we may note that normative expressions like, "one ought not to steal," can be understood either as expressing a *normative prescription* or a *normative proposition* (or both).[34] Taken as expressing a normative prescription, "One ought not to steal" directs one to refrain from stealing; and to accept this prescription is to commit oneself to refrain from stealing. Taken as expressing a normative proposition, it asserts that stealing violates the criterion (or set of criteria) that defines the moral point of view (i.e., that defines what "morally right" and "morally wrong" mean); and to accept this proposition as true does not commit one to acting in any particular way. Accepting a certain criterion (or set of criteria) as definitive of the moral point of view does not commit one to prescribing (in Hare's sense) from that point of view.

Thus, one who accepts the principle of utility as specifying *the* criterion of (moral) right and wrong is thereby committed only to accepting a certain normative proposition— i.e., that acts are right if and only if they maximize the general happiness. Moreover, this will be a proposition about what it is for an act to be (morally) right or wrong— about what it means to say that an act is (morally) right or wrong. What *substantive* moral propositions one accepts will depend on what factual judgments one accepts concerning which acts maximize (or fail to maximize) the general happiness. And even when one is led thereby to accept some substantive moral principle like "stealing is wrong," one is not committed to accepting this as a normative *prescription*. Indeed, one who accepts the principle of utility as definitive of "right" and "wrong" in the moral sense is

[34] See his *Norm and Action* (London: Routledge & Kegan Paul, 1963), pp. 104-05.

left perfectly free to employ some other criterion—say, self-interest—to govern his own universalizable prescriptions. Thus, he can admit that stealing is morally wrong (i.e., he can accept the normative *proposition* that, morally, stealing ought not to be done), even though he also accepts the normative *prescription* that, all things considered, one ought to steal when one can thereby promote one's own advantage.

If all of this is correct, then there really are no good reasons for rejecting the view that there is some particular proposition expressed by anyone who claims of some act that it is morally wrong. Such a propositional account of moral judgments and beliefs is neither guilty of the sorts of confusions alluded to by those who charge that it commits "the naturalistic fallacy" nor is it guilty of violating the requirements of neutrality and autonomy.

4. Evaluative Judgments

At this point a defender of the thesis of internalism may reply that, even if it is true that to accept (or assent to) what is expressed in saying, "X is morally wrong" is to accept a certain proposition as being true, and even if one can accept this proposition as true without also having a con-attitude toward X, we cannot claim that believing X to be morally wrong consists *merely* in accepting this proposition as true. This is because believing X to be morally wrong involves making (or having made) an evaluative judgment, and having some pro- or con-attitude is a necessary condition of making a genuinely *evaluative* judgment. Thus, unless a person has a con-attitude attitude toward X, he himself cannot be said to believe that X is wrong. He can at most be said to believe that X is wrong in an inverted-commas sense—i.e., that not doing X is required in order to conform to the moral standards that people generally accept. This is so because evaluating is not the same as, and cannot be reduced to, describing.

When one makes an evaluation (or accepts a certain evaluation as correct), one is doing something more than asserting or accepting a certain description as holding true of a certain state of affairs. The process of evaluation is something that is essentially connected with such things as choosing, giving one's approval of, and recommending—processes which manifest pro- and con-attitudes.

The central claim made in this argument is a variation of what I have called the thesis of internalism. It holds that *having some pro- or con-attitude is a necessary condition of making a genuinely evaluative moral judgment*. But the underlying claim is a claim about the nature of evaluative judgments in general. Let us begin, then, by first considering nonmoral evaluative judgments.

Sometimes, when one makes an evaluative judgment, one is applying certain generally accepted criteria or standards. Moreover, these standards seem to be objective in character—or, at least, to have a kind of inter-subjective validity. In some cases this is because the standards have been laid down by some authoritative body, such as the American Quarter Horse Association. Thus, judges in horse shows are expected to observe certain standards—and not simply their own personal preferences—in making their evaluations. In most cases, however, the standards to be employed are determined, not by legislative fiat, but by the fact that people are known to have certain typical interests and purposes in choosing among things of a certain kind. Thus, when one is evaluating such things as hammers and automobiles, cheeses and wines, or philosophers and football players, one must apply standards determined by the interests or purposes of those whom one is apt to be advising. Sometimes, then, when a person says (sincerely) that such and such is good, he is not necessarily expressing his own pro-attitudes or preferences; rather, he is expressing a judgment guided (via certain standards) by the pro-attitudes or preferences of others—namely, those who employ him as judge or wine-taster, or who ask for his advice or recommendation.

Now, as applied to these sorts of cases, the thesis about evaluation that we are considering does not seem to be correct. For this thesis holds that, unless one has a pro-attitude toward the kind of thing in question in virtue of its satisfying such standards, and unless one is prepared oneself to choose things satisfying these standards when one is choosing among things of this sort, one cannot—in saying, "This is good"—be expressing a genuinely evaluative judgment or belief. This, it seems to me, is a mistake. One can hold this view only if one adopts what I shall try to show is a stipulative and question-begging definition of "evaluative."

To see this it may be useful to draw a distinction, suggested by Nowell-Smith, between two kinds of evaluative judgments: judgments of preference and judgments of appraisal.[35] Sometimes, when one says that something is good (say, for example, a certain kind of wine), one is expressing one's own preference for it and commending it to others as well. In such cases one is expressing a judgment of preference. Making such an evaluative judgment involves having a pro-attitude toward wines insofar as they satisfy certain standards. But in other cases one need not be expressing any pro-attitude toward, or preference for, this sort of wine. One may simply be claiming that this wine satisfies those standards (answering to the recognized tastes and interests that people have with respect to wines) that are generally accepted as governing the appraisal of wines. In such cases one is simply applying those standards that are customarily used for appraising wines and that one knows to govern the preferences of those whom one is advising.

But it would be a mistake to conclude that in the latter cases one is not making a genuinely evaluative judgment

[35] See his *Ethics* (Baltimore: Penguin Books, 1954), p. 170.

but is merely describing and using "good" in an inverted-commas sense. And it would also be a mistake to conclude that in such cases one cannot be said to believe oneself that such wines are good, but can be described merely as believing that such wines are generally believed by others to be good. Consider a professional wine-taster. If he says, "This is a good wine," he is not necessarily expressing a personal preference or attempting to persuade others; he is evaluating in accordance with agreed upon standards. And it is surely wrong to insist that if these standards do not reflect his own preferences, then he is merely classifying or describing rather than grading or appraising. For, not only does he understand the point or purpose of applying the grading labels; he intends to advise those whose preferences are reflected by the generally recognized standards. Thus, the professional wine-taster is to be contrasted with a person who calls a certain wine good simply because he has heard the experts call it good, even though he himself is not competent to apply these standards—and, perhaps, does not even know what they are. Perhaps the latter person may be said to be using "good" in an inverted-commas sense and saying merely that this is the sort of wine that the experts call good. But this is not the case with the professional wine-taster. He is making a genuinely evaluative judgment.

Thus, it may be that the professional wine-taster does not himself prefer the sort of wine that he himself judges to be good according to the generally accepted criteria. Perhaps he himself much prefers wines that he judges to be inferior according to these standards. Or perhaps he does not like any wines very much, preferring beer to wine. If he now expresses his own personal (but universalizable) preference for wine Y over wine X (or for beer over wine) by saying, "Wine Y is better" (or, "Beer is better"), he will then be making an evaluative judgment of (personal) preference rather than a (mere) judgment of appraisal. J. O. Urmson calls this sort of evaluative judgment a standard-setting, as opposed to a standard-using judgment.[36] He will now be recommending different standards for judging or appraising wines. However, his making this sort of standard-setting judgment is in no way incompatible with his also making the other sort of standard-using judgment. Moreover, both may be said to be genuinely evaluative judgments.

Suppose we ask now whether he himself believes wines of type X to be good. Suppose, moreover, that he himself prefers beer to wine or, at least, much prefers wines of type Y. Does it follow that he himself does not believe wines of type X to be good? I do not think that it does. Suppose, however, that he expresses his own preference for wines of type Y by telling us that he himself does not believe wines of type X to be good. If he says this without making clear that he is merely expressing his own personal preference and is not judging in accordance with the generally recognized standards (which reflect tastes quite different from his own), he will surely be just as misleading as if he says that wines of type X are good when he himself does not prefer such wines. For the fact remains that he does judge wines of type X to be good according to the generally recognized standards (he does not disagree with other professional wine-tasters in this respect). Hence, he does judge (appraise) wines of type X to be good in the standard-using sense.

What I should like to suggest here is that we need to distinguish between two kinds of evaluative judgments or beliefs and to recognize that a person's (merely) standard-using evaluative judgments (his non-preferential appraisals) may conflict with his standard-setting (or preferential) evaluative judgments. To insist that what he really believes (or what he himself judges) is the one rather than the other, or to try to reduce standard-using evaluative judgments to

[36] See *The Emotive Theory of Ethics*, p. 67.

mere descriptive judgments, is simply to ignore this distinction.

As I mentioned earlier, when our professional wine-taster tells us that a certain wine is good, there is an important sense in which he may also be said to be advising us. But in order for this to be true it is not necessary that he have a pro-attitude toward this wine. If one thinks that he must have such a pro-attitude, then perhaps one is failing to distinguish between two kinds of advising. As others have pointed out, we must distinguish between *advising* someone *to* choose or do something, which seems to involve an intention that the advisee choose or do it, and *advising* someone *about* the merits (pros or cons) of making a certain choice or acting in a certain way.[37] The latter kind of advising does not require any intention upon the part of the adviser that the advisee so choose or act. Thus, our professional wine-taster is certainly advising, in one sense, those who have employed him or asked for his advice—even though he may not care whether they follow his advice or not. He is nevertheless advising them about the merits of this wine. Indeed, I am not even sure that he cannot be said to be recommending this wine to them or (knowing that their tastes differ from his) advising them to choose it. In the latter case this may involve his having a pro-attitude toward their getting the kinds of wine that they prefer, but it need not involve a pro-attitude on his part toward these wines.

It also seems to me that, while advising about (as opposed to advising to) is not so common in moral contexts as in prudential ones, it is possible in moral contexts as well—i.e., a person who is himself indifferent about the moral rightness or wrongness of actions may nevertheless advise others about the moral propriety or impropriety of acting in a certain way. But this view is disputed by Nowell-

[37] See H.L.A. Hart and A. M. Honore, *Causation in the Law* (Oxford: Clarendon Press, 1959), p. 51.

Smith, who argues that, while it is possible to make non-moral appraisals that consist merely in applying certain generally accepted criteria, without making a preferential evaluative judgment (and thus being prepared to choose or prescribe a certain course of action), this is not possible in the case of moral appraisals. Thus, while criticizing "any theory which says that to appraise is always to praise, advise, commend, etc." because "on some occasions a man may be simply *applying* the criteria that he and others customarily use for these purposes," he insists that "moral appraisals are . . . connected with choosing or advising in a way that non-moral appraisals need not be."[38] Why does Nowell-Smith think that moral appraisals are so different?

> The reason is that, whatever may be the case with other types of appraisal, moral appraisals must be universal. Anyone who makes a moral appraisal even of a remote character must be willing to apply the same criteria universally. And it follows from this that he must be willing to apply them in practical contexts.[39]

Suppose, he says, that after reading Cicero I judge Verres to be a villain. If this is a genuine moral judgment, then I must be prepared to condemn anyone whose behavior is like that of Verres in the relevant respects. And this means that I must be prepared to condemn myself if I act as Verres does. But what if I am not averse to villainy—except perhaps when I am the victim of it? What if I admire and desire to emulate the sort of person who is not afraid to act in a villainous manner in order to promote his own advantage? Does this prevent me from judging that Verres is a villain and, furthermore, that "anyone [including myself] who oppressed the poor, robbed the rich, took bribes, and cheated the treasury, and all for his own personal profit" would be a villain? It is not clear why my judgment

---

[38] *Ethics*, p. 177.
[39] *Ibid.*

must express my own preference merely in order to be universal. That one's moral judgments must express one's own preferences follows not from their being implicitly universal, but from their being, in Hare's sense, prescriptive. But that moral judgments are prescriptive in this sense is just what I wish to contest.

Suppose that one is a Harean fanatic who believes that one ought always to act in such a way as to promote one's own advantage—even if this involves hurting, killing, deceiving, or cheating others. One might then express one's view by saying that, although Verres is a villain, he is nevertheless a good man (meaning by this, as Hare seems to, that he is the sort of man that one ought to emulate). One would thereby be expressing one's own preferential evaluative judgment. But this—as I shall go on to argue—is perfectly compatible with one's also making the non-preferential evaluative judgment that Verres is a *morally* bad man.

5. *The Moral Point of View*

This brings us now to the topic of moral evaluation. There is indeed a difference between moral evaluative judgments and nonmoral ones, but it is not the one pointed out by Nowell-Smith. Nowell-Smith thinks that it is impossible to believe that X is the morally better man and yet to prefer emulating Y, because (like Hare) he holds that moral judgments are to be distinguished from nonmoral judgments in terms of their dominance or overridingness. This way of drawing the distinction between the moral and the nonmoral has been much criticized, and I shall subject it to further criticism in the next chapter. Many philosophers find that it has counter-intuitive consequences. It implies, for example, that if someone is prepared to prescribe universally that no one ever step on the lines of a pavement, and is prepared to accept this requirement as a dominant or overriding one, then this is for him a moral principle—

173

perhaps even a basic one. And it implies that if someone finds red blood on green grass so beautiful that he is willing to universally prescribe that such an effect be brought about at all costs—even at the cost of killing innocent persons, then he may be described as believing that this is *morally* required and not just a matter of aesthetic preference. Since many people may consider prudential, religious, or aesthetic considerations to be more important than what would normally be taken to be moral considerations, this view seems to me to blur, rather than clarify, the lines between the moral and the prudential or religious or aesthetic.

In the next chapter I shall argue that moral judgments are to be distinguished from nonmoral judgments in terms of the kinds of grounds or reasons given to support them. The full articulation and defense of this view must wait until then, but a nice, succinct statement of this view can be found in the following passage from W. K. Frankena's *Ethics*.

> It seems to me that what makes some normative judgments moral, some aesthetic, and some prudential is the fact that different points of view are taken in the three cases, and that the point of view taken is indicated by the kinds of reasons that are given. Consider three judgments: (a) I say that you ought to do X and give as the reason the fact that X will help you succeed in business; (b) I say that you should do Y and cite as the reason the fact that Y will produce a striking contrast of colors; and (c) I say that you should do Z and give as the reason the fact that Z will keep a promise or help someone. Here the reason I give reveals the point of view I am taking and the kind of judgment I am making.[40]

In order to understand further the kind of difference that obtains between moral evaluations and many, but not all,

[40] *Ethics*, p. 110.

nonmoral evaluations, it may be useful to employ a distinction, suggested by J. O. Urmson, between evaluations of things *as things of a certain kind* and evaluations of things *from a certain point of view*.[41] When we make an evaluative judgment of something as a thing of a certain kind—e.g., as a member of a certain class of things, or as something that serves a certain function or fulfills a certain role—we are guided by certain generally acknowledged and agreed-upon criteria which, as I suggested earlier, reflect the typical interests and purposes that people have in choosing among things (or persons) of that sort. This characterization holds true of many—if not most—nonmoral evaluations. But it does not hold true of all nonmoral evaluations; and (as Urmson himself argues) it does not hold true of moral evaluations.

Let us, once again, first consider nonmoral evaluative judgments. The kinds of nonmoral evaluative judgments that we have so far considered all seem to fit Urmson's characterization of evaluations of things as things of a certain kind. But to show that not all evaluations fit this mold, Urmson asks us to consider the judgment, "This is a good thing from the farmer's point of view," said with reference to, perhaps, a period of weather or the constructing of a road. As Urmson points out, when we judge a road to be a good thing from the farmer's point of view, we seem to be making a different kind of evaluation of it than when we judge it to be a good road (i.e., good *qua* road). That they are different is indicated by the fact that different kinds of reasons seem to be relevant in each case. Thus, as Urmson points out, whether or not a road is well sign-posted would seem to be irrelevant to the question of whether it is a good thing from the farmer's point of view (since this is of negligible importance to farmers), but this is quite relevant to the question of whether it is a good road. Similarly, that it serves as a barrier against flooding would seem

[41] See *The Emotive Theory of Ethics*, pp. 98 ff.

to be quite relevant to whether it is good from the farmer's point of view, but not so to whether it is a good road.

In the case of evaluations of things as things of a certain kind, the criteria of evaluation seem to be determined by the interests or purposes that people typically have in choosing among things of that kind. This is not true of evaluations of things from a point of view. So it is tempting to think that they are determined instead by the interests or purposes of a certain class of evaluators, such as farmers. But this is not necessarily the case. As Urmson points out, "there are abstract points of view which anybody may adopt."

> Thus, any of us may look at a problem from the agricultural point of view without being farmers. Moreover, something may be bad from the agricultural point of view (leading perhaps to low quality crops) but good from the farmers' point of view (leading perhaps to higher profits). . . .[42]

Other examples of abstract points of view are the economic point of view, the aesthetic point of view, and, of course, the moral point of view. If the criteria to be employed in making evaluative judgments from such abstract points of view are not determined by the interests or purposes that people typically have in choosing among things of a certain kind, and if they are not determined by the interests or purposes that characterize a particular group of persons, how are they determined? The answer that suggests itself is that they are determined by the definition of what it is to judge from that point of view. Or, to put it in another way, what criteria one employs to govern one's evaluations determines from what point of view one is evaluating. To evaluate morally, then, is to evaluate from a certain abstract point of view; for, if the view suggested

[42] *Ibid.*, p. 104.

earlier is correct, to evaluate morally is to evaluate on the basis of certain criteria.

I shall not attempt here to answer the very difficult question: in terms of what criteria is the moral point of view to be defined? One very plausible answer is that given by D.A.J. Richards, who (following the suggestions of John Rawls) holds that to evaluate actions morally is to evaluate them from the point of view of their conformity or nonconformity with those principles of action that would be agreed upon by rational contractors in a certain hypothetical position of choice, characterized by equal liberty and a veil of ignorance. Richards further claims that to say (or judge) that an act is morally required (ought to be done) is to assert (or accept as true) the proposition that this act is required in order to conform one's behavior to such principles.[43] However, I am not now concerned with whether this or any other definition of what it means to say that X is morally required is the correct one. The question that I am here concerned with is whether *any* such purely propositional analysis of moral judgments can be said to be adequate. The objection we have been considering, it will be recalled, is this: even if it is true that to accept (or assent to) what is expressed in saying "X is morally wrong," is to accept a certain proposition as true, and even if one can accept this proposition as true without also having a con-attitude toward X, we cannot hold that believing X to be morally wrong consists merely in accepting this proposition as true.

Thus, this objection might continue, even if we grant that to evaluate morally is to evaluate from a certain point of view and that to evaluate from this point of view is to apply certain criteria, we cannot identify believing (or judging) an act to be morally wrong merely with the belief that this act violates (or fails to satisfy) these criteria. For unless a person makes the moral point of view his own "internal

[43] See *A Theory of Reasons for Action*, pp. 80 and 104.

point of view" (to use Hart's terminology)[44]—i.e., unless he regards the fact that an act violates these criteria as a reason for not doing it, he cannot make genuinely evaluative judgments about the moral wrongness of actions. In order to make genuinely evaluative judgments (or have evaluative beliefs) about the moral wrongness of actions, not only must a person be prepared to apply these criteria in determining whether an act is wrong; he must also have a con-attitude toward acts that fail to satisfy them. Unless he adopts such a critical attitude toward these criteria, he can make moral judgments only from an external point of view, and in this case he cannot be said to make any genuinely evaluative judgments. If he judges an act to be morally wrong only from an external point of view, he can be said to judge only that this act would be judged to be wrong by those who do have such a critical attitude toward these criteria. But he himself cannot be said to believe that it is morally wrong in a genuinely evaluative sense; rather, he judges it to be wrong in a purely descriptive sense.

Once again I must say that this view seems to me to simply beg the question at issue—namely, whether the thesis of internalism is true, for it employs a stipulative and question-begging definition of "evaluative." I have already attacked this view in connection with nonmoral evaluative judgments. I shall now argue that this view must also be rejected in connection with moral judgments. I submit that in order to make a genuinely evaluative moral judgment it is sufficient that one judge from the moral point of view merely in the sense of applying the criteria that define this point of view in order to govern one's appraisals of actions. One must, of course, distinguish (as Frankena has pointed out) between saying, from the moral point of view, "X is wrong," and saying, "X is wrong from the

---

[44] See H.L.A. Hart, *The Concept of Law* (Oxford: Clarendon Press, 1961), pp. 55-56.

moral point of view."[45] Having a certain conative disposition to avoid doing X is a necessary condition of the
former but not of the latter. Yet it seems to me that in both
cases one may be expressing a genuinely evaluative judgment. Once again, it is a mistake to try to reduce the latter
of these two judgments to a merely descriptive judgment
that uses "wrong" only in an inverted-commas sense.

As I argued earlier, genuinely evaluative judgments can
be made even by the professional wine-taster who dislikes
wines himself. Such a person can apply criteria which he
knows to govern the choices of others and can advise them
and guide them even though he is not *prescribing* in Hare's
sense—i.e., is not thereby committing himself to choosing
to drink the wines he recommends. But it would surely be
false to suggest that he is therefore merely describing and
not evaluating wines. For not only does he use the grading
labels, he understands the point or purpose of the grading
and intends to advise others even though he does not share
their preferences. Thus, I can see no grounds for claiming
that he is merely classifying, rather than grading, wines.
Similarly, even the so-called "amoralist"—i.e., the person
who is himself indifferent to matters of moral right and
wrong—can make genuinely evaluative judgments about
what is morally right and wrong. Indeed, if the "amoralist"
is a very subtle thinker, he might be called upon by those
who are morally concerned to advise them about the moral
propriety or impropriety of such things as abortion or "reverse discrimination." And if the "amoralist" understands
(at least, intellectually) the criteria that define the moral
point of view and understands (intellectually) the feelings
and attitudes that make others concerned about whether
their behavior conforms to these criteria, then he may choose
(perhaps for a fee) to advise them and hence engage in the
process of moral evaluation. If he now employs these cri-

---

[45] This remark is attributed to Frankena by Urmson in the work cited
above. I have been unable to locate it in Frankena's writings.

teria to govern his judgments about what is right and wrong, he will be judging from the moral point of view. Although he will not say, "X is wrong," from the moral point of view (at least, not in the sense in which Frankena understands this), he will say "X is wrong from the moral point of view," (i.e., "X is *morally* wrong"). And this, I submit, is all that is necessary in order for him to be evaluating, as opposed to merely describing.

Indeed, it seems to me to be even less plausible to suppose that having certain pro- or con-attitudes is a necessary condition of evaluative judgments made from a certain point of view than it is to suppose that this is true of evaluative judgments of things as things of a certain kind. For one thing, it is important to notice that the same kind of thing can be favorably evaluated from one point of view and unfavorably evaluated from another point of view. To use Urmson's example: "The planting of the hard shoulder of motorways with flowers would be a good thing from the aesthetic point of view (aesthetically), but economically (from the economic point of view) could not be justified."[46] Thus, a person who prefers saving money over creating beauty might agree that planting the flowers would be aesthetically good, but nevertheless not prefer to have them planted and not be prepared to vote for or recommend this proposal. But surely this does not mean that he himself does not really believe that this would be an aesthetically good thing. Similarly, there is no reason why a person could not judge it to be a morally bad thing to slaughter people on the lawn merely in order to create the aesthetically pleasing contrast of red on green even though he himself prefers the creation of beauty to the avoidance of moral wrong-doing.

Of course, these examples only show that having a preference for X over Y is not a necessary condition of judging X to be good (or better than Y) from a certain point of view.

[46] See *The Emotive Theory of Ethics*, p. 105.

One might still contend that having some pro-attitude—even though it might be overridden by some other pro-attitude—is a necessary condition of judging X to be good from a certain point of view. But we must remember that, just as we may sometimes be asked to look at a problem and judge it from the other fellow's point of view—even when we do not share his point of view (which in this case would be defined by his tastes and interests)—so we may be asked to look at and judge a problem from some abstract point of view—such as, for example, the aesthetic (or economic) point of view—even though we ourselves have no interest whatsoever in beauty (or saving money).

There is also another point to be made. When one is making evaluative judgments of things as of a certain kind, one must either allow one's judgment to be governed by criteria that reflect the interests or purposes that people typically have in choosing among things of that kind (in which case one will be making a standard-using judgment of appraisal) or, if one's own interests and purposes are peculiar in this regard, one must adopt and employ criteria which reflect them (in which case one will be making a standard-setting judgment of preference). In both cases, however, one must express one's judgment in the same way—by saying, "This is a good X." Hence, in cases where a person's tastes and interests differ from those of most people, he has no other way of expressing his own personal (but universalizable) preference except by saying, "No, *this* is a good (or better) X." Because of this we are tempted to say that the person's standard-setting judgment must reflect what he himself believes (or what he really believes)—in cases where it conflicts with his standard-using judgment about the same thing. Now, as we have seen, the same kind of thing can be favorably evaluated from one point of view and unfavorably from another point of view—and by the same person. But in this case one can express these different judgments in different ways: for example "This painting is good from the economic point of view (i.e., it is a very good investment) but, aesthetically, it is very poor," or, "Verres was certainly an immoral (i.e., morally bad) man, but this is a dog-eat-dog world and, therefore, I admire and think it good to emulate a man like that." Thus, in these cases the question, "Which does he really believe, that X is good or that X is bad?" does not arise.

It is also important here to remember the observation made earlier—namely, that it may well be a conversational implicature of our saying, "Jones believes X to be morally wrong," that Jones disapproves of X. This may explain why we are hesitant to say this of Jones if we know that he is indifferent to matters of (moral) right and wrong. For it would be misleading for us to say this in this case, even though it is true that Jones judges X to be wrong from the moral point of view (and, hence, accepts as true the proposition that X is morally wrong). It must also be admitted that it would be misleading (if not just false) to say that such a person has a morality (or has moral principles). To have a morality is not just to have certain convictions about what is morally right and wrong—i.e., not merely to accept as true certain propositions about what is right and wrong; having a morality involves having a conative disposition to act on these convictions. Thus, to say that Jones has a morality (or has moral principles) seems not merely conversationally to implicate that he has a certain conative disposition; its seems logically to imply this. But then it must also be pointed out that it is not necessary to have a morality in this sense in order to judge from the moral point of view and make genuinely evaluative judgments about what is morally right and wrong. The morally indifferent person differs from the morally concerned person, not in moral judgment (at least, not necessarily), but in conative disposition. The trouble is not that such a person lacks conviction, but that he lacks concern—concern (or, at least, an equal concern) for the interests and welfare of others.

Fortunately, most people do have at least some concern for the interests and welfare of others. Thus, any definition of "right" and "wrong" (in the moral sense) that, for example, makes harming others count necessarily as a wrong-making feature of acts will be able to account for why all but the abnormal have at least some motivation for avoiding that which they believe to be morally wrong. This is all that is necessary to explain the "moving appeal" of moral judgments. I have argued that to go further than this, so as to deny even the possibility of moral indifference, is both unnecessary and false.

It is unnecessary because we can explain why it seems paradoxical to suppose that someone believes X to be wrong but fails to have any con-attitude toward X without resorting to the hypothesis that to say that Jones believes X to be wrong logically implies that Jones has a con-attitude toward X (the thesis of internalism). We can explain this equally well on the hypothesis that saying that Jones believes X to be wrong conversationally implicates that Jones has a con-attitude toward X. It is false because it is simply a plain matter of fact that some people (those we call "psychopaths," for example) *are* indifferent to matters of moral right and wrong. As we noted earlier, this indifference can manifest itself in either of two ways: a refusal to make any moral judgments in the first place (which results in amoral behavior) or a failure to be motivated by whatever judgments one does make. And it is important to recognize (as I pointed out in Chapter Three) that noncognitivist analyses of moral beliefs not only imply that the latter is impossible, they also make amoral wrongdoing problematic.

Thus, if moral indifference is to be adequately explained, we require a cognitivist analysis of moral beliefs. In this chapter I have attempted to defend such analyses against the charges that they cannot explain why it is a non-contingent fact that to say, "X is wrong," is to condemn or express disapproval of X, and that such analyses are guilty of committing the "naturalistic fallacy" by violating the requirements of neutrality and autonomy. I have also argued that one can make judgments from the moral point of view without adopting that point of view, in the sense of prescribing from it, and that such judgments must nevertheless be considered genuine moral judgments; so that even the so-called "amoralist" can make genuine moral judgments and give expert moral advice to others—if he chooses to do so.

SEVEN

* * * * *

PREFERENTIAL WICKEDNESS

In Chapter One I argued that the conception of wickedness as preferential wickedness provides a more adequate reflection of the way in which we ordinarily conceive of wickedness than does the conception of wickedness as perverse wickedness. For we do not ordinarily conceive of the agent of a wicked act as failing to believe that what he does is wrong. "He knows very well that it is wrong," we are inclined to say. We do not think that, although he prefers the avoidance of moral wrongdoing to the realization of his other ends, he himself believes that what he does is morally right. This suggests that, were it not for some false, or bad, moral belief, he would not choose to act as he does. He kills someone in order to take his wallet, for example, because he believes that this sort of act is morally right (either required, or at least permissible). According to this conception, the agent of a wicked act is not lacking in conscientiousness (i.e., the desire to avoid wrongdoing), rather, he is lacking in moral conviction (i.e., the belief that what he does is wrong).

The alternative is to view the agent of a wicked act as believing that what he does is wrong, but doing it in spite of this because he prefers the pursuit of some other desired end to the avoidance of moral wrongdoing. This is the conception of wickedness as preferential wickedness, which seems to me to offer us a better account of what we ordinarily (i.e., when not philosophizing) take wickedness to consist in. But many philosophers would claim that preferential wickedness is impossible, that the very notion of it is incoherent. It makes no sense to suppose that someone thinks that it is morally wrong to do some act and yet prefers, all things considered, to do it, for this is incompatible with his thinking that, morally, he ought not to do it.

According to many of those who adopt a noncognitivist analysis of moral beliefs, a person cannot be said to believe that an act is morally wrong unless he has not only a universalizable pro-attitude toward (or universally prescribes) its avoidance, but also has a *dominant* pro-attitude toward (or prescribes an *overriding* principle requiring) its avoidance.[1] According to this view it is dominance or overridingness that distinguishes moral judgments and principles from other kinds of evaluative (or normative) judgments and principles. It is a necessary condition of accepting a principle of action as a *moral* principle that one think that one ought not to allow that principle to be overridden by one's other normative principles.[2] Thus, if one accepts a principle of action according to which a certain kind of act is not to be done but one chooses to perform an act of this

---

[1] As I have already pointed out, this view is defended by Nowell-Smith and by Hare (in the works cited above). More recently, it has been defended by Neil Cooper in *The Diversity of Moral Thinking* (Oxford: Clarendon Press, 1981).

[2] Strictly speaking, this applies only to principles specifying moral requirements (obligations). To apply it to principles specifying acts of supererogation (what it is morally good, but not obligatory, to do) one must amend this criterion in the manner suggested by Cooper: "A man's moral principles are practical principles which he thinks ought to override or which he thinks it would be a good thing to override nonmoral normative principles" (*ibid.*, p. 107). When I later discuss overridingness as a criterion for distinguishing between moral and nonmoral judgments and principles, I shall, for the sake of simplicity, discuss only judgments and principles about what one ought to do.

kind nevertheless because its performance is required by some other principle that one also accepts and one thinks that it is better (or that one ought) to act on the second principle, even though it means violating the first, then it follows that the first principle cannot be one of one's moral principles and hence that one cannot believe that it is morally wrong to do the act.

A closely related, but weaker, thesis concerning the supremacy of moral principles has been defended by some who adopt a cognitivist analysis of moral beliefs. These philosophers hold that to say that a person is morally required not to do a certain act implies that he has an overriding reason not to do it.[3] This follows from a correct analysis of what it means to say that a person is morally required to do something. Hence, if one believes that it is morally wrong to do X, then one must also believe, if one's beliefs are to be consistent, that one has an overriding reason not to do it. If one thinks that it is morally wrong to do X but nevertheless prefers (in the sense of thinking that it is better for one or that one ought, all things considered) to do X, one's thinking will be incoherent. On this view it is not the very notion of preferential wickedness that is incoherent (as it is for those noncognitivists who make overridingness a necessary condition for having a moral belief); the incoherence in this case resides in the conjunction of the moral belief with this sort of preference. Overridingness is here said to be a necessary condition of a requirement on action being a moral one (as opposed, say, to a requirement of etiquette or prudence), whereas

[3] This thesis has been defended by the following: Kurt Baier in *The Moral Point of View* (Ithaca: Cornell University Press, 1958), in his "Moral Reasons," in *Midwest Studies in Philosophy*, vol. 3, 1978, pp. 62-73, and in "Moral Reasons and Reasons to be Moral," in A. I. Goldman and J. Kim, eds., *Values and Morals* (Dordrecht, 1978), pp. 231-56; by G. R. Grice in *The Grounds of Moral Judgment* (London: Cambridge University Press, 1967); and by D.A.J. Richards in *A Theory of Reasons for Action* (Oxford: Clarendon Press, 1971).

the other thesis takes overridingness to be a necessary condition of *believing* a requirement to be a moral one. Nevertheless, this view is equally unwelcome to anyone who wishes to conceive of wickedness as preferential wickedness, for we do not wish to allow that preferential wickedness is possible only so long as we suppose that the agent has inconsistent beliefs.

Thus, it is incumbent on one who wishes to defend the conception of wickedness as preferential wickedness to challenge both of these views about the supremacy of moral judgments and principles. This will be the main purpose of the present chapter.

1. The Supremacy of Moral Principles

It is often said that moral considerations are the most important kind of considerations bearing on how we ought to act—or, at least, that what a person takes to be moral considerations are, for him, the most important kind of considerations. To suppose that someone thinks that he ought to subordinate moral considerations to other kinds of considerations—such as, for example, prudential, aesthetic, political or even religious considerations—seems paradoxical and inconsistent with the notion that he believes the former to be moral considerations. If someone professes to believe that some other consideration is more important than the demands of morality, we must take him to be referring, not to what he himself believes to be morally required, but rather to what is generally believed to be morally required (the requirements of the positive morality of his social group). If, on some particular occasion, he allows some nonmoral consideration (such as the demands of artistic achievement) to carry more weight than something which he himself recognizes to be a moral consideration (such as the suffering of human beings), this will be a case of weakness of will. It cannot be said that, although he himself believes that what he does is morally wrong, he nevertheless chooses to let some other consideration override this consideration because he prefers this to the avoidance of moral wrongdoing, for this would be inconsistent with holding that he himself believes that what he does is morally wrong. Thus, on this view, preferential wickedness is not possible.

One way of construing the importance that we attach to moral considerations is in terms of the notion of overridingness. A person thinks that moral considerations are more important than other kinds of considerations just in case he thinks that moral considerations ought to override other kinds of considerations when they conflict. And, as we have seen, those philosophers who appeal to overridingness in order to distinguish moral judgments and principles from other kinds of normative judgments and principles hold that it is a necessary truth that a person thinks that he ought to let the consideration that his act would be morally wrong (i.e., would violate his moral principles) override other kinds of considerations. On this sort of view one cannot deliberately choose to let a moral principle be overridden by some other principle of action without ceasing to accept it as a moral principle.

To accept a principle as overriding is to believe that, in cases where it conflicts with some other principle, one ought to act on it even though it means violating the other principle. If one thinks that one is justified in violating a certain principle in order to observe some other principle, this entails that one does not accept the first principle as an overriding one. It is an essential characteristic of a moral principle that one does not (barring weakness of will) allow one's moral principles to be overridden, whereas one may allow one's other normative principles to be overridden. Hare uses the following examples to illustrate this.[4] Con-

---

[4] See *Freedom and Reason* (Oxford: Clarendon Press, 1963), pp. 168-69. In his more recent book, *Moral Thinking* (Oxford: Clarendon Press, 1981), Hare modifies his earlier account of the overridingness of moral principles so as to allow for *prima facie* moral principles, which can be overridden,

sider first the case where a moral principle conflicts with some other kind of principle. Suppose you believe that, so far as matters of aesthetics are concerned, one ought not to juxtapose scarlet and magenta; and suppose that your wife gives you for your birthday a magenta cushion to put on the scarlet sofa in your room at college. In this case a person who also believes that, so far as moral requirements are concerned, one ought not to hurt one's wife's feelings will think that this consideration takes precedence and hence that, all things considered, one ought to keep the cushion on the sofa. Here one allows the aesthetic judgment to be overridden by the moral judgment.

Suppose, however, that a moral principle comes into conflict with another moral principle? In this case, Hare suggests, one does not allow one's principle to be overridden by another moral principle; rather, one modifies one of them to keep them from conflicting. For example, suppose that one believes that it is wrong to tell lies but also believes that it is wrong to reveal secrets to the enemy in time of war. One can conceive of circumstances in which these two moral considerations come into conflict. In this case, one may modify the first principle so as to build into it an exception permitting lies when necessary to avoid revealing secret information to the enemy. If so, one judges that it is not morally wrong to tell a lie in such circumstances. By way of contrast, in the previous case one is not inclined to say that one ought not to juxtapose scarlet and magenta except when doing so is necessary to avoid hurting one's wife's feelings. One does not think that this is aesthetically bad except when so necessitated. Rather, one thinks that it is aesthetically displeasing even in these circumstances, but that this aesthetic consideration ought to be overridden by the moral consideration.

---

as well as what he calls "critical moral principles," which cannot be allowed to be overridden. However, he still insists that the former must be justified by appealing to the latter. See pp. 60-61.

If this view is correct, then one cannot judge that, all things considered, it would be morally wrong to do a certain act and yet believe that one ought, all things considered, to do it. Having the latter belief is logically incompatible with believing that the act is morally wrong. For to believe that an act is morally wrong is to believe that it is wrong (ought not to be done), all things considered.

Critics have replied that it makes perfectly good sense to suppose that someone not only does, but thinks that he ought to, put self-interest above the requirements of morality.[5] Similarly, it seems possible for a person to put the demands of art or the needs of the state above the requirements of morality. It is no doubt true that most people do put moral considerations above other kinds of practical considerations. But this can be explained by the fact that they care more about such things as alleviating suffering than they do about creating great works of art or establishing some ideal social order. Most people not only think that it is wrong to cause unhappiness for others, they also prefer to forgo certain gains for themselves rather than cause such unhappiness. Most people care more about alleviating suffering than they do about observing good manners, and most people also think that the former is more important than creating great works of art. This is merely a contingent fact, however, and there are unfortunately some people who are so devoted to the pursuit of some nonmoral end or ideal that they are even willing to violate moral requirements when necessary.

Defenders of the view we have been considering will reply in turn that it does indeed make sense to suppose that someone thinks that something else is more important than the requirements of morality, but only if we mean the

[5] See, for example: P. R. Foot, "When Is a Principle a Moral Principle?" *Proceedings of the Aristotelian Society*, suppl. vol. 28, 1954, pp. 95-110; W. K. Frankena, "The Concept of Morality," *University of Colorado Studies* (Series in Philosophy, No. 3, 1967), pp. 1-22; and G. J. Warnock, *Contemporary Moral Philosophy* (London: Macmillan and Co., 1967).

requirements of some positive morality—what is required by the moral principles generally accepted in his social group, or perhaps what is required by the principles of some widely accepted traditional morality, such as that associated with the Judaic-Christian religious tradition.[6] Still, it might be asked, why cannot someone think that something else is more important than even what he himself takes to be morally required? Why cannot someone think that the creation of great beauty is more important than the avoidance of moral wrongdoing—at least with respect to some kinds of wrongdoing, such as causing a certain amount of unhappiness to one's wife or children? Why cannot someone think that a certain amount of immorality is justified if it is necessary to preserve the existence of the state? The answer that will be given is that, if we really wish to describe what he himself believes to be morally required or permissible, we should describe him as believing (in the one case) that one is morally justified in causing a certain amount of unhappiness in order to produce a great work of art, or (in the other case) that, because the existence of the state is essential for the salvation of mankind, one is morally justified in engaging in deception and depriving some innocent persons of their freedom and perhaps even their lives if this is necessary to preserve the state.[7]

According to this view, then, a person's moral principles are, by definition, those that express his basic preferences among the ends he values, whatever these happen to be. It makes no sense, then, to speak of a person as deliberately subordinating his moral values to other kinds of values; for, if he indeed does so, we must describe him as believing that this is what one morally ought to do. The point is that we cannot identify certain values as moral values apart from the preferences (the dominant pro-attitudes) of those

[6] See Neil Cooper, *The Diversity of Moral Thinking*, pp. 35-40 and 96-97.
[7] *Ibid.*, pp. 98-101.

who accept them as values. What makes a value a moral value for someone is not its content but the role it plays in that person's life. Any value—the existence of a certain kind of state or social order, the creation of great works of art, even the pursuit of self-interest—can be accepted by someone as a moral value so long as he is willing to allow it to play a dominant role in his life.

There are, then, two different ways of looking at the matter in the case of a person who appears to subordinate moral considerations to some other kind of practical consideration. We can say that, although he believes that what he does is morally wrong, he values some other consideration (the demands of artistic achievement, say, or the requirements of self-interest) more highly than the requirements of morality; or we can say that, although he believes that what he does is considered morally wrong by most people, he himself believes that it is morally right, because he believes that the particular wrong-making feature in question is outweighed by some other (morally) desirable feature of the act.[8] How, then, are we to decide which of these is the correct description?

The basic issue that is here being raised is: How are moral judgments and principles to be distinguished from non-moral ones? According to the proponents of overridingness as the criterion for distinguishing between the moral and the nonmoral, moral judgments and principles cannot be distinguished from nonmoral ones in terms of their content; they can be distinguished from them only by purely formal criteria—i.e., by those which impose no restriction on the kinds of action that can be claimed to be morally required. Any normative principle, no matter what sort of actions it prescribes, can be a moral principle—or perhaps it is better to say that any normative principle can be treated by someone as a moral principle so long as he adopts the

[8] Of course, he may also simply deny that the first consideration really is a wrong-making consideration.

proper attitude toward it (is willing to prescribe it universally and accept it as overriding, for example). This sort of
theory is often contrasted with theories that impose some
material restriction on what can count as a moral consideration. Such "material" conceptions of morality (as they
are called) hold that only certain kinds of factual considerations are relevant to (i.e., count as reasons for or against)
moral judgments and principles.[9] Let us now see what can
be said for and against each of these definitions of "moral."

2. The Moral and the Nonmoral

We have been considering overridingness as a necessary
condition of accepting a normative principle as a moral one
(and as the distinguishing feature between moral and other
kinds of normative principles). As I pointed out earlier,
many philosophers find this view to have counterintuitive
consequences. It implies, for example, that it makes sense
to suppose that, if someone has perverse enough desires
or preferences, he might believe that it is morally wrong,
in and of itself, to step on the lines of a pavement. It also
allows that one might intelligibly claim that there is a basic
(nonderivative) moral obligation to create the effect of red
(blood) on green (grass), no matter what the consequences
for the interests of others. And, as I pointed out in Chapter
One, it implies that it makes perfectly good sense for an
extremely rugged individualist to claim that it is immoral
to commit acts of Good Samaritanism. I myself find these
consequences quite counterintuitive. But what is one to say
when the defenders of the view here being criticized do
not admit that they are counterintuitive? They may admit
that the beliefs and claims described above are perverse
and certainly false, but they will deny that they are unin-

[9] This terminology was suggested by W. K. Frankena. See his "The
Concept of Morality."

telligible; such judgments may be false, or bad, moral judgments, but they are still moral judgments, they will insist.

Perhaps all one can do at this point is to show that there is another way of looking at the matter and then leave it up to each reader to decide which way of looking at the matter offers the more plausible explication of what he takes a moral principle to be. In the previous chapter, I stated that I find much more plausible the sort of view that distinguishes between moral and nonmoral judgments in terms of the kinds of reasons that are thought to be relevant to determining their truth or falsity (acceptability or unacceptability) by those who accept them. To make a moral judgment, I suggested, is to judge from the moral point of view, and to judge from the moral point of view involves evaluating on the basis of certain criteria. To specify what these criteria are would be to elaborate an ethical theory—something which cannot be done here.

However, at least this much can be said. Moral considerations—i.e., considerations relevant to determining the acceptability or unacceptability of moral judgments—must include considerations of harm and benefit to human beings (and, perhaps, to animals too). I am not convinced that any form of utilitarianism can adequately account for considerations of justice or fairness, but I do not see how anyone can deny that the consideration of harm or benefit to other human beings is at least relevant (if not decisive) to the question of the moral rightness or wrongness of actions, and, moreover, that causing harm to others (and some kinds of failing to benefit others) counts as a wrong-making characteristic of actions. I do not see how anyone who claims to know what it means to say that it is *morally* wrong to do something can deny that an act's causing pain, injury, or death to someone is at least *a* reason for judging it to be morally wrong. Indeed, it is in terms of such criteria as these that most people are taught the meaning of "morally wrong," I have argued. We are not first taught the meaning of "morally wrong" and then taught that such acts are morally wrong; rather, such criteria define, for the ordinary person, what it means to say that an act is morally wrong. Proponents of a more Kantian viewpoint also seem to be correct in arguing that the moral point of view is necessarily incompatible with the point of view of egoism. Our concept of a moral principle is the concept of a normative principle that places a certain restriction on the pursuit of his own self-interest by each individual in order to avoid unfairly frustrating the interests of others; and the notion of fairness here employed seems best explicated in terms of those restrictions or requirements on action that one would be willing to have everyone abide by—or, better still, that could be agreed to by all rational contractors, given Rawls's veil of ignorance and the circumstances of equality.

The view that I am here advocating holds that in order to make a moral judgment one must employ certain criteria of evaluation, since this defines what it is to judge from the moral point of view. It is this, and not overridingness, that distinguishes moral from nonmoral practical judgments. The chief objection that has been made to this view is that it is just a form of naturalism in a different guise; and indeed it must be admitted that it is, for it holds that certain factual considerations necessarily count for or against certain moral judgments. But whether this constitutes a legitimate objection to it is another question. Indeed, this dispute about the meaning of "moral" turns out to be just another outbreak of the old feud between the naturalists (descriptivists) and the prescriptivists. Prescriptivists insist that no one is required to employ certain criteria of evaluation just in order to be making moral judgments; rather, one is free to employ any criteria whatsoever so long as one is prepared to accept the consequences of universally prescribing in accordance with them. Naturalists insist, on the other hand, that certain descriptive features of actions are necessarily relevant to their moral evaluation. Anti-naturalists like Hare argue that this not only illegitimately

commits us to accepting certain substantive moral principles, it also robs us of our freedom to form our own moral
opinions. But, as I argued in the previous chapter, these
charges are misguided. To hold, for example, that an act's
causing pain to someone necessarily counts in favor of its
moral wrongness is not to assert a substantive moral principle (not to adopt a moral position) but rather to say something about what it is to judge that an act is *morally* wrong.
Nor does it commit one to making any *prescriptions* about
how one ought to act. It may commit one to accepting the
proposition, say, that it is morally wrong to cause another
person pain just for the sake of one's own amusement, but
this does not in itself commit one to prescribing that such
acts be avoided.

It is worth pointing out that, although the sort of view
that I am here defending has been described as proposing
a material (or content-based) definition of "moral," this
description is somewhat misleading. Advocates of this view
can agree with advocates of a purely formal definition that
practically any normative principle, no matter what its content, can be accepted as a moral principle. Whether one
treats it as moral or not depends on what one thinks are
reasons for or against accepting it. Thus, if one holds that
it is wrong to step on the lines of a pavement and if one's
reason for thinking this is that this will cause great harm
by bringing on a plague, then one may be said to accept
this principle as a moral one. If, however, one simply abhors
the sight of such a thing and hence prefers that it not be
done, no matter what human interests are thereby frus-
trated, and this is why one thinks it wrong to step on the
lines of a pavement, then one cannot be said to be treating
this principle as a moral one. This view can also allow that
one and the same principle can be treated by one person
as a moral principle and by someone else as a maxim of
prudence or mere rule of etiquette. Thus, as Kant pointed
out, the principle that one ought not to cheat others can
be accepted by one person as a moral principle and by

someone else as a maxim of prudence. This will be so if the former accepts it on the grounds that cheating is unfair and the latter accepts it on the grounds that cheating does not pay.

What really distinguishes this sort of theory from those that propose a so-called formal definition of "moral" is that it imposes certain restrictions on the kind of facts that can count as considerations for or against moral judgments. Only certain kinds of things (e.g., causing pain, failing to prevent suffering, causing another to be deceived, etc.) count. One cannot make anything one likes count just by making certain universal prescriptions. Thus, bringing about the effect of red on green cannot, in and of itself, count as a moral consideration, even if one is prepared to universally prescribe that this be brought about, no matter what the cost in terms of suffering and death.

There is only one respect in which this view imposes restrictions on the content of moral principles. It does rule out principles which are simply inconsistent with the moral point of view. Thus, principles such as that one ought to harm rather than benefit others or that one ought to do whatever will promote one's own interests, no matter how this affects the interests of others, could not possibly be accepted as moral principles by anyone.[10] But why should anyone object to this? Well, Hare objects to defining "moral" in such a way that "a man shows that he is not making a moral judgment if he is not prepared to abandon a principle when it conflicts with the most pressing interests of large numbers of people" because, he argues, "to put this restriction upon the use of the term 'moral' is to write some kind of utilitarianism into its definition."[11] However, I have

[10] But, as I pointed out in Chapter One, even a principle directing one to maximize unhappiness might be accepted by someone as a moral principle if he has perverse beliefs about what is harmful or beneficial for human beings—if he believes, for example, that experiencing pain and suffering makes one stronger and wiser.

[11] See *Freedom and Reason*, p. 163.

already argued that in the sense in which this is true there is nothing objectionable about it, since we are not committed to any *substantive* moral principles by such a definition.

Hare argues further that if we define the term "morally ought" in such a way that it "is bound by the restriction that one cannot think that one [morally] ought to do something which utterly disregards other people's interests," as well as by the requirements of universalizability and prescriptivity, then we make it impossible to sensibly discuss certain important issues.[12] He considers the case of a fanatical Nazi who is so devoted to the ideal of a purely Aryan society that he prefers the realization of this ideal, no matter what the cost in terms of the frustration of other people's (and even his own other) interests. His belief that he ought to exterminate Jews in order to realize this ideal may be mistaken or perverse, but it is still, Hare suggests, a moral belief. By refusing to call it a moral belief we simply refuse to acknowledge our moral disagreement with him. Thus, although he is disagreeing with us on the most fundamental sort of issue that people can disagree about, we have no way of expressing this disagreement.

What Hare fails to see, however, is that we do have a way of expressing this difference. We can make use of the concept that Hare (mistakenly) wishes to identify with the notion of a moral ought—namely, that expressed by an "ought" not bound by the above restriction but only by the requirements of universalizability, prescriptivity, and overridingness. That is to say, we can make use of the term "ought" merely to express our own personal but universalizable preferences. (And here, as Hare argues, we are free to employ any criteria of evaluation that we like, so long as we are willing to make universal prescriptions in accordance with them.) Thus, we can say that although the Nazi thinks that we ought to pursue this ideal even

---

[12] *Ibid.*, pp. 165-66.

though it involves moral wrongdoing (doing something that we *morally* ought not to do), we think that we ought not to pursue it, given that it involves moral wrongdoing. Indeed, it is Hare's way of drawing the distinction between the moral and the nonmoral that leaves us with no way of raising an issue that many would say is the most fundamental of all issues for moral philosophers: why ought one to do what he morally ought to do? Why ought we to attach any weight at all to moral considerations, or, at least, why ought we to give them an overriding weight in determining what to do? On Hare's view that important question becomes senseless.[13]

It is more plausible to argue that, even if considerations regarding the effects of one's actions on the interests of others are necessarily relevant to their moral evaluation, such considerations do not exhaust the class of moral considerations. Hare claims, for example, that there are "two distinct grounds on which we can commend or condemn actions, one of which is connected with the interests of other people, and the other with ideals of human excellence," and he argues that "one reason why it is wrong to confine the term 'moral question' by a terminological fiat to questions concerning the effect of our actions on other people's interests, is that such a restriction would truncate moral philosophy by preventing it saying anything about ideals."[14]

Now it must be admitted that the term "ethical" is commonly applied to views advocating purely personal ideals of human excellence that are not concerned with conduct toward others nor based on a consideration of their interests. Certainly, it seems correct to call the ideals of the Stoics and Epicureans ethical ideals, and it does not seem inappropriate to apply the term "ethical" to ideals advocating such things as a life of contemplation, asceticism,

---

[13] This is pointed out by Frankena in "The Concept of Morality."
[14] *Freedom and Reason*, pp. 147 and 149.

and submission to God, and perhaps even the acquisition, of power and dominance. Moreover, the terms "ethical" and "moral" are interchangeable in most people's minds. Thus, Hare may well be correct in claiming that the question of whether to become a stockbroker or an army officer is, in one sense of the term, a moral question—even if it is acknowledged that this choice will not make any real difference to other people's interests; and it may also be correct, therefore, to call moral the considerations thought to be relevant to such a choice—e.g., that the life of a stockbroker is dull and sedentary whereas that of an army officer is exciting and prestigious.

To admit this is, however, a far cry from admitting that it makes sense to suppose that someone might think that stepping on the lines of a pavement is something that is in and of itself morally wrong, or that one has a basic moral obligation to create the effect of red (blood) on green (grass). These seem to be purely aesthetic considerations that form no part of any ideal of human excellence. The same seems to me to be true of such ideals as that of a purely Aryan society or a society made up of only blond, blue-eyed people. Hence, insofar as someone places a higher value on the creation of such a society (or on creating the effect of red or green) than on either the avoidance of human suffering or making himself in some sense a better person or human being, such a person must be said to be subordinating moral to nonmoral considerations.

It also seems to me that some ideals of human excellence cannot serve as grounds of moral judgments, since to appeal to such ideals would be incompatible with judging from the moral point of view. Thus, an egoistic ideal specifying that it is good for one to promote one's own advantage, regardless of the effect on the interests and welfare of others, would preclude us from allowing adverse effects on the interests of others to count against the moral rightness (permissibility) of actions. The same might be said of other ideals, such as those specifying that it is good for a person to dominate others and keep them under one's complete control or to have more than one's fair share.

Perhaps the fairest way of settling this dispute about the meaning of "moral" is for both sides to acknowledge that our ordinary use of this term reflects two quite different concepts, and that what we have here are not two competing conceptions of morality (i.e., alternative explications of the same concept) but rather (equally correct) explications of two concepts of morality. (Indeed, this is a point that both sides seem willing to concede.) Thus, in one sense (the broader sense, as it is called) moral principles are, for each person, those principles by which, in the end, he chooses to guide his life. In this sense, what one morally ought to do is what one ought, all things considered, to do; moral considerations are all inclusive. In the narrow sense, on the other hand, moral principles are to be identified with a particular kind of principle—namely, those which place certain restraints on the pursuit of self-interest, so as to make each person's pursuit of his own good as compatible as possible with that of everyone else. In this sense, moral considerations are restricted to certain kinds of considerations—namely, utility and justice.

So long as it is recognized by both parties to this dispute that each of these concepts is equally legitimate, this seems to me to be a perfectly acceptable compromise, for it allows what I wish to argue for: that preferential wickedness is possible. It allows that there is a legitimate (and, I would add, important) sense of "moral" and "morally" such that a person may believe (himself and not merely in an inverted-commas sense) that he morally ought not to do something but nevertheless prefer (in the sense of thinking that he ought, all things considered) to do it.

3. The Categorical Nature of Moral Principles

Some philosophers have defended the thesis of the supremacy or overridingness of moral principles on the ground that moral requirements are categorically binding. Indeed, it is precisely this, they argue, that distinguishes moral requirements from other requirements on action. Whereas other kinds of normative principles express "oughts" that are hypothetical or conditional, in the sense that they apply to one only given that one has certain aims, moral principles express "oughts" that apply to one, no matter what one's desires and interests happen to be. Moreover, whereas the oughts expressed by other normative principles—such as technical and prudential oughts and those indicating the requirements of etiquette—can be defeated, not only by pointing out that one lacks the relevant concerns but also by the fact that they conflict with moral requirements, moral oughts can neither be made irrelevant by lack of certain concerns nor defeated by other practical requirements. Thus, if one morally ought to do something, one has not just *a* reason but a conclusive or overriding reason to do it.

This thesis about the overridingness of moral judgments and principles differs from the one previously considered, since it takes overridingness to be a consequence of the nature of moral requirements rather than a consequence of the nature of moral beliefs. Whereas the other view explains the supremacy of moral principles on the ground that treating a principle as overriding is a necessary condition of accepting it as a moral principle, this view explains the overridingness of moral principles by claiming that the content of moral principles is such that anyone (whether he himself accepts these principles or not) has an overriding reason to act in accordance with them. Hence, this view does not yield the paradoxical consequences that result when one allows that any principle—no matter what its nature or content—counts as a moral principle so long as someone universally prescribes it and accepts it as overriding.

What is it, then, about moral principles that makes them categorically binding, according to proponents of this view? Before answering this question, we should point out that the claim that moral principles are categorically binding can be understood in two quite diffferent ways. It can be taken to mean either or both of the following:

(1) Moral principles are categorically binding in the sense that what one is morally required to do does not depend on what one's desires and interests happen to be—i.e., the fact that one morally ought to do something is not contingent on the fact that doing it promotes one's interests or realizes some object of one's desires.

(2) Moral principles are categorically binding in the sense that one has reason to comply with them no matter what one's particular desires and interests happen to be—i.e., if one morally ought to do something, then one has reason to do it, regardless of whether or not it promotes the satisfaction of one's desires and interests.

These two claims are quite different, even though many moral philosophers (including Kant, I think) have tended to conflate them. The first is a claim about the conditions under which one is morally required to do something, whereas the second is a claim about the conditions under which one has reason (or is rationally required) to do something. Now, as I shall argue later, it is perfectly consistent to hold that what one morally ought to do does not depend on what one's desires and interests happen to be, while insisting that what one has reason to do does depend on this. Notice also that it is only the second of these two claims that implies that the agent of a preferentially wicked act has inconsistent beliefs (since he believes both that, morally, he ought to do X, and that, all things considered, he ought not to do X). But, whereas the first of these claims seems to me to be quite true, the second seems to me to be false. Let us now see what can be said in its behalf.

A number of contemporary moral philosophers have argued (1) that the mere fact that one morally ought to do something entails that one has a reason to do it, irrespective of whether or not it promotes the satisfaction of one's desires and interests, and (2) that such "moral" reasons are superior in justificatory weight to any reasons one might have, in terms of promoting one's desires and interests, for not doing it. These conclusions follow—or so it is argued—from the very nature of moral requirements.

It has been suggested, for example, that moral requirements are identical with those requirements on action whose observance is in the interest of everyone alike—not in the sense that it is always in everyone's long-range interest to do what he is morally required to do (for this often involves a genuine sacrifice in terms of the agent's own interests), but rather in the sense that it is in everyone's interests that everyone obey such requirements. Moral requirements place certain restrictions on each person's pursuit of his own self-interest, such that everyone is made better off by the presence, rather than the absence, of such restrictions. It follows that everyone has reason to make a contract with everyone else to observe such requirements.[15]

Thus, G. R. Grice holds that a class of actions is morally required just in case it is in the interest of everyone alike to make a contract with everyone else to do actions of that class. And he argues that it follows from this that such a requirement must be a rational requirement (since "it is a requirement which is more conducive to everyone's interests than its absence, and we could not have better grounds than that for claiming practical rationality for it") and hence that everyone has reason to comply with such requirements.[16]

Unfortunately, this argument rests on an equivocation between two senses of "rational requirement." In calling a requirement on action rational we might mean that it is

---

[15] This sort of account of morality was defended by Thomas Hobbes in his *Leviathan*. More recently, it has been defended by Kurt Baier and G. R. Grice (see the works cited above).

[16] See *The Grounds of Moral Judgment*, p. 133.

a requirement that it is rational for us to choose, agree upon, or contract for; or we might mean that it is rational for us to comply with this requirement. Now, it may plausibly be maintained that moral requirements are rational requirements in the first of these two senses, but it does not follow from this that we have a reason to comply with such requirements even when this does not promote our interests, let alone that we have a reason to comply that overrides considerations of self-interest. From the fact that everyone has reason to expect to benefit if everyone observes moral requirements (taking this to be a necessary truth about moral requirements), it follows that everyone has reason to want to live in a society governed by moral principles and to promote the realization of such a society by advocating such principles and encouraging others to observe them through setting an example for others (when necessary) by one's own observance of such principles. One can admit all this, however, without having to agree that everyone has reason to observe such principles even when doing so is not in one's overall interest.

If one wishes to argue that moral requirements provide us in and of themselves with overriding reasons for acting, a more promising line of argument is to hold that this follows not merely from the nature of moral requirements but from this together with a correct analysis of what it is to have a reason for doing something. One might argue that a correct account of the nature of reasons for action requires that we recognize moral principles as an independent source of reasons for action—and of reasons for action that override other kinds of reasons for action. Thus, D.A.J. Richards argues that, although there is a certain class of reasons for action that depend on what the agent's desires and interests happen to be, there is another class of reasons of which this is not true. The principles of morality, he says, "define a large class of reasons for action . . . which apply quite apart from a particular agent's wants and desires (e.g., even to an amoralist who has no desire to regulate his life by the principles of morality, and who has other desires whose rational pursuit involves contravening moral principles).''[17]

According to Richards, to say that a certain act is morally required is to say that it is required by those principles that perfectly rational, egoistic persons would agree on (as standards regulating their conduct toward one another) in a certain hypothetical position, characterized primarily by equality and a veil of ignorance.[18] Now why should we suppose that principles so defined specify a class of reasons for action? We have already seen that Grice's argument will not do. From the fact that it would be rational for egoistic men to make a contract to observe these principles it does not follow that it is always rational for them to act on such principles. Richards admits, however, that it would not be rational for a wholly self-interested wearer of Gyges's ring to observe such principles, but he insists that such a person nevertheless has a reason (even a conclusive reason) for acting morally.[19] Failure to see this, he says, results from confusing rationality and reasonableness. What is rational is what is required by the principles of rational choice, given the relevant agent's desires, whereas what is reasonable is what is required by certain moral principles— namely, those which specify duties and obligations, as opposed to acts of supererogation.[20]

This appeal to the concept of reasonableness seems to me simply to beg the question, since it defines reasonableness in terms of the concept of morality. Moreover, it is not clear to me that everyone does have a reason, let alone an overriding reason, to do what is reasonable *in this sense*. Suppose, for example, that there is a serious fuel shortage and it has been determined that the fuel supply can be made to last the winter only if everyone (or virtually

---

[17] See *A Theory of Reasons for Action*, p. 280.
[18] *Ibid.*, pp. 80 and 228.
[19] *Ibid.*, pp. 282, 290.
[20] *Ibid.*, pp. 76, 229, and 280.

everyone) turns down his thermostat to 65 degrees. In that case there is certainly a sense in which it is reasonable for each of us to set our thermostats at 65 degrees, and, moreover, it would be unreasonable for me to expect everyone else to do this while I keep mine set at 72 degrees. Yet, if I am certain that everyone else will turn his thermostat down and that keeping mine at 72 degrees will not make any difference, and *if I have no desire to play fair*, why do I have even *a* reason, let alone an overriding one, to turn down my thermostat? I do not see how appealing to this distinction between rationality and reasonableness is going to convince the kind of moral skeptic who doubts that any person necessarily has reason to do that which he morally ought to do; for such a skeptic will not admit that any person, regardless of his desires and interests, has reason to act reasonably (at least, not in Richards's sense).

Another argument for recognizing moral requirements as an independent source of (overriding) reasons for action can be found in the most recent writings of Kurt Baier. Baier argues that any theory of reasons for action that limits reasons to self-anchored ones (i.e., those determined by the desires of the agent) has unacceptable consequences. He attempts to show this by appealing to the well-known example of the prisoner's dilemma:

> The story is that two prisoners, A and B, accused of jointly committed crimes are told that if both confess they will receive 10 years in prison, if neither confesses, 2 years, and if one confesses while the other does not, the one who confesses will get off scot free, while the other will get 20 years.[21]

Assuming that neither desires to sacrifice his freedom for the sake of the other's and that each desires to receive the least possible sentence, then, *if all reasons are self-anchored,* it would seem to follow that the rational course of action

---

[21] "Moral Reasons," p. 70.

for each is to confess. This yields the paradoxical result that they are less well off by acting rationally (confessing) than if they act otherwise (do not confess).

This result can be avoided, Baier suggests, if we recognize moral requirements as an independent source of reasons. And he gives a further argument to establish that they indeed are such an independent source of reasons for action. If everyone recognizes moral requirements as providing reasons for acting that override self-anchored reasons, everyone will be better off (in terms of the satisfactoriness of their lives). This shows, Baier contends, that moral requirements ought to be so regarded, and hence that they really are a source of such reasons.

This argument rests on two very questionable assumptions. The first of these is the theory of soundness for reasons of action that Baier adopts—namely, that whether or not some fact about an act (e.g., the act's being morally required) counts as a reason for doing that act depends on the consequences of its being generally regarded as such, and that if the consequence of everyone's regarding it as such makes everyone better off, then it really is such a reason for acting.[22] This seems to me to commit one to a not very plausible kind of pragmatic theory of truth; the belief that P (e.g., that the fact that an act is morally required is an overriding reason for doing it) is true just in case everyone's believing P will make everyone better off.

The other questionable assumption behind this argument is the criterion of adequacy for any theory of reasons for action that Baier employs. It must be the case, he thinks, that people will do better for themselves, in terms of the satisfactoriness of their lives, if they do what they have reason to do rather than follow some other course of action. If a theory of reasons allows that a group of perfectly rational people could lead a life that is worse than a group

[22] *Ibid.*, pp. 68 and 73. Also, see "Moral Reasons and Reasons To Be Moral," pp. 240 and 244.

of people who are less perfectly rational, then such a theory cannot be correct, for surely it must be a good thing to be rational.[23] It is this view that lies behind the claim that in the case of the prisoner's dilemma a theory of reasons that limits itself to self-anchored reasons yields a paradoxical consequence. But why should we assume that rationality will always guarantee the best outcome?[24] Why should we assume that a group of perfectly rational but utterly selfish persons will do better for themselves than a group of less rational but less selfish persons? One can admit that it must be a good thing for everyone to be rational without also holding that everyone's being rational must by itself (without their also having certain other-regarding concerns and a sense of justice) guarantee a satisfactory social life. Hence, I am not convinced that this criterion of adequacy is a valid one.

It is, of course, not possible to consider here all of the arguments that have been proposed in an attempt to establish the rationality of acting in accordance with moral principles. Instead, let me now try to explain why I think this attempt is both misguided and unnecessary.

4. Morality and Rationality

Much of the impetus for the view that moral principles must, in some sense, be overriding comes, I think, from the idea that it must be rational to act morally. One of the major preoccupations of moral philosophers, from Plato and Aristotle to the present, has been to convince us that there is a perfect coincidence between acting morally and acting rationally. The idea that it might be rational for someone (on some occasion) to act immorally or (what is perhaps

[23] See "Moral Reasons," p. 68 and "Moral Reasons and Reasons To Be Moral," pp. 240 and 244.

[24] For an argument that this assumption is false see Lawrence H. Davis, "Prisoners, Paradox, and Rationality," *American Philosophical Quarterly*, vol. 14, 1977, p. 230.

worse) irrational to act as one morally ought has seemed totally absurd to them. But if moral behavior must also be rational behavior, then not only must one have *a* reason to do what one morally ought to do, one must have a conclusive (or overriding) reason to do it. Yet, the attempts made to establish this latter claim have, in my view, not succeeded. Indeed, it seems to me that no one has succeeded in demonstrating that every one has even *a* reason to do what he morally ought to do.

Why, then, do so many philosophers want to insist that everyone must have (at least some) reason to do that which he morally ought to do—or, at least that everyone must acknowledge that he has a reason to do that which he believes that he morally ought to do? I shall now try to show that this desire to demonstrate the rationality of morality is based on a number of false assumptions.

To many moral philosophers, it seems paradoxical to suppose that someone might acknowledge that X is morally wrong and yet deny that he has any reason not to do X. Here again one hears it said that, although someone might refuse to acknowledge that he has a reason to do what is commonly thought to be morally wrong, he cannot refuse to admit that he has a reason not to do X if he himself acknowledges that X is wrong. Some argue that acknowledging that one has a reason not to do X is a necessary condition of believing X to be morally wrong; so that a person simply cannot (correctly) be said to believe (himself) that X is morally wrong if he does not acknowledge that he has a reason not to do it. (This may be thought of as another version of internalism—especially if one regards a person's acknowledging that he has a reason, i.e., some justification, for doing something as a motivating factor.) Others would allow that it is possible to deny that one has a reason not to do what one acknowledges to be morally wrong, but that such a person has inconsistent beliefs, since X's being morally wrong for P to do entails that P has some reason not to do X.

Both of these views find support in the observation that it seems paradoxical to say, "I know that X is morally wrong, but what reason do I have not to do X?" Now one need not deny that this seems paradoxical. The question is: do either of these two views give the correct explanation of the paradoxical character of this remark? Notice that it may also seem paradoxical for someone to say, "I know that X is illegal, but what reason do I have not to do X?" But we are not inclined to say that this is because believing that one has a reason not do to X is a necessary condition of acknowledging X to be illegal, or because its being illegal for one to do X entails that one has a reason not to do X. Rather, this remark seems paradoxical because we assume that most people want to avoid doing what is illegal, and normally our purpose in telling someone that to do X is illegal is to point out to him that he (therefore) has a reason not to do X. (One might even go so far as to suggest—) although this may be going too far—that saying that X is illegal conversationally implicates that there is a reason not to do X.) Thus, if someone replies by saying, "Yes, I know that X is illegal," we will take this as an expression of his agreement not only that X violates the law but also that he therefore has a reason to avoid X (even though he may go on to point out that this consideration is outweighed by the fact that X is morally required). But suppose that this remark is made by a professional thief who has figured out a way to do X without being detected. In this case, his remark, "I know it's illegal, but what's that to me?" makes perfectly good sense.

It may also seem paradoxical for someone to say, "I know that X is a bad move since it will allow my Queen to be captured, but what reason do I have not to make this move?" If so, this is because our purpose in evaluating chess-moves as good or bad (and in advising chess players) is to promote the goal of winning the game. Moreover, anyone who does want to win the game he is playing will have a reason to avoid bad moves. But if one is playing only because one has promised to play with someone and if one has now become quite tired of playing, then one may have no reason not to (and every reason to) make a bad move. Here again it makes perfectly good sense for such a person to say, "Yes, I know it's a bad move, but what's that to me?"

However, it might seem paradoxical for him to say, "I know it's a bad move, but I don't see that there is any reason for not making this move." In fact, this remark may strike one as self-contradictory, for it cannot be denied that from the point of view of winning the game there is a reason not to make this move. But to say this is only to say that, if one wants to win, one has a reason not to make this move. Hence, it does not follow either that refusing to acknowledge that one has a reason not to make this move is incompatible with believing it to be a bad move (one that one ought not to make) or that it is inconsistent to admit that this is a bad move while denying that one has any reason not to make it.

I shall now argue that we can give a similar account of, "I know that it is morally wrong, but what reason do I have not to do it?" It has sometimes been argued that "P morally ought not to do X" entails "P has a reason not to do X," since if P morally ought not to do X then P has at least a moral reason not to do X.[25] This is fallacious. To say that P has a moral reason not to do X is to say no more than that, other things being equal, P morally ought not to do X—that it is (*prima facie*) morally wrong for P to do X. This entails only that from the moral point of view there is a reason for P to avoid doing X; and this means only that, if P is concerned to avoid moral wrongdoing, P has a reason not to do X. Thus, the remark above seems paradoxical because if P morally ought not to do X then, of course, there is a moral reason for his not doing X. But this does not mean that he has a reason to avoid doing X

[25] See, for example, Gilbert Harman, *The Nature of Morality* (New York: Oxford University Press, 1977), pp. 84-86.

no matter what his concerns are. Nor does it mean that one cannot, or even that it is inconsistent to, deny that one has a reason not to do X if one acknowledges that X is morally wrong.

Another reason that so many moral philosophers have wanted to demonstrate that everyone has a reason to avoid moral wrongdoing is this: if we can demonstrate that what someone does is morally wrong without also establishing that he has a reason not to do it, then moral arguments are empty and meaningless. For even if we could rationally convince someone that what he proposes to do is morally wrong, we might still fail to convince him that he has any reason to refrain from doing it. In this case his moral judgment will have no influence on his conduct.

Now perhaps it *is* pointless and futile to try to convince someone who has no desire to avoid moral wrongdoing that what he proposes to do is morally wrong. Nevertheless, it seems to me that it is not too overly optimistic to suggest that most people are concerned to avoid moral wrongdoing—even if, because of weakness of will or placing some other value above this, they often end up doing what they believe to be wrong. This fact about human beings seems to me enough to ensure that moral judgments will have some influence on people's conduct.

It is true that the account of moral judgments that I have been defending here does not *guarantee* the practicality of moral judgments, in the sense that it does not entail that it is necessarily the case that any person has a reason to do what he morally ought to do—or even that everyone must acknowledge that he has a reason to do that which he believes he morally ought to do. According to the view that I have been suggesting, there are objective criteria for determining what is morally right and wrong. These criteria are definitive of what it is to judge from the moral point of view and, hence, of what it is to believe that an act is *morally* right or wrong. Thus, anyone who wishes to consider the question of the moral wrongness of acts must employ these criteria. He is not free to employ any criteria he likes just so long as he is willing to make the proper universal prescriptions. It follows that what he must acknowledge to be morally right and wrong does not depend on what his particular desires and preferences happen to be. But what he has reason to do does depend on this.

One criticism that has been made of this kind of view is that it guarantees the objectivity of moral judgments at the price of robbing them of any necessary influence on people's conduct, since it allows one to acknowledge that one morally ought not to do something without also acknowledging that one has some reason not to do it.[26] And I am willing to admit that this view does preclude moral judgments from having this kind of necessary influence on people's conduct. Although moral judgments will have an influence on those who are morally concerned, they will fail to have an influence on those whom we call "amoral." It must be pointed out, however, that those who try to guarantee the practicality (in this sense) of moral judgments also pay a price—namely, that of robbing moral judgments of their objectivity. For, if whether or not we are logically compelled to accept a given moral judgment depends in the end on what our particular desires and preferences happen to be, then this means that moral judgments are, in an important sense, subjective. On such a view, we cannot rationally convince someone that what he proposes to do is morally wrong—even if it is a case of torturing someone solely for the sake of amusement—provided that he has perverse enough preferences and can therefore make the necessary universal prescriptions.

So, what good does it do us to guarantee that a person must acknowledge that he has a reason not to do X if he judges that X is morally wrong, if we cannot rationally convince him that X is morally wrong? Moreover, as we

[26] See Cooper, *The Diversity of Moral Thinking*, p. 68, and Hare, *Moral Thinking*, p. 71.

saw in the discussion of amorality, anyone (even those without perverse preferences) can escape being influenced by moral judgments simply by refusing to make moral judgments. There is simply no way to convince the "amoralist" that he ought to even consider whether what he does is morally right or wrong, let alone that he ought not to do it if it is morally wrong.

It has also been argued that, unless we hold that a person has a reason to do that which he morally ought to do, we cannot condemn him for not doing it.[27] How can we blame him for not doing something if he had no reason to do it? This argument is also fallacious. If a person has no concern to avoid moral wrongdoing, then he will have no reason to avoid acts simply because they are morally wrong. But surely this lack of concern is not an excusing circumstance. As I argued earlier (in Chapter Three), this lack of moral concern is itself indicative of a lack of concern for the interests of others—something that we rightly consider to be a serious character defect. Thus, far from its being the case that we cannot blame someone for doing something if he had no reason not to do it, the fact that a person has no reason not to do that which is morally wrong is evidence that he has a morally bad character. Indeed, it seems to me that it is simply the mark of a thoroughly immoral person that, if such a person were to possess Gyges's ring, he would have no reason to avoid moral wrongdoing.

Such a person is immoral, but he is not necessarily irrational. But then it seems to me to be quite sufficient that we can charge such persons with immorality; it seems entirely unnecessary to beat them over the head with the further charge of irrationality. Indeed, those who insist that we must try to convince people that immorality is also somehow irrational seem to me to show a kind of disrespect for morality. For they seem to think that it is not enough

[27] This argument is suggested by Harman. See *The Nature of Morality*, pp. 97-98 and 107-09.

to accuse the wrongdoer of immorality; we must also be able to accuse him of irrationality—or, at least, of acting contrary to reason in some sense. And this suggests that the first charge is not quite serious or important enough.

5. Preferential versus Perverse Wickedness

In Chapter One I argued that the conception of wickedness as preferential wickedness offers us a better account of how we ordinarily (when not philosophizing) conceive of wickedness. There I tried to show that the conception of wickedness as perverse wickedness leads one into insuperable difficulties when given one interpretation (the cognitivist version) and yields unacceptable consequences when given the other interpretation (the noncognitivist version). In this chapter I have attempted to answer the charges that preferential wickedness is logically impossible (the view of those who make overridingness a necessary condition of moral beliefs) and that it involves incoherent beliefs on the part of the agent (the view of those who claim that everyone has an overriding reason to do what is morally required). In these arguments I have emphasized the differences between these two conceptions of wickedness. Thus, it may be worth noting at this point that they are, nevertheless, two ways of conceiving of one thing—namely, wickedness. In order to explain how this is so, let us now observe what these two conceptions of wickedness have in common.

On both conceptions the agent of a wicked act can be described as believing that he ought to act as he does. But whereas on the conception of wickedness as perverse wickedness the agent believes that he morally ought to act as he does, on the conception of wickedness as preferential wickedness the agent believes that, although morally he ought not to do it, all things considered he ought to do it. Thus, although in both cases the agent may be described as having a bad, or perverse, belief about how one ought to act, in the case of perverse wickedness this will be a bad moral belief, whereas in the case of preferential wickedness this will be a morally bad belief.[28] In both cases, however, the agent is conceived of as preferring (in the sense of thinking it best, or that he ought all things considered) to act as he does. Thus, on either conception of wickedness it results from the same basic defect on the part of the agent—namely, bad preferences or values. Suppose, for example, that he kills another in order to take his money. On both conceptions he does so because he prefers a gain for himself to the preservation of another's life, and this preference may be viewed as reflecting the fact that he places a greater value on the pursuit of self-interest than on avoiding harm to others. In other words, he thinks that one ought (or, at least, that it is good) to promote one's own advantage even at the cost of another person's life.

Given this, it may seem that the differences between these two conceptions of wickedness are not very important and that nothing much hinges on which of them we adopt. What difference does it make whether we describe the agent's belief that one ought to kill another if this will really be to one's advantage as a bad moral belief or a morally bad belief? Here I can only repeat what I have already said. It is essential to our notion of wickedness as a more evil or blameworthy kind of wrongdoing that the agent of a wicked act does not desire to avoid moral wrongdoing, since this would mean that he has the same redeeming quality as the agent of a morally weak act. For this reason, it seems better to conceive of the agent of a wicked act as willingly doing something that he himself believes to be morally wrong.

[28] A qualification is necessary here. In some cases the agent of a wicked act may be described as believing merely that what he does is morally permissible. In this case his belief that he *ought* to do it (since it is not morally wrong and yet serves some other purpose) will be based on other than moral considerations. Still, he does believe that it is morally all right, and this is a bad moral belief.

EIGHT

* * * * *

BLAMEWORTHINESS

I have been discussing different ways of conceiving of immoral behavior and the different forms that such behavior can take on. These are all forms of blameworthy behavior. Immoral behavior is not just a case of doing something that is *wrong*—in the sense of the sort of act that one ought not to choose to do—it is morally *bad* behavior as well. Such behavior reflects adversely on the agent. Although (as we shall see) to be guilty of such behavior does not necessarily mean that one is a bad person or has a bad character, it does always count as a bad mark against one. The agent of an immoral act is thought to be deserving of blame in virtue of having done it. But what makes one deserving of blame? What does blameworthiness consist in?

It is also thought that some kinds of immoral behavior are worse than others, and that the agent is more deserving of blame for some kinds of immoral behavior than for others. Thus, Aristotle claimed—and most of us would agree—that wicked behavior is worse than morally weak behavior. Why is this? What is it about wickedness that makes it more blameworthy? And what about the other forms of immorality that we have been discussing? Where do amorality, moral indifference, and moral negligence fit into the scale of moral badness? These are some of the questions that I shall now try to answer.

219

1. Blameworthiness and Moral Defects

It used to be rather commonly thought that to say that X is blameworthy (or deserves to be blamed) for having done A is to say no more than that it is right to blame X for A—where blaming is taken to be some act of reproving X, such as scolding or upbraiding. This view is now generally rejected on two grounds. First, acts of blaming require an independent justification over and above that given for the claim that blame is deserved. Thus, even though we are quite justified in holding someone blameworthy for having done something, it might be wrong for us to scold him since he already condemns himself much too severely. Secondly, it might be right to blame someone (in this sense) even though he does not deserve to be blamed. This will be especially true if one adopts a utilitarian standard of rightness; but it may also be true because, although it is unjust to blame him, utilitarian considerations are overriding in this case.[1] Some critics of this view also claim that when a person deserves blame, what he deserves is not some way of acting toward him but rather our having a certain kind of attitude toward him.

Thus, another view that has been suggested is that to be blameworthy is to be worthy of certain kinds of negative attitudes, such as remorse on the part of the agent toward himself and indignation on the part of others.[2] On this view X is blameworthy for A if and only if blaming attitudes toward X are fitting or appropriate, given that X has done A. This view seems more plausible, but it will not tell us very much unless we are also given some account of what

---

[1] The concept of blameworthiness here being criticized is proposed by Moritz Schlick in *Problems of Ethics* (New York: Dover Publications, Inc., 1939, 1962), and by Nowell-Smith in *Ethics* (Baltimore: Penguin Books, 1954). For further criticisms see R. B. Brandt, "Blameworthiness and Obligation," in A. I. Melden, ed., *Essays in Moral Philosophy* (Seattle: University of Washington Press, 1958), pp. 3-39, and Jonathan Glover, *Responsibility* (New York: Humanities Press, 1970), esp. pp. 50-52 and 68-70.

[2] See Brandt, "Blameworthiness and Obligation," pp. 16-17.

makes attitudes of disapproval toward X on account of A fitting or justified. Here it has been suggested that blaming attitudes are justified just insofar as X's doing A is a manifestation of some character defect—i.e., insofar as A was due to X's having a faulty character.

But although it seems correct to say that X's doing A must be due to some shortcoming on X's part, this need not be a defect of character. It is sufficient that A be due to a certain kind of defective or faulty state of mind on X's part. For example, it might be due to the fact that, on this occasion at least, X failed to resist some temptation, or failed to be moved by the plight of another. (These examples show that a state of mind can be faulty because of what it is lacking, e.g., strength of will or concern for others.) This does not mean that X must be a weak-willed, or unsympathetic, person. Thus, an imputation of blame need not always be an indictment of the agent as a person. As E. L. Beardsley points out, what makes a moral offender blameworthy "is something about his state of mind *on that occasion* when he committed his offense."[3] Thus, it is somewhat misleading to characterize judgments of blameworthiness as judgments about the worth of agents, as opposed to judgments about the worth of actions.

What kind of defective or faulty state of mind makes a person deserving of blame? R. B. Brandt adopts the view just rejected—namely, that it must be a manifestation of some defect of character, and he supports this claim by appealing to what we commonly accept as excuses. If we examine these, he says, we will find that "most of them function to show that in the circumstances the act did not manifest a character worse than standard."[4] Now although this account of the rationale behind excuses is better than the one which holds that their function is to show that in the circumstances acts of blaming would serve no useful

[3] "Blaming," *Philosophia*, vol. 8, 1978, p. 580.
[4] "Blameworthiness and Obligation," pp. 13-14.

purpose (since this rationale is at least on the right track), it is still not quite correct. The various excuses that we accept do serve to show that the "fault" does not lie in some shortcoming on the part of the agent but rather in the fact that, given the circumstances, the agent either literally could not have done otherwise or, at least, could not reasonably be expected to have done otherwise.[5] But, as we have seen, to say that the agent was at fault—or even that what was done was his fault—is not to imply that his character is faulty.

Although Brandt is wrong about the rationale behind excuses, his suggestion that we look at this as the key to discovering what makes a person blameworthy is promising. But on this score Jonathan Glover seems to me to come closer to the mark when he suggests that the commonly recognized excuses reflect our conviction that it cannot be fair to blame someone for doing something if he could not help doing it.[6] For what these excuses do seem to show is that, given the circumstances, the agent either literally could not avoid what he did or else could have avoided this only at the cost of making some unreasonable effort or sacrifice. And in the latter cases we are often also inclined to say of the agent that he could not help it or that he really had no choice. A person may claim, for example, that he was forced to cooperate in the theft because the others threatened to kill him if he did not. And if we consider the threat to be genuine we will be inclined to excuse him, since we do not think it reasonable to require him to sacrifice his life in order to avoid stealing. Here we do not consider his unwillingness to sacrifice his life to be a defect on his part. Suppose, however, that someone steals something merely because he wants it and cannot afford to buy it. Here his unwillingness to do without it rather than steal

---

[5] Strictly speaking, this applies only to what I shall later call exculpating, as opposed to mitigating, excuses.

[6] *Responsibility*, p. 73.

it is a faulty state of mind, for we think it quite reasonable to expect people to make this kind of "sacrifice." His preference for stealing in this case makes his act a case of wickedness. If, however, this were a case of extreme need (stealing a loaf of bread for one's starving child) we would again have an excuse—if not a justification.[7]

There would also appear to be cases where it is unreasonable to expect people to be able to control their desires and emotions. Thus, we might be inclined to excuse the husband who stumbles upon an adulterous engagement between his wife and another man, and then proceeds to assault the man in a jealous rage. If we think that almost any man would have done the same in the circumstances, that hardly any of us could have successfully controlled our rage, then we do not consider his lack of self-restraint a shortcoming or fault in him. Perhaps there are also cases of temptation that are such that hardly anyone could have resisted. But when a person fails to control his desires and emotions in circumstances where most people are able to exercise self-restraint, then his lack of self-control counts as a shortcoming that justifies blame.

In cases where ignorance is appealed to as an excuse, we find that, if the excuse is valid, the agent could not have avoided the act, given his ignorance, and could not reasonably be expected to have avoided the ignorance. If it turns out that it was reasonable to expect him to have taken certain precautions in order to avoid being ignorant of, or mistaken about, a certain morally relevant fact, then

---

[7] In cases like this the distinction between an excuse and a justification may be difficult to maintain. Suppose that your child has been kidnapped, and the criminals tell you that they will kill your child unless you steal some diamonds for them. Does the threat made on the life of your child constitute an excuse—or a justification—for your stealing the diamonds? If this really is the only way to save your child's life, would you not be justified in stealing the diamonds? If so, your act could not even be said to be morally wrong. (Does it make any difference if it is your own life that is at stake?)

his ignorance is not excusing and we have a case of moral negligence.

Some excuses (exculpating ones) serve to remove blameworthiness entirely, whereas others (mitigating ones) merely reduce blameworthiness. The former show that, given the circumstances, it would be unreasonable to expect the agent to have avoided the offense. The latter show that, given the circumstances, it would have been very difficult for him to have avoided it. However, the line between excuses that completely remove blameworthiness and those that merely reduce the degree of it is not easy to draw. An impoverished person who steals some food in order to alleviate his hunger is certainly less blameworthy than one who steals something merely because he does not wish to have to pay for it. But it is difficult to say just how desperate he must be before we excuse him completely. Similarly, the fact that someone was very emotionally upset when he made the thoughtless remark that so deeply hurt another makes him less blameworthy than if he had not been so upset, and at some point (e.g., if he is undergoing severe emotional turmoil) it may excuse him completely.

What an examination of the nature of excusing circumstances reveals is this. When a person has both the capacity and the opportunity to avoid doing something that is morally wrong and avoiding it does not involve making an unreasonable effort or sacrifice, then he is blameworthy—although the degree of blameworthiness may be lessened by the difficulty (as determined by the degree of effort or the magnitude of the sacrifice involved) of avoiding it. When this is the case, the wrongdoing is his fault because it is due to some shortcoming on his part. He is to blame for it both in the causal sense (since we cannot blame it on the circumstances) and in the moral sense.

I have argued that the defective or faulty state of mind that makes a person deserving of blame need not be a manifestation of some character trait, and that Brandt is mistaken in thinking that this is what is revealed by an examination of the rationale behind excuses. All that is shown is that the act must be due to some shortcoming on the part of the agent. However, nothing further is revealed about the nature of these shortcomings. Some have suggested that the defective state of mind that makes a person blameworthy will always be some bad desire or intention—or, at least, either this or the absence of some good desire or intention.[8] This, I shall argue, is a bit of an oversimplification. I shall suggest that when the agent is deserving of blame for what he has done it will be due to one of three main kinds of shortcomings: bad preferences, lack of moral concern, and lack of self-control. These are the three main sources of immorality.

Before discussing this matter further, however, I should like to make a few remarks about the alleged undermining of all judgments of blame by the thesis of determinism. Although I have no new solutions to offer with respect to resolving this long-standing controversy, it may be useful to clarify my position on this subject.

2. The Thesis of Determinism

Let us suppose that for every human act (indeed, for every event) there is a set of antecedent conditions which, together with the truth of the relevant causal laws, entails the occurrence of the act.[9] This means, it is said, that no one can ever do anything other than what he does; and since it is agreed that no one deserves blame for doing something if he could not have done otherwise, it follows that no one can ever be said to be blameworthy.

[8] See Beardsley, "Blaming," pp. 577-78, and Glover, *Responsibility*, p. 198.

[9] For interesting discussions of different versions of this thesis see Glover, *Responsibility*, pp. 21-48, and Wesley C. Salmon, "Determinism and Indeterminism in Modern Science," in Joel Feinberg, ed., *Reason and Responsibility* (Encino and Belmont, Calif.: Dickenson Publishing Co., 1971), pp. 316-32.

A number of philosophers have claimed that this argument rests on an equivocation, because the sense in which determinism implies that no one could have acted otherwise is not the sense in which this is incompatible with someone's being blameworthy. And, according to the way in which I have defined blameworthiness, this would seem to be the case. On this account what is necessary (though not sufficient) for blameworthiness is that the agent had both the opportunity and the ability to do otherwise, should he have desired or chosen to do so. The thesis of determinism implies only that, given certain antecedent conditions and the truth of certain causal laws, no other act was possible. But this does not mean that the agent lacked either the opportunity or the capacity to act otherwise, should he have chosen to do so.[10] Thus, so-called soft-determinists argue that the truth of determinism is perfectly compatible with blameworthiness.

Hard-determinists reply that this position rests on an inadequate conception of moral responsibility and blameworthiness. To be blameworthy for a given act, it is not sufficient that the agent had the ability and opportunity to avoid it, should he have desired or chosen to do so; it must also be the case that he had the ability or capacity to desire or choose differently; *and*, if determinism is true, no one can ever desire or choose differently. What one chooses to do is determined by what one's desires are, and what one's desires are is determined ultimately by influences over which one has no control—namely, inherited traits and social environment. Thus, it is argued, moral responsibility for actions "requires not only that the agent was not coerced, [it] also requires that the agent *originally chose his own character*—the character that now displays itself in his choices and desires and efforts."[11]

---

[10] This point is well explained and argued for by Glover, *Responsibility*, pp. 74 ff.

[11] Paul Edwards, "Hard and Soft Determinism," in Sidney Hook, ed., *Determinism and Freedom* (New York: Collier Books, 1961), p. 123.

Notice that what is at issue here is not whether or not determinism is true. It is not even a question about how to interpret the thesis of determinism or about what its implications are. Disagreement about whether anyone is ever really blameworthy stems not so much from these things as it does from disagreement about the conditions requisite for moral responsibility. Is it really necessary that one could have desired or chosen otherwise, or that one originally chose one's own character? Some have argued that it is not just that these conditions are not satisfied; they are, in principle, incapable of being satisfied; the notions of being able to desire differently and being able to choose one's own character are unintelligible and meaningless.[12] But if it is logically impossible to satisfy the conditions requisite for moral responsibility, we do not need the thesis of determinism to prove that no one is morally responsible.

Perhaps, however, the notion of being able to desire or choose differently can be given a sense (although I am not sure that I can say the same about choosing one's own character). Most of us are able to alter or modify our desires and intentions through reflection. If I find myself desiring or intending to do something that I know to be bad for me (such as smoking cigarettes), I can often moderate the motivational influence of such a desire by reminding myself of why it is that the satisfaction of this desire would have bad consequences. I can also be rationally persuaded by others to alter many of my desires and intentions (if I choose to listen to what they say). In many cases my desires can be not only modified but extinguished. In this sense, then, people do have the capacity to change their desires and intentions and, hence, to choose differently than they actually do.

[12] See Sidney Hook, "Necessity, Indeterminism, and Sentimentalism," in *Determinism and Freedom*, pp. 187 ff., and John Hospers, "What Means This Freedom?" in *Determinism and Freedom*, pp. 140-42.

We also have some idea of what it would be like to lack this capacity, for there are some people in whom this capacity is impaired—at least in certain respects. The alcoholic, it seems, cannot control his desire to drink in the way in which others obviously can.[13] The kleptomaniac differs from the ordinary thief precisely in this respect— namely, that he cannot (at least, not without extremely great difficulty) extinguish or modify his desire to steal. This kind of impaired capacity is also characteristic of those who suffer from various other neuroses, such as compulsive hand washing. Indeed, it has been claimed that this is "the defining characteristic of neurotic behavior: it is unchangeable by any rational considerations."[14] These are all examples of what has been called "psychological compulsion." But it is important to notice that this sort of psychological compulsion is not characteristic of everyone, nor does the thesis of determinism imply that it is.

A somewhat different kind of affliction, consisting in a more general impairment of the capacity to modify one's desires and intentions by reflecting on their consequences, is often attributed to the psychopath. It is said that he is in general unable to resist the impulses and temptations of the moment. All of these unfortunate people suffer from an impairment of a capacity that we believe normal human beings to possess. The thesis of determinism does not imply that even normal people lack this capacity, nor does it imply that there is no difference between sick, neurotic, and compulsive behavior, on the one hand, and ordinary cases of weakness of will, on the other hand. As I argued earlier, the agent of a morally weak act fails adequately to control some impulse or emotion, not because he lacks the

[13] "The test for self-control, which differentiates between my intention and that of the alcoholic, is that my intention can be altered by providing reasons that give me a sufficiently strong motive, while his can only be altered, if at all, by some form of manipulation such as behaviour therapy or drugs." (Glover, *Responsibility*, p. 100.)

[14] Hosper, "What Means This Freedom?" p. 131.

capacity to do so, but because he is not concerned enough about avoiding moral wrongdoing to exercise this capacity as fully as he might.[15]

Perhaps, then, all that is necessary in order for one to be deserving of blame is that one possess this capacity that we believe all normal human beings to have. But here again we find that the hard determinist is unwilling to accept this. Once we recognize that "the so-called normal person is equally the product of causes in which his volition took no part," then we cannot help concluding that "if, unlike the neurotic's, his behavior is changeable by rational considerations, and if he has the will power to overcome the effects of an unfortunate early environment, this again is no credit to him; he is just lucky."[16]

One might respond by asking why we must suppose that those who are fortunate enough to have this ability cannot fail to exercise it. And if they can have this ability but fail to exercise it, then why are they not to blame for this? The hard determinist will no doubt reply that when they fail to exercise this general ability, this too is determined by their genetic and environmental programming. They differ from people who do not even have this capacity (or have it only to a limited degree) much in the way that more sophisticated computers differ from less sophisticated ones. They have the ability to do certain things—make certain calculations (in the case of computers) or exert a certain degree of effort (in the case of humans)—that the others lack the ability to do, but there are limits to their ability. Just as there may be calculations that are too complicated for even the more sophisticated computer, so there are certain temptations too great for the normal person to cope with. Perhaps even normal persons are programmed to make an effort only up to a certain point; so that if a greater effort is required to resist the impulse or control

---

[15] On this point I agree with Glover. See his *Responsibility*, p. 100.
[16] Hospers, "What Means This Freedom?" p. 135.

the passion, they too will fail. Who can say that this is not so?

For this reason it has been suggested that, if we adopt the perspective of ultimate causes, all moral distinctions break down and we view everyone as moral equals. It is when we adopt this perspective that we are inclined to say: "There but for the grace of God go I." The question now is whether this perspective is compatible with, or rather invalidates, the judgments arrived at when we adopt the more limited perspective of moral responsibility. E. L. Beardsley argues that, although judgments made from the latter perspective do not tell the whole story, they nevertheless tell a useful and important story. And she contends that, although judgments made from the perspective of ultimate causes may *supplement* the judgments made from the perspective of moral responsibility, they cannot *supplant* these judgments.[17] Similarly, R. B. Brandt argues that, although certain blaming attitudes may have to be altered or reduced in strength in order to retain their appropriateness when we acquire knowledge of prior causes, they are not wholly dissolved by this knowledge. He gives the following examples.

(1) For instance, if we are angry at ourselves for some self-centered act, the experience may become less poignant if we reflect that probably our self-centeredness is the result of long periods of sickness as a child, when we were a center for family concern. Such thoughts seem to make us less bitterly remorseful, more sadly receptive of ourselves. But the attitude is not wholly dissolved by such reflection, if the thing that has been injured is something highly prized.

(2) Take, for instance, the German, who, we learn, heartily assisted in torturing and murdering Jews dur-

[17] See her "Determinism and Moral Perspectives," in *Reason and Responsibility*, pp. 459 ff. (reprinted from *Philosophy and Phenomenological Research*, vol. 21, 1960, pp. 1-20). The idea of distinguishing between these two perspectives was suggested to me by this article.

ing the war, with no excuse. We may form theories as to how he got that way: his father, the old Prussian household, the tradition of race hatred. And these reflections mellow our indignation, as Spinoza insisted long ago. Nevertheless, we shall not be able to embrace him with warmth when we next see him—any more than we can stifle our admiration for Anne Frank by assuring ourselves that it is only bad luck that we are not all of us made of stuff as stern as she.[18]

I am not sure that Brandt is correct in thinking that these examples show, not only that such attitudes as remorse and indignation "do not wholly dissolve when we reflect on the causal origin of the behavior that arouses them," but also that "we may with some reason suppose [these attitudes] to be objectively justified even if determinism is true."[19] I am inclined to think that some kinds of blaming attitudes are not justified if determinism is true: self-righteous indignation and holier-than-thou contempt, for example. Still, I am also inclined to agree with Brandt and Beardsley that viewing human behavior from the perspective of ultimate causes does not invalidate all blaming attitudes. For one thing, as Brandt points out, ". . . some attitudes are solely concerned with what their object is now. If we like a person because he has a sense of humor, this attitude is not undermined by the information that he inherited it from his mother."[20] Similarly, our feeling of repugnance for the German described by Brandt is not affected by the knowledge of how he came to be this way, because what we despise is the sort of person he is now. It is precisely what he has become (for whatever reasons) that disgusts us. It is, of course, quite true that, given the proper antecedent conditions, anyone of us could become just like him. This is what makes us shudder: to think that

---

[18] *Ethical Theory* (Englewood Cliffs, N.J: Prentice-Hall, Inc., 1959), p. 526.
[19] *Ibid.*
[20] *Ibid.*, p. 524.

we might be like this. The thought of becoming such a person revolts us, and rightly so.

This brings up another point. It is important to us to have certain ideals of what people should be like. We approve of self-control and concern for others, and we disapprove of selfishness and lack of self-restraint. We consider honesty and generosity to be admirable and praiseworthy traits of character, and we consider greediness and callousness to be reprehensible. Moreover, we cannot help disapproving of and being disappointed by those who fail to live up to our ideals, anymore than we can help admiring and desiring to emulate those who exemplify them. And so long, at least, as these attitudes are directed at individuals *qua* exemplars of these good or bad qualities, rather than at individuals *qua* individuals, these attitudes would seem to be justified. Thus, viewing things from the perspective of ultimate causes need not undermine all of our feelings of approval and disapproval. However, it should temper some of them; and it may even show us that some of these feelings (e.g., contempt, self-righteous indignation, hatred, feelings of moral superiority, etc.) are totally unjustified.

If this is correct, then viewing things from the perspective of moral responsibility retains its importance for us even if we admit the truth of determinism. For we cannot do without ideals of what human beings should be like, anymore than we can do without principles to guide our particular actions. This means that it is necessary for us to evaluate human behavior not only as right or wrong but also as good or bad, admirable or reprehensible. It means, also, that the perspective of moral responsibility is not wholly undermined or invalidated by the perspective of determinism.

3. *The Roots of Immorality*

Our discussion of different types of immoral behavior has revealed that there are three main kinds of shortcomings in virtue of which persons may be said to be blameworthy for what they do: bad preferences, lack of moral concern, and lack of self-control. These may also be thought of as the principal sources of immorality. The first is the source of wicked behavior, whether interpreted as perverse or preferential wickedness. The second manifests itself either in the failure to make moral judgments in the first place, in which case it results in amoral behavior, or in the failure to act on those moral judgments that one does make, in which case it results in morally indifferent behavior. The third is the source of both moral negligence and moral weakness, depending on whether the agent fails to prevent his desires and emotions from interfering with his making the judgment that his act is wrong or interfering with his acting on this judgment.

We began our discussion of the various ways of conceiving of immoral behavior by noting the inadequacy of Aristotle's assumption that all cases of immorality can be reduced to two types: wickedness and moral weakness. We have seen that there are cases of immoral behavior where the agent fails to believe that what he does is wrong, but which are not cases of (perverse) wickedness; and we have seen (although this is more controversial) that there are cases of immoral behavior where the agent believes that what he does is wrong, but which are not cases of moral weakness. We also noted that the twofold classification of immoral behavior into those cases where the agent fails to believe and those where he believes that what he does is wrong reflects the common-sense conviction that there are two main reasons why someone might fail to avoid doing something that is morally wrong: lack of knowledge (or belief) and lack of (sufficient) motivation.

As our subsequent discussion has indicated, however, a greater variety of sources of wrongdoing is revealed when we look more deeply and ask why the agent fails to believe that his act is wrong or why he lacks sufficient motivation to avoid a wrongdoing that he himself acknowledges. In each case we find that there are three main kinds of shortcomings that can account for this. Combining these two ways of classifying immoral behavior—that in terms of the absence or presence of the belief that the act is wrong and that in terms of the type of moral defect or shortcoming involved—we can now represent the six main types of immoral behavior that we have been discussing by the following schema.[21]

		The agent's belief-state	
		does not believe wrong	does believe wrong
The agent's moral defect	bad preferences	perverse wickedness	preferential wickedness
	lack of self-control	moral negligence	moral weakness
	lack of moral concern	amorality	moral indifference

It might be suggested that if we look even deeper we shall find that there is really only one ultimate source of immoral behavior—namely, bad desires. This seems most plausible with respect to cases of wickedness, since in cases of wickedness (on either interpretation) the agent desires to do just what he does—for example, to steal, break a promise, kill someone who stands in his way, etc.[22] But one might hold that all immoral behavior derives ultimately from bad desires. In cases of moral negligence and moral weakness, one might argue, the trouble stems from the fact

[21] Strictly speaking, the distinction between perverse and preferential wickedness is not a distinction between two types of immoral behavior, but rather a distinction between two different ways of conceiving of one type of immoral behavior.

[22] However, if we conceive of wickedness as perverse wickedness, the agent does not himself believe such acts to be wrong. Hence he cannot be said to desire to do something that (he believes) is wrong.

that the agent has certain bad desires which he finds himself unable to control. It is his lust, or greed, or envy, or excessive desire to impress others, that does him in. Even in cases of amoral and morally indifferent behavior, although here the trouble seems to be a lack of a good desire rather than the presence of some bad desire, it might be argued that indifference to matters of right and wrong also has its ultimate source in bad desires. Perhaps it is because the agent is so consumed by the desire to promote his own advantage that he has no desire to avoid wrongdoing; perhaps, that is, he cares so much about his own interests that there is no room left in his heart for concern about the interests of others.

This way of looking at these matters oversimplifies and distorts, and it is not even very helpful for an understanding of wickedness. Most of the desires that motivate wicked behavior are not desires that we consider bad in themselves—such as the desire to humiliate or the desire to hurt someone. When a person chooses to steal something, for example, the desire that normally motivates him is simply the desire to possess a certain object. Insofar as we suppose that the agent could have satisfied this desire by purchasing the object or gaining it in some other morally permissible manner, we have no reason to suppose that the desire itself is bad. Similarly, when a person breaks a promise or kills someone who stands in his way, the desire that motivates him is usually a desire to achieve some end or goal that can be promoted by the promise-breaking or killing. And there need be nothing bad or evil about desiring this end. What is bad is the fact that the agent prefers to satisfy this desire even at the cost of promise-breaking or killing someone. For this reason I have suggested that it is bad preferences, rather than bad desires, that cause wicked behavior.

W. D. Ross has suggested that most wicked acts are the result, not of bad desires, but of selfishness; and if we think of selfishness not just as a trait of character but also as

235

something that can characterize on occasion even the acts of someone who is not a selfish person, this statement seems correct.[23] For selfishness, so conceived, consists in preferring to promote one's own good rather than to avoid harming or frustrating the interests of others—even when the gain for oneself is slight and the loss for others is great. And it is true that in the case of most wicked acts the preference that causes the act is an instance of this more general kind of preference.

Some wicked acts do seem to be caused by bad desires, however. Someone might torture another human being, for example, and be motivated by the desire to hurt that human being. But even here it is possible to find bad preferences at the root of the trouble. Perhaps the agent desires to torture someone because the sight (or even the thought) of someone in pain gives him a certain thrill, or because his causing another to feel pain makes him feel powerful and dominant. It may be that the agent does have some concern to avoid harming others, but, nevertheless, prefers to get this thrill (or to feel dominant and powerful) even at the cost of frustrating the interests of others. If so, the wicked act is, once again, caused by a bad preference. Suppose, however, that the agent has no concern whatsoever to avoid harming his victim. Suppose that he not only fails to desire that his victim not feel pain, he desires that his victim does feel pain. Suppose, moreover, that it is the latter desire and no other that ultimately motivates him. In this case what attracts him is precisely what makes his act wrong—i.e., its causing pain to someone. This comes close to desiring to do what is wrong as an end in itself, which might be thought of as the most evil desire of all.

Such desires are not easy to understand. It is tempting to think that they are always symptomatic of some pathological condition. The notion of a desire to do what is

[23] See *The Right and the Good* (Oxford: Clarendon Press, 1930), pp. 166-67.

morally wrong as such is especially problematic. For those who adopt a noncognitivist analysis of moral beliefs this desire may seem more paradoxical than lack of the desire to avoid wrongdoing. But it proves puzzling even for those who offer a cognitivist account of moral beliefs. What does such a desire really come to? What is it a desire for? We cannot construe it as a desire to flout social conventions, to spite God, or to advance one's own interests at the expense of the interests of others; for then it is not a desire to do wrong as an end in itself. The most plausible suggestion is that it is to be cashed out as the desire to do certain acts simply in virtue of what it is about these acts that makes them wrong—e.g., causing pain or injury, deceiving another, violating a trust, etc. Thus understood, the desire to do what is wrong is really a class of desires, including the desires to cause pain, to kill, to humiliate, to deceive, to cheat, etc.

Suppose now that a person is motivated by the desire to kill or humiliate or deceive another as an end in itself. In this case I am inclined to think that what we have here is an extreme case of lack of moral concern. The agent not only fails to be negatively motivated by those features of the act that make it wrong; he is positively attracted by these features. Here the trouble is not that the agent has bad priorities; the trouble is that he has *only* a morally bad desire (such as the desire to hurt someone) and hence lacks any compensating morally good desire (such as the desire to avoid frustrating the interests of others). Thus, insofar as he does believe that his act is morally wrong, he will be completely unmoved by this belief. If he does wrong, it will be a case of morally indifferent wrongdoing rather than a case of preferential wickedness (although, as I shall point out in the next section, this does not make it any less evil or "wicked," in a broader sense of this term). If he fails to believe that his act is wrong, it will be a case of amoral wrongdoing. Here the trouble is still lack of moral concern, for he would not have avoided the act even if he did believe it to be wrong; in this case lack of moral concern accounts for lack of moral belief—for his not having bothered to make any moral judgment. If one wants to construe his act as a case of *perverse* wickedness, one must suppose that the bad desire accounts not only for his failing to believe that his act is wrong but also for his believing that his act is right. But, as I have already argued, to suppose this is both implausible and unnecessary.

In any case, enough has been said to show that bad desires are not the sole source of immoral behavior. Wicked behavior is caused by bad preferences rather than by bad desires. And although bad desires may sometimes preclude one's having any moral concern and thus give rise to amoral or morally indifferent wrongdoing, one can also have a lack of moral concern without having any bad desires. One can simply not care that what one does causes pain to another, for example. Finally, morally negligent and morally weak behavior stem not from having bad desires (i.e., desires that make one especially prone to wrongdoing) so much as from one's failing adequately to control one's desires. Those who avoid wrongdoing often have these same desires. Moral negligence and moral weakness result, rather, from a failure to exercise certain capacities of rational self-control in circumstances in which it is not unreasonable to expect one to do so, and where many others have succeeded in doing so.

If one wishes to find some single, ultimate source of all immoral behavior, a more promising candidate is lack of moral concern. If we ask why the agent of a wicked act prefers to act as he does—prefers, for example, to kill another person rather than not have something he wants— the answer seems to be that he is just not concerned enough about preserving the life of another human being. He fails to be sufficiently concerned about the very feature of his act that makes it wrong. If we ask why the agent of a morally negligent or a morally weak act fails to exercise certain capacities of self-control, the answer that once again suggests itself is: because he did not care enough. Thus, it is plausible to hold that there is only one ultimate moral shortcoming—lack of moral concern—and that all blameworthiness reduces to it.

The notion of moral concern is closely related to the notion of conscientiousness. Indeed, they may seem to one to be identical. However, as conscientiousness is commonly conceived of, it is a narrower notion than moral concern. For example, R. B. Brandt defines a conscientious person as "one strongly motivated to avoid doing anything he thinks wrong, and who is willing to make considerable sacrifice to do what he thinks is right."[24] This definition identifies moral concern with a concern to avoid doing what one believes to be morally wrong and to do what one believes to be morally required, and it suggests that lack of moral concern consists in being insufficiently motivated by the thought that it would be morally wrong to do something. But, as we have seen, lack of moral concern not only can account for one's doing what one believes to be wrong; it can also lead to one's not believing that it is wrong—either because one does not even bother to make any moral judgment (amorality) or because one mistakenly but negligently believes that it is right (moral negligence). Thus, moral concern includes more than a concern to avoid doing that which one believes to be morally wrong, since moral concern must also be able to account for why we make moral judgments—why we have come to believe that our act is morally wrong in the first place.

One might think of conscientiousness as consisting simply in a strong desire to avoid wrongdoing. One could then hold that lack of this could account both for one's not doing what one judges to be wrong and for one's not judging one's act to be wrong (as in cases of amoral and morally negligent wrongdoing). However, this desire to avoid wrongdoing as such is almost as puzzling as the desire to

[24] *Ethical Theory*, p. 469.

do what is wrong for its own sake. What does such a desire amount to? Kant viewed it as a kind of abstract desire to act only on rules of conduct that one would be willing to have everyone act on. Moreover, he seems to have thought that one could be motivated simply by the mere idea of duty, or the moral law—i.e., that nothing else was necessary to account for a person's wanting to conform his behavior to moral requirements than his bare understanding of what a moral requirement is. This seems to me to be a mistake. I have argued that it is not impossible for someone to understand what it is for an act to be morally wrong but not care whether his acts are morally wrong. Moreover, I have suggested that whether or not a person does care about this will depend on whether or not he cares about the interests of others. And it is really this concern for the interests of others that I wish to identify with moral concern. In any case, it is this concern that accounts for one's concern to avoid moral wrongdoing (and not *vice versa*, as Kant seems to suggest).[25]

Now if one does understand the notion of moral concern in this way, then to say that all immoral behavior results from a lack of moral concern is not very far from the truth. Lack of moral concern does seem to lie behind all immoral behavior, and it is important to recognize this for a full understanding of the nature of immorality. Nevertheless, to say this is still something of an oversimplification, for there are important differences that it ignores or, at least, obscures. Insofar as the agents of morally weak and morally negligent acts can be said to be lacking in moral concern (otherwise they would have tried harder, taken greater precautions, etc.) they are not nearly so lacking as the agents of wicked and amoral (including morally indifferent) acts.

[25] See, for example, *The Critique of Practical Reason* (New York: The Liberal Arts Press, 1956), pp. 85 ff., and *The Doctrine of Virtue* (New York: Harper & Row, 1964), pp. 116 ff. For Kant's general views on the nature of conscientiousness, see *Fundamental Principles of the Metaphysics of Morals*, Section I.

This is reflected in the fact that the agents in the former cases are inclined to feel remorse for what they have done. And it is also reflected in the fact that we generally consider them to be less blameworthy than wicked or amoral agents. Thus, to simply attribute all immorality to lack of moral concern, without noting the role played by lack of self-control in certain forms of immoral behavior, is to ignore important differences relevant to our moral assessments of such behavior.

The differences between wicked behavior and amoral wrongdoing (in the broad sense) are perhaps not so great. As we have seen, both can be contrasted with the two forms of "akratic" wrongdoing (as they might be referred to) and, thus, both can be considered cases of wickedness—in a broader sense of this term, in which it designates all forms of willful and compunctionless wrongdoing. Yet even here there are important differences that should not be ignored. Although it is true that the agent of a wicked act is not as morally concerned as he should be, the trouble with him is not so much that he is lacking in moral concern as that he has a false sense of priorities—he prefers, for example, to promote his own advantage rather than to avoid frustrating the interests of others. Moreover, it seems worse for the agent to be completely lacking in moral concern, as in cases of amoral and morally indifferent wrongdoing. Thus I have chosen to distinguish between wrongdoing due to bad preferences and that due to (complete) lack of moral concern.

4. Comparative Blameworthiness

As we have just noted, judgments of blameworthiness are often comparative in nature. Some kinds of acts (e.g., killing) seem to be worse than others (e.g., stealing), and hence we are inclined to consider a person more blameworthy for doing the one kind of act than for doing the other. We can also compare acts of the same kind with respect to blameworthiness. A person who steals because he succumbs to some very strong temptation is considered less blameworthy than one who steals merely to avoid having to pay for some item; and a person who steals in order to help the poor, whose needs are being ignored, is less blameworthy than one who steals for selfish reasons. Reflection on these kinds of judgments reveals that there are three main perspectives from which such comparative judgments can be made.

The kind of act. It is generally believed that certain kinds of acts are, in and of themselves, worse than others. For example, it is thought to be worse to kill someone than to steal from someone, worse to injure someone than to insult someone. It is also thought (although this is more controversial) that it is worse to kill ten persons than to kill one person.[26] In these cases what makes one kind of act worse than another is the fact that the one brings about (or perhaps fails to prevent) a greater harm; and one harm may be greater than another either qualitatively (i.e., because of the kind of harm—e.g., loss of life is worse than loss of property) or quantitatively (e.g., loss of ten lives is worse than loss of one). But many have claimed that, even where the same kind of harm is involved, some kinds of acts are worse than others. Thus, it is said to be worse to kill someone than to let someone die, worse to injure someone than to fail to prevent someone's being injured. Here, it is said, the former are more reprehensible because, in general, violations of stricter duties are worse than violations of less strict duties. However, I am inclined to doubt this last claim.

If one holds that killing someone is a violation of a stricter moral requirement than is letting someone die, this mean that it is more difficult to justify killing someone than letting

[26] For an interesting examination of this assumption see John M. Taurek, "Should the Numbers Count?" *Philosophy & Public Affairs*, vol. 6, 1977, pp. 293-316.

someone die. For example, the fact that one could save another person's life only by risking one's own might be held to justify letting this other person die. But if one were suffering from severe heart disease and were therefore in danger of dying, this would not justify killing someone else, even if this were the only way to obtain a new heart. All that follows from this is that circumstances that justify (i.e., make not wrong) acts of letting die do not always justify acts of killing. This does not mean, however, that in circumstances where both are wrong they are not equally blameworthy. Given circumstances where both are wrong, then, given similar motives and intentions, they are equally bad or reprehensible, it might be argued.[27]

All of these comparative judgments seem to be subject to an other-things-being-equal proviso. A person is not necessarily more blameworthy for killing someone than for stealing from someone. It depends on the circumstances and the motives and intentions of the agent. Consider the woman who kills the brute of a husband who has physically and verbally abused her for years and who has threatened to kill her and her children if she sues for divorce. Is she more blameworthy than someone who swindles a poor man out of his life savings? Considering such things as the circumstances and the agent's state of mind adds another dimension (actually, two more dimensions) to judgments of comparative blameworthiness. It involves making judgments from the perspective of the kind of shortcoming or defect that causes the act and that of possible mitigating conditions (either circumstances or motives) that lessen the degree of blameworthiness.

---

[27] See Michael Tooley, "An Irrelevant Consideration: Killing versus Letting Die," and James Rachels, "Active and Passive Euthanasia," both in Bonnie Steinbock, ed., *Killing and Letting Die* (Englewood Cliffs, N.J.: Prentice-Hall, Inc., 1980), pp. 56-62, and 63-68. Rachels's paper is reprinted from *New England Journal of Medicine*, vol. 292, 1975. I am indebted to Heidi Malm, who is writing a dissertation on this subject, for helping me to clarify my thinking on this matter.

The kind of shortcoming. Since some kinds of defective states of mind seem to make one more blameworthy than others for having done a certain act, a consideration of the agent's state of mind may be relevant insofar as it indicates the kind of shortcoming that the act was due to.[28] Aristotle held that one is more blameworthy for performing a wicked act than for an act of moral weakness; and, at least so long as one is speaking of the same kind of act in each case, this seems correct. Other things being equal, it is worse to prefer stealing something from one's neighbor rather than not have it than it is to prefer not to steal but fail to prevent one's desire for the stolen item from overriding one's preference. It is also worse to deliberately hurt someone's feelings by making a remark that one hopes will amuse others (because one prefers to amuse them rather than to avoid hurting the other person's feelings) than it is to do this unwittingly for lack of having thought about the effect that one's amusing remark might have on the person whose feelings were hurt.

However, although it seems true that a person is more blameworthy for having performed a wicked act than for having performed a morally weak or morally negligent act of the same type, it does not seem to be true that any wicked act is more blameworthy than any morally weak or morally negligent act. This is because not all preferences are equally bad and some instances of lack of self-control are worse than others. It is worse to prefer stealing one's neighbor's diamonds rather than buy some than it is to prefer breaking a luncheon engagement rather than miss an important lecture that one has just heard about. Thus, some bad preferences are worse than others for much the same reasons that some bad desires are worse than others. We can also note important differences between cases of

---

[28] A consideration of the agent's mental state may also be relevant insofar as it indicates the presence of a compensating good motive that lessens the degree of blame. I shall discuss this shortly.

wrongdoing due to lack of self-control. Among cases of moral negligence, cases of moral recklessness and self-deceptive wrongdoing seem worse than the others, because in these cases the wrongdoing is, in a certain sense, willful. In cases of moral recklessness the agent is aware of the risk of wrongdoing but deliberately disregards this, and we have seen that cases of self-deceptive wrongdoing involve a kind of willful moral blindness or ignorance. Because of this, these species of moral negligence seem almost as bad in general, or as kinds of immorality, as wickedness.

Indeed, particular instances of these species of moral negligence may even be worse than some instances of wickedness. Consider, for example, a person who is considering what to do about an elderly and sickly parent who has become a burden to him. It may be that this person so desires to relieve himself of this burden that he successfully deceives himself into thinking that death is really in the parent's own best interests and thus performs what he takes to be an act of euthanasia. If killing the parent (or allowing the parent to die) is clearly unjustified and if this person would easily recognize this if he assessed the situation correctly (i.e., without being led by his desire to ignore certain features and exaggerate the importance of others), this would seem to be a pretty bad act—i.e., one for which the agent is highly blameworthy. Now compare this act with a person's failing to visit a sick friend in the hospital because, even though he believes this to be wrong, he prefers to stay at home and watch television. The first act seems somehow worse, and the agent seems somehow more blameworthy. Perhaps this is because we think that the first act is so much worse as a kind of act that this consideration outweighs the fact that the second act is more clearly a case of willful or intentional wrongdoing (and hence manifests a worse kind of shortcoming). It is not clear, however, to what extent judgments made from these two different perspectives are really commensurable. So, perhaps our judgment is based rather on the fact that this particular bad preference (preferring to watch television rather than visit a sick friend) is not a very bad preference, since it is only a mild form of selfishness, whereas the self-deception that gives rise to the other act seems particularly serious or bad.

For much the same reasons, certain instances of moral weakness may also seem worse than certain cases of wickedness. For example, suppose that someone refuses to prevent an innocent person from being killed, because in order to do so he would have to reveal certain information that would embarrass him. Although he believes it to be morally wrong not to save this person, he cannot bring himself to face the embarrassment that it would cause him. Here again this seems worse than refusing to visit a sick friend because one prefers to watch television, not just because this act is so much worse as a kind of act (considering the harm involved), but because this particular instance of lack of self-control (failing to prevent one's fear of being embarrassed from interfering with one's saving a human life) is an especially bad instance of weakness of will. However, it does seem to be true that, in general, acts of wickedness are worse than acts of moral negligence or moral weakness.

If we now compare wickedness with amoral and morally indifferent wrongdoing, the latter seems worse. This is true even if we conceive of wickedness, as I have suggested, as preferential wickedness. It seems worse to have no moral concern at all than to have some but nevertheless value something else more.[29] Hence, I am inclined to think that,

---

[29] If we conceive of wickedness as perverse wickedness, amoral and morally indifferent behavior seem even more worse than wickedness. For, in this case the agent of a wicked act prefers to avoid moral wrongdoing to realizing any conflicting ends but (mistakenly) believes that what he does is morally right. And even though (according to the noncognitivist version, at least) this perverse belief is itself a manifestation of a morally bad preference, it is still better for a person to have some concern for the

in general, amoral and morally indifferent wrongdoing are more blameworthy than wickedness. But here again, when we compare different kinds of wrong acts, there appear to be exceptions. Just as not every bad preference is equally bad, so some instances of lack of moral concern are not as bad as others. This is because it seems possible for a person to be morally indifferent in some respects but not in others. For example, a person may be quite concerned about hurting or injuring others but not at all concerned about deceiving them (telling lies or breaking promises, for example), except when this is harmful to them in some other way. Suppose, then, that such a person tells a lie that promotes some end of his, because he does not think that telling this lie will hurt anyone (although he acknowledges that it is nevertheless wrong). This particular morally indifferent act does not seem to be very reprehensible (provided there really is good reason to think that the lie is harmless), even though it reflects a complete lack of concern about its wrong-making feature. Now consider the following case of wickedness. A person steals some rare object from his neighbor because his neighbor will not sell it to him. He does not want his neighbor to be deprived of this object and wishes that he (the thief) could find another like it somewhere else; but, given that this is not possible, he prefers that his neighbor be deprived of what belongs to him rather than that he (the thief) not have it. I fail to see why this act is less blameworthy than the morally indifferent act just considered, even though the agent is in this case not completely lacking in concern about the feature of his act that (even he believes) makes it wrong.

Thus, the most that can be said about the comparative blameworthiness of the different forms of immoral behavior is this. Given acts of the same kind—e.g., stealing, failing to help someone in need, etc.—done in similar cir-

---

welfare of others, but prefer his own good when these conflict, than it is to have no concern at all for the welfare of others.

cumstances, then, other things being equal (i.e., apart from the possible mitigating conditions to be discussed shortly), amoral and morally indifferent acts are more reprehensible or blameworthy than wicked acts, and the latter are more blameworthy than morally negligent and morally weak acts. Moreover, even when we compare different kinds of wrong acts, this same ranking seems to hold in general—although here there appear to be exceptions.

What about comparisons between different types of immoral behavior due to the same shortcoming? It might be thought that, in general, moral indifference is worse than amoral wrongdoing and moral weakness worse than moral negligence, because in the former cases the wrongdoing is conscious and intentional. But it may be doubted whether the fact that one's wrongdoing is conscious or intentional or not is relevant in itself (i.e., apart from what it reveals about the agent's possible defects) to assessments of comparative blameworthiness. Thus, although the agent of a morally indifferent act knowingly does what is wrong, whereas the amoral agent is ignorant that what he does is wrong, when we consider that the latter may be ignorant only because he does not care to know (and hence does not even consider) whether what he does is right or wrong and, in any case, would not be inclined to avoid it even if he did believe it to be morally wrong, the amoral agent seems just as bad. Similarly, what seems most important in comparing moral weakness with moral negligence is that in both cases the agent desires and prefers to avoid wrongdoing, and fails to avoid wrongdoing only because he fails to exercise certain capacities of rational self-control. The fact that moral negligence is a case of unconscious and unintentional wrongdoing does not seem to make it less blameworthy, since this does not mean that the morally negligent agent is any more concerned to avoid wrongdoing than is the morally weak agent. Indeed, as we have seen, certain forms of moral negligence—namely, moral recklessness and self-deceptive wrongdoing—are not only

not clearly cases of unconscious or unintentional wrongdoing; they seem to be in some sense more *willful* than
typical cases of moral weakness—where the agent does
what is wrong in spite of himself and, in this sense, against
his will (resolve).

Mitigating conditions. The third perspective from which
comparisons in terms of blameworthiness can be made is
the vantage point of mitigating conditions (should there be
any). Given two morally wrong acts of the same kind due
to the same shortcoming, one may still be less blameworthy
than the other because of the presence of mitigating conditions. These seem to be of two types: adverse circumstances and good motives.

Adverse circumstances sometimes make it merely very
difficult to avoid moral wrongdoing, without making it
impossible or making it unreasonable to expect the agent
to have avoided it.[30] A person who has grown up in poverty
and been deprived of most of the nice things in life may
find it much more difficult to resist the temptation to steal
something, especially if there is little chance that he will
ever be able to afford such a thing. Insofar as this is the
case, we consider such a person less blameworthy for stealing than those who have no such excuse. Again, a person
suffering from emotional trauma due to some unusually
stressful condition in his life may be somewhat excused for
doing something to hurt the feelings of another. Under
such circumstances it is often very difficult to control one's
anger, for example, and it is difficult to advert to the harm-

[30] The presence of such circumstances constitutes a mitigating, rather
than an exculpating, excuse. For a useful discussion of mitigating circumstances see E. L. Beardsley, "Moral Worth and Moral Credit," *The Philosophical Review*, vol. 66, 1975, pp. 304-28. I owe to Beardsley the suggestion that, when we consider possible mitigating conditions, we are
judging from a different perspective than when we consider the kind of
act or the shortcoming (defect) that causes it. She also seems to me to be
correct in claiming that judgments of comparative blameworthiness made
from these different perspectives are not really commensurable.

ful consequences of one's acts for others. A person is also not as blameworthy if he fails to be morally concerned (i.e., care about the interests of others) under such conditions. It may even be that adverse conditions make some bad preferences less reprehensible than they might otherwise be. For example, if a person has been deprived of love and encouragement, so that he feels very insecure, we may partially excuse him for showing partiality toward his friends.

Blameworthiness can also be reduced by the presence of good motives. These too seem to function either as mitigating excuses or, at least, as compensating or countervailing factors. For example, an employer may give a job to someone who is much less qualified than the other applicants, and we may think that this is not only unfair but, all things considered, wrong. Nevertheless, if we find that the employer was motiviated by pity for a person whose life had been particularly unfortunate, we shall consider him less blameworthy than if he had been motivated, say, by racism or sexism. Similarly, the thief who steals in order to help the unfortunate will be considered less blameworthy than the thief who steals in order to benefit himself.

Comparison of acts in terms of blameworthiness can be made from any one of these three perspectives. And, as we have seen, act X may be more reprehensible than Y when judged from one of these perspectives and less reprehensible than Y when judged from another perspective. In such cases we may think that the greater reprehensibility of X, when compared with Y from one perspective, is outweighed by the greater reprehensibility of Y, when compared with X from a different perspective. But it is not clear to me that comparisons made from these different perspectives are really commensurable.

5. Cognitivist versus Noncognitivist Perspectives: Concluding Remarks

As we have seen, how one conceives of immorality depends, at least in part, on how one conceives of the nature of moral beliefs. If one adopts a noncognitivist account, according to which having a moral belief necessarily involves having some pro- or con-attitude, then one cannot allow that moral indifference is a possible form of immorality. And if one adopts the kind of view which holds that believing an act to be morally wrong entails having a dominant, or overriding, con-attitude toward acts of that sort, then preferential wickedness will not be a possible form of immorality for one, either—so that one must then conceive of wickedness as perverse wickedness.

I have also argued that wickedness does not seem so bad in comparison with other forms of immorality, such as moral weakness, when we conceive of it as perverse wickedness rather than as preferential wickedness. Thus, how one conceives of the nature of moral beliefs also has implications for judgments of comparative blameworthiness. Wickedness seems less reprehensible when we conceive of the agent as failing to believe that what he does is wrong and believing instead that it is right. For, in this case, although he willingly does something that is morally wrong, he does not willingly do something that he believes is morally wrong. Although he knowingly and intentionally does what he does (e.g., he steals or refuses to prevent a death) and although this is something that is morally wrong, he does not knowingly and intentionally do it under the description of its being a morally wrong act. Now, as we saw when comparing amoral wrongdoing with moral indifference and moral negligence with moral weakness, the fact that wrongdoing is conscious and intentional rather than the reverse is not in itself very important. However, in this case the fact that the (perversely) wicked agent does not consciously and intentionally do what is morally wrong is significant, because it allows for the possibility that he really prefers to avoid doing what is morally wrong and, hence, would be inclined not to act as he does if he believed such acts to be morally wrong. (Indeed, on the kind of noncognitivist analysis of moral beliefs that we have been considering, this is necessarily true.) Perhaps if we were somehow able to persuade him afterwards that what he did was morally wrong, he would then feel remorse.

When wickedness is viewed in this way, it does not seem so obviously worse than moral negligence and moral weakness. On this conception the agent of a wicked act no more willingly does what is wrong than does the agent of a morally negligent act. Of course, the former is guilty of a worse kind of shortcoming or defect. The "sin" of the latter is negligence—i.e., a failure to take reasonable precautions to avoid being ignorant that one's act is in violation of one's own moral principles; whereas the "sin" of the former consists in having a bad preference (or bad value-priorities), which manifests itself, according to the noncognitivist, in his accepting a bad moral principle. But although this is some reason for thinking that wickedness is worse than moral negligence, wickedness seems much more worse than moral negligence when we conceive of it as preferential wickedness. For in that case the agent of a wicked act willingly does something that he himself believes to be morally wrong. This not only makes wickedness a much more purposive kind of wrongdoing; it also rules out the possibility that the agent of a wicked act has the saving grace of conscientiousness (which may be thought of as a kind of mitigating factor). If, instead, we conceive of wickedness as perverse wickedness, it is also difficult to understand why it is worse than moral weakness. If we allow that the agent of a wicked act prefers to avoid moral wrongdoing just as much as does the morally weak agent and fails to avoid wrongdoing only because he fails to realize that what he does is wrong, then it is not clear why he is worse than the morally weak agent, who chooses to do something in spite of the fact that he himself believes it to be morally wrong. Moreover, as I have already suggested, if we were afterwards able to convince him that he was mistaken in thinking that acts of this sort are morally right, he might even come to feel remorse.

The noncognitivist will no doubt reply that, given the

wicked agent's preferences, it is not possible to convince him rationally that what he does is morally wrong. His conviction that acts of this sort are morally right is just a reflection of his own basic preferences. Moreover, it is in this respect that the wicked agent is worse than the morally weak agent, for at least the latter does not have bad value-priorities. Nevertheless, this does not seem to me how we ordinarily conceive of wickedness. We do not conceive of it on the model of perverse wickedness. Rather, we think that the most evil or reprehensible kind of wrongdoing consists in willingly and intentionally doing something that one believes to be morally wrong, either because one simply does not care that it is morally wrong or because one prefers the pursuit of some other end to the avoidance of moral wrongdoing.[31] Any analysis of the nature of moral beliefs that does not allow for even the possibility of these forms of immoral behavior is, it seems to me, defective. Hence, I am inclined to consider these implications of noncognitivist accounts of moral beliefs as good reasons for rejecting these accounts.

The primary purpose of this book has been to explore the nature and variety of immoral behavior; but the secondary purpose has been to show that no purely noncognitivist account of the nature of moral beliefs can adequately account for the nature and variety of immorality. Such accounts not only force us to misconstrue the nature

---

[31] I have allowed, however, that certain kinds of amoral wrongdoing may be just as bad as cases of deliberate wrongdoing, because in these cases, although the agent does not intentionally do something that he himself believes to be morally wrong, he fails to believe that it is wrong only because he is so unconcerned about moral wrongdoing that he does not even bother to consider whether what he does is morally right or wrong. Moreover, although such an amoral agent cannot be said intentionally to do something that he himself believes to be wrong, he does intentionally do something that he realizes might very well be wrong (something that he might come to believe is wrong if he considered this question). Thus, unlike the agent of a perversely wicked act, the amoral agent cannot be said to have the saving grace of conscientiousness.

of wickedness, making it appear much less reprehensible than it actually is; they also prevent us from recognizing the most blameworthy forms of immorality. I have argued that, of the three main kinds of shortcomings that render people blameworthy, the most serious and reprehensible is utter lack of moral concern. For this reason, amoral and morally indifferent acts are, in general, more blameworthy than wicked acts—no matter whether we conceive of wickedness as perverse or as preferential in character. But, if one adopts a noncognitivist analysis of moral beliefs, lack of moral concern becomes difficult, or impossible, to explain.

We have already noted that such analyses rule out morally indifferent behavior as logically impossible, since such analyses make having some con-attitude toward an act a necessary condition of believing it to be wrong. We have also noted that such accounts make amoral behavior difficult, if not impossible, to explain. The agent of an amoral act fails to believe that what he does is wrong because he does not even consider the question of whether or not what he does is morally wrong; and he fails to consider this because he does not really care whether or not it is morally wrong. In this case it is not that he both believes that what he does is wrong and yet fails to care (that is impossible on any noncognitivist account); rather, he does not care *if* what he does should happen to be wrong. But on a purely noncognitivist analysis of moral beliefs it is also difficult to understand what this more general lack of moral concern comes to. On a cognitivist account, not caring whether one's acts are right or wrong is not caring whether or not a certain state of affairs (or certain kinds of facts) obtains— e.g., not caring whether or not one's acts should fail to maximize happiness, or not caring whether or not they should happen to be instances of certain kinds of acts, such as killing or hurting or lying. But on a noncognitivist account, the notion of not caring whether or not one's acts should happen to be morally wrong makes no sense. For on such analyses there is nothing there (no possible fact existing antecedently to and independently of one's moral beliefs) for one to either care or not care about.

Some have suggested that noncognitivism also makes moral weakness logically impossible. I have argued that this is a mistake. It is true that certain kinds of noncognitivist analyses—Hare's, for example—seem to rule out genuine moral weakness as a form of immoral behavior. For on such accounts cases of moral weakness are cases of psychological impossibility, and hence it would seem that the agent cannot be considered blameworthy in such cases. But, as others have pointed out, it is not necessary to make the connection between moral beliefs and action as tight as Hare does. While insisting that having some con-attitude toward an act is a necessary condition of believing it to be wrong, one can allow that such con-attitudes may differ in strength and need not be particularly strong on some occasions. In this way a noncognitivist could even accept my explanation of moral weakness as being due to the agent's not caring enough that his act is wrong—except that we should now say, not that he does not care enough that his act is wrong, but that the care (con-attitude) embodied in this belief that his act is wrong is not strong enough. Nevertheless, problems arise for the noncognitivist when one considers the standard noncognitivist criterion for distinguishing between moral and nonmoral evaluative, or normative, judgments—namely, dominance (or overridingness). This criterion seems to rule out the possibility that the con-attitude embodied in one's believing that an act is wrong might not be sufficiently strong to enable one to resist or overcome a contrary attitude—or, as I would prefer to say, might not be strong enough to prompt one to take the measures necessary to control a competing pro- or con-attitude. However, Neil Cooper has argued that this is not so. He argues that, although believing that an act is morally wrong involves accepting a universalizable and overriding principle prescribing its avoidance, this does not entail that one wants to avoid acts of this kind more *intensely* than one wants to do anything else. It only entails that one wants to avoid doing this act in *preference* to anything else.[32]

The trouble with this solution, however, is that it is difficult to see what this distinction comes to on a noncognitivist analysis of evaluative judgments. Insofar as we can distinguish preferring X to Y from wanting X more strongly than Y, we must equate preferring X to Y with believing that X is better than Y (or that one ought to choose X rather than Y). But whereas a cognitivist can clearly distinguish believing that X is better than Y from wanting X more strongly than Y, it is not clear how this is to be done on a noncognitivist analysis of evaluative beliefs. Thus, I am inclined to think that moral weakness does turn out to be more problematic than it ought to be if one adopts a noncognitivist analysis.

I have argued in this book that the dichotomy (suggested by Aristotle) between wickedness and moral weakness oversimplifies and distorts the nature of immorality, and that we must distinguish wickedness (which, I have also argued, is better conceived of as preferential wickedness) both from *akratic* and amoral (in the broad sense) wrongdoing. I have further argued that *akratic* wrongdoing, as Aristotle conceived of it, must be further subdivided into morally weak and morally negligent wrongdoing, and that amoral (in the broad sense) wrongdoing includes both morally indifferent wrongdoing and amoral wrongdoing proper. Finally, I have argued that all of these forms of immorality—especially moral indifference and preferential wickedness—are possible, and, indeed, that the most serious and blameworthy kind of wrongdoing consists in the agent's deliberately doing something that he himself believes to be morally wrong, either because he prefers this to sacrificing

---

[32] See *The Diversity of Moral Thinking* (Oxford: Clarendon Press, 1981), p. 93.

some other end or because he simply does not care if what he does is morally wrong. If these arguments are correct, then we have good reason to reject, or at least seriously doubt, any analysis of moral beliefs that makes one of these types of immorality impossible or problematic.

BIBLIOGRAPHY

*

Aristotle. *Nicomachean Ethics,* translated by W. D. Ross, in Richard McKeon, ed., *The Basic Works of Aristotle,* pp. 935-1126. New York: Random House, 1941.—*De Anima,* translated by J. A. Smith, in *The Basic Works of Aristotle,* pp. 534-603.

Austin, John. *Lectures in Jurisprudence.* London: John Murray, 1873.

Austin, J. L. *How To Do Things with Words.* Oxford: Clarendon Press, 1962.

Baier, Kurt. *The Moral Point of View.* Ithaca, N.Y.: Cornell University Press, 1958.—"Moral Reasons," in *Midwest Studies in Philosophy,* vol. III, 1978, pp. 62-73.—"Moral Reasons and Reasons to be Moral," in A. I. Goldman and J. Kim, eds., *Values and Morals,* pp. 231-56. Dordrecht, Holland: D. Reidel Publishing Co., 1978.

Beardsley, E. L. "Determinism and Moral Perspectives," *Philosophy and Phenomenological Research,* vol. 21, 1960, pp. 1-20.—"Moral Worth and Moral Credit," *The Philosophical Review,* vol. 66, 1975, pp. 304-28.—"Blaming," *Philosophia,* vol. 8, 1978, pp. 573-83.

Benson, John. "Wants, Desires, and Deliberations," in G. W. Mortimore, ed., *Weakness of Will,* pp. 200-15. Reprinted from *Aristotelian Society,* suppl. vol. 42, 1968.

Bentham, Jeremy. *An Introduction to the Principles of Morals and Legislation.* New York: Hafner Library, 1948 (originally published, 1789).

Brandt, R. B. "Blameworthiness and Obligation," in A. I. Melden, ed., *Essays in Moral Philosophy,* pp. 3-39. Seattle: University of Washington Press, 1958.—*Ethical Theory*. Englewood Cliffs, N.J.: Prentice-Hall, Inc., 1959.—"Some Merits of One Form of Rule-Utilitarianism," *University of Colorado Studies*, Series in Philosophy, No. 3, 1967, pp. 39-65.

Broad, C. D. "Some of the Main Problems of Ethics," in Feigl and Sellars, eds., *Readings in Philosophical Analysis*. New York: Appleton-Century-Crofts, Inc., 1949, pp. 547-63.

Cleckley, H. *The Mask of Sanity*. St. Louis: C. V. Mosby, 1941.

Cooper, Neil. "Oughts and Wants," in G. W. Mortimore, ed., *Weakness of Will*, pp. 190-99. London: Macmillan and Co., 1971. Reprinted from *Aristotelian Society*, suppl. vol. 42, 1968.—*The Diversity of Moral Thinking*. Oxford: Clarendon Press, 1981.

Davidson, Donald. "How is Weakness of the Will Possible?" in Joel Feinberg, ed., *Moral Concepts*, pp. 93-113. London: Oxford University Press, 1969.

Davis, Lawrence H. "Prisoners, Paradox, and Rationality," *American Philosophical Quarterly*, vol. 14, 1977, pp. 319-27.

Demos, Raphael. "Lying to Oneself," *Journal of Philosophy*, vol. 57, 1960, pp. 588-95.

Duff, Antony. "Psychopathy and Moral Understanding," *American Philosophical Quarterly*, vol. 14, 1977, pp. 189-200.

Edgerton, Henry W. "Negligence, Inadvertence, and Indifference: The Relation of Mental States to Negligence," *Harvard Law Review*, vol. 39, 1926, pp. 549-69. Reprinted in Herbert Morris, ed., *Freedom and Responsibility*, pp. 246-50. Stanford, Calif.: Stanford University Press, 1961.

Edwards, Paul. "Hard and Soft Determinism," in Sidney Hook, ed., *Determinism and Freedom*, pp. 117-25. New York: Collier Books, 1961.

Fingarette, Herbert. *Self-Deception*. London: Routledge & Kegan Paul, 1969.

Foot, Philippa. "When Is a Principle a Moral Principle?" *Proceedings of the Aristotelian Society*, suppl. vol. 28, 1954, pp. 95-110.—"Moral Arguments," *Mind*, vol. 67, 1958, pp. 502-13.

Frankena, W. K. "Obligation and Motivation in Recent Moral Philosophy," in A. I. Melden, ed., *Essays in Moral Philosophy*, pp. 40-81.—"The Concept of Morality," *University of Colorado Studies*, Series in Philosophy, No. 3, 1967, pp. 1-22.—*Ethics*. Englewood Cliffs, N.J.: Prentice-Hall, Inc., 1973.

Gauthier, D. P. "Hare's Debtors," *Mind*, vol. 77, 1968, pp. 400-05.

Gensler, H. J. "The Prescriptivism Incompleteness Theorem," *Mind*, vol. 85, 1976, pp. 489-96.

Glover, Jonathan. *Responsibility*. New York: Humanities Press, 1970.

Grice, G. R. *The Grounds of Moral Judgment*. London: Cambridge University Press, 1967.

Grice, H. P. "Logic and Conversation," in Cole and Morgan, eds., *Syntax and Semantics, Vol. 3, Speech Acts*. New York: Academic Press, 1975.

Haksar, Vinit. "Aristotle and the Punishment of Psychopaths," *Philosophy*, vol. 39, 1964, pp. 323-40.—"The Responsibility of Psychopaths," *Philosophical Quarterly*, vol. 15, 1965, pp. 135-45.

Hardie, W.F.R. *Aristotle's Ethical Theory*. Oxford: Clarendon Press, 1968.

Hare, R. M. *The Language of Morals*. Oxford: Clarendon Press, 1952.—*Freedom and Reason*. Oxford: Clarendon Press, 1963.—*Essays on the Moral Concepts*. London: Macmillan and Co., 1972.—*Moral Thinking*. Oxford: Clarendon Press, 1981.

Harman, Gilbert. *The Nature of Morality*. New York: Oxford University Press, 1977.

Harrison, Jonathan. "When Is a Principle a Moral Principle?" *Proceedings of the Aristotelian Society*, suppl. vol. 28, 1954, pp. 111-34.—*Our Knowledge of Right and Wrong*. London: George Allen & Unwin, Ltd., 1971.

Hart, H.L.A. *Punishment and Responsibility*. New York: Oxford University Press, 1968.—and Honore, A. M. *Causation in the Law*. Oxford: Clarendon Press, 1959.

Hobbes, Thomas. *Leviathan*, ed. by Michael Oakeshott. Oxford: Basil Blackwell, 1960 (originally published, 1651).

Hook, Sidney. "Necessity, Indeterminism, and Sentimentalism," in Sidney Hook, ed., *Determinism and Freedom*, pp. 180-92. New York: Collier Books, 1961.

Hospers, John. *Human Conduct*. New York: Harcourt, Brace & World, Inc., 1961.—"What Means This Freedom?" in Sidney Hook, ed., *Freedom and Determinism*, pp. 126-42. New York: Collier Books, 1961.

Lukes, Stephen. "Moral Weakness," in G. W. Mortimore, ed., *Weakness of Will*, pp. 147-59. London: Macmillan and Co., 1971. Reprinted from *Philosophical Quarterly*, vol. 15, 1965.

Kant, Immanuel. *Foundations of the Metaphysics of Morals*, translated by Lewis W. Beck. New York: Liberal Arts Press, 1959 (originally published, 1785).—*Critique of Practical Reason*, translated by Lewis W. Beck. New York: Liberal Arts Press, 1956 (originally published, 1788).—*The Doctrine of Virtue*, translated by Mary J. Gregor. New York: Harper & Row, 1964 (originally published, 1797).

Mathews, Gwynneth. "Weakness of Will," in G. W. Mortimore, ed., *Weakness of Will*, pp. 160-74. London: Macmillan and Co., 1971. Reprinted from *Mind*, vol. 75, 1966.

McCord, W., and McCord, J. The *Psychopath*. Princeton, N.J.: Van Nostrand, 1964.

Milo, Ronald D. "Bentham's Principle," *Ethics*, vol. 84, 1974, pp. 128-39.

Moore, G. E. *Principia Ethica*. Cambridge: Cambridge University Press, 1903.

Nowell-Smith, P. H. *Ethics*. Baltimore: Penguin Books, 1954.

Perry, R. B. *Realms of Value*. Cambridge, Mass.: Harvard University Press, 1954.

Prichard, H. A. *Moral Obligation: Essays and Lectures*. Oxford: Clarendon Press, 1912.

Rachels, James. "Active and Passive Euthanasia," in Bonnie Steinbock, ed., *Killing and Letting Die*, pp. 63-68. Englewood Cliffs, N.J.: Prentice-Hall, Inc., 1980. Reprinted from *New England Journal of Medicine*, vol. 292, 1975.

Richards, D.A.J. *A Theory of Reasons for Action*. Oxford: Clarendon Press, 1971.

Ross, W. D. *The Right and the Good*. Oxford: Clarendon Press, 1930.—*Aristotle*. New York: Meridian Books, Inc., 1959 (first published, 1923).

Russell, Bertrand. "The Elements of Ethics," in Sellars and Hospers, eds., *Readings in Ethical Theory*. New York: Appleton-Century-Crofts, Inc., 1952, pp. 1-32.

Salmon, Wesley C. "Determinism and Indeterminism in Modern Science," in Joel Feinberg, ed., *Reason and Responsibility*, pp. 316-32. Encino and Belmont, Calif.: Dickenson Publishing Co., 1971.

Santas, Gerasimos. "Plato's Protagoras and Explanations of Weakness," in G. W. Mortimore, ed., *Weakness of Will*, pp. 37-62. London: Macmillan and Co., 1971. Reprinted from *The Philosophical Review*, vol. 75, 1966.

Schlick, Moritz. *Problems of Ethics*. New York: Dover Publications, Inc., 1939, 1962.

Searle, John. *Speech Acts*. London: Cambridge University Press, 1970.

Seavey, Warren A. "Negligence—Subjective or Objective?" *Harvard Law Review*, vol. 41, 1927, pp. 1-28. Reprinted in Herbert Morris, ed., *Freedom and Responsibility*, pp. 251-62. Stanford, Calif.: Stanford University Press, 1961.

Sharp, F. C. *Ethics*. New York: The Century Co., 1928.

Smith, M.B.E. "Indifference and Moral Acceptance," *American Philosophical Quarterly*, vol. 9, 1972, pp. 86-93.

Stevenson, C. L. "The Emotive Meaning of Ethical Terms," in Sellars and Hospers, eds., *Readings in Ethical Theory*, pp. 415-29. New York: Appleton-Century-Crofts, Inc., 1952. Reprinted from *Mind*, vol. 46, 1937.—*Ethics and Language*. New Haven, Conn.: Yale University Press, 1944.

Stocker, Michael. "Act and Agent Evaluations," *Review of Metaphysics*, vol. 27, 1973, pp. 42-61.

Taurek, John M. "Should the Numbers Count?" *Philosophy and Public Affairs*, vol. 6, 1967, pp. 293-316.

Terry, Henry T. "Negligence," *Harvard Law Review*, vol. 29, 1915, pp. 40-50. Reprinted in Herbert Morris, ed., *Freedom and Responsibility*, pp. 243-46. Stanford, Calif.: Stanford University Press, 1961.

Thalberg, Irving. "Acting Against One's Better Judgment," in G. W. Mortimore, ed., *Weakness of Will*. London: Macmillan and Co., 1971, pp. 233-46. First published in *Theoria*, vol. 21, 1965, pp. 242-54.

Tooley, Michael. "An Irrelevant Consideration: Killing vs. Letting Die," in Bonnie Steinbock, ed., *Killing and Letting Die*, pp. 56-62. Englewood Cliffs, N.J.: Prentice-Hall, Inc., 1980.

Torrance, S. B. "Prescriptivism and Incompleteness," *Mind*, vol. 90, 1981, pp. 580-85.

Urmson, J. O. *The Emotive Theory of Ethics*. New York: Oxford University Press, 1971.

Von Wright, G. H. *Norm and Action*. London: Routledge and Kegan Paul, 1963.

Warnock, G. J. *Contemporary Moral Philosophy*. London: Macmillan and Co., 1967.

Watson, Gary. "Scepticism About Weakness of Will," *The Philosophical Review*, vol. 86, 1977, pp. 316-39.

Wertheimer, Roger. "Understanding the Abortion Argument," *Philosophy and Public Affairs*, vol. 1, 1971, pp. 67-95.

Williams, Norman and Sheila. *The Moral Development of Children*. London: Macmillan and Co., 1970.

Wilson, John, Williams, Norman, and Sugarman, Barry. *Introduction to Moral Education*. Baltimore: Penguin Books, 1967.

Wright, Derek. *The Psychology of Moral Behavior*. Baltimore: Penguin Books, 1971.

INDEX

✳

Glover, Jonathan, 220, 222, 225n, 226n, 228n
golden-rule argument, 70, 74
Grice, G. R., 187n, 205, 207
Grice, H. P., 144, 148n

Haksar, Vinit, 61n
Hardie, W.F.R., 96n
Hare, R. M., 14, 15n, 47-50, 53, 65-76, 80, 112n, 130, 146-47, 153-59, 162-64, 173, 186n, 189, 196, 198-201, 255
Harman, Gilbert, 213n, 216n
Harrison, Jonathan, 44-45, 53n
Hart, H.L.A., 84, 88, 96n, 171n, 178
Hobbes, Thomas, 49, 205n
Honore, A. M., 171n
Hook, Sidney, 227n
Hospers, John, 33n, 40-41, 46, 228n, 229n
hypocrite, moral, 113

ideals, 199-201, 232
ignorance, of facts, 9, 31, 40-41, 110; of right and wrong, of moral principles, see moral ignorance
illocutionary force, 148-51, 155
impulsiveness, 86, 98, 109, 114
incontinence, 91-97. See also akrasia; akratic wrongdoing; weakness of will
indecisiveness, 19n, 120, 123, 135
indifference, to right and wrong, see moral indifference
intemperance, 119, 123
internalism, 14, 140-51, 164, 166-67, 178, 183, 211
intuitionism, 34, 42, 65, 151-53
irresolution, 119-20, 123

Kant, Immanuel, 7, 74, 137, 196-97, 204, 240

knowledge, having versus exercising, 92-94

Lukes, Stephen, 112n, 130n

McCord, J., and McCord, W., 61n
Malm, Heidi, 243n
Mathews, Gwynneth, 118n, 122, 131n
metaethical theory, 14, 17-18, 26, 158
Milo, Ronald D., 42n, 161n
Milton, John, 7n
Moore, G. E., 152n, 153-54, 160
moral beliefs (judgments, principles), contrasted with nonmoral beliefs (judgments, principles), 14-17, 47-53, 172-77, 186-202, 255. See also morality, concept of
moral blindness, 100n, 109-10, 245
moral concern, see conscientiousness
moral concern, lack of, 5, 12, 17, 27, 35, 38, 56, 63, 74-81, 216, 225, 233-34, 238-41, 246-47, 250, 253, 257; and moral negligence, 12, 137-38, 238-39; and moral weakness, 12, 121, 132-34, 137-38, 228, 233-34, 238; and non-cognitivist analyses of moral beliefs, 59, 75-76, 79-80, 140, 183, 252-54; and wickedness, 6, 12, 35, 38, 238, 240. See also amoral wrongdoing; moral indifference
moral deafness, 74, 80
moral education, 27-28
moral ignorance, 6, 18, 25, 58-65; and amoral wrongdoing, 77-78, 248; and moral negligence, 82-97, 106-13, 224, 245; and perverse wickedness, 29-36, 39-46, 109
moral indifference, 5-8, 11-12, 26-

LIBRARY OF CONGRESS CATALOGING IN PUBLICATION DATA

Milo, Ronald D. (Ronald Dmitri), 1935-
  Immorality.

  (Studies in moral, political, and legal philosophy.)
  Bibliography: p.
  Includes index.
  1. Immorality. I. Title. II. Series.
BJ1411.M55 1984   170   84-42564
ISBN 0-691-06614-0 (alk. paper)